Quit Kissing My Ashes

Quit Kissing My Ashes

A Mother's Journey Through Grief

JUDY COLLIER

Forty-Two Publishing
Baton Rouge, Louisiana

Printed in the United States of America

Publisher's Catalog-in-Publication
(*Provided by Quality Books, Inc.*)

Collier, Judy.
    Quit kissing my ashes : a mother's journey through
grief /Judy Collier. – 1st ed.
    p. cm.
    LCCN 2001126621
    ISBN 0-9710107-0-6

    1. Spiritualism. 2. New Age movement.   I. Title.

BF1261.2.C65 2002   133.9
                        QB101-701036

Published by Forty-Two Publishing, P.O. Box 14295,
Baton Rouge, LA 70898
Cover design by Foster & Foster
Interior design and typography by Publishing Professionals,
New Port Richey, Florida

This book is dedicated with love to my daughters, Jill and Jamie. After all that has transpired the past five years, I am thankful they still call me "Mom."

I am grateful that both Jill and Jamie have been there for me. Though both have felt Kyle's death in different depths, their understanding of my need to keep their brother in my life has let me know how truly special my daughters are.

Jill and Jamie, without your being who you are, the happiness and contentment I have found would not be possible. I love you very, very much.

A special thank you to my "sounding board," without whose encouragement this book would not have been possible. No one else could or would have put up with hearing my stories over and over and over again. Thank you, Jim. I love you with all my heart.

Contents

Acknowledgments

The following souls have enriched my journey beyond any words of expression. Each has been there for me when they were needed, helping me to grow spiritually and enabling me to accept the path that God has blessed me with. I take this opportunity to give heartfelt thanks to them.

Mary Jo McCabe, truly a "gift" from God. Your compassion and ability to connect the spiritual with the physical has given me a peace concerning Kyle's whereabouts. Your messages have given me a greater understanding of not only the purpose of our lives here on earth, but the knowledge that we are all indeed connected to each other and a loving God whose light will shine upon us throughout eternity. Because of you, I *know* I will be with Kyle again. You, more than anyone else, have enabled me to look forward to the future, and I am blessed for that.

John J. Edward, the best medium ever. Your messages given not only to Jim and me, but also to others who loved Kyle, have enabled me to think of death not as an end, but as a wondrous beginning. Your accurate descriptions of things known just to Kyle, often given in a humorous way, let us know that our son not only survived his death, but more importantly is exactly the same person we knew when he was with us physically. Your portrayal of events that have occurred after Kyle's "graduation" have given us *proof* our son is still involved in our lives, knowing *everything* that is happening on the earthly plane. I will be forever grateful for the many opportunities you have given us to connect with our son.

Linda Hullinger, a classmate who became a very special teacher to me. Your willingness to help me and your openness in sharing your personal and innermost experiences have given further proof that everything happens for a reason. I will always laugh while thinking of our many trips when I excessively worried about

Kyle's ability to bring other children to the meetings. His continuing to be a big part of my earthly existence, because of your desire to help others, has let me know what a special and "gifted" soul you truly are.

Sister Rita Coco, for giving me comforting words and hope for the future. You were the starting point for this miraculous journey, and your acceptance of the wonders of the spirit world led me to search, without any reservations, for answers to questions unknown to me.

Janice Hurst, for being Cory's Mom and understanding everything I say. The pain you have experienced because of Cory's untimely and tragic death has enabled me to share my pain with you in a way that few others would understand. You've been a sounding board who lets me speak from my heart. And because of our continued obsession with our sons, Cory and Kyle will probably really be upset when we finally get to join them.

Kathy Hayes, for being Barlow's Mom and letting Barlow "hang out" with Kyle. I know that Barlow and Kyle made sure that we "hooked up" with each other after their deaths. Barlow's ability to pop up unannounced at various events has given me added insight into the spiritual world. I look forward to the day I can meet your son face to face. And by then, no telling what he and Kyle will have been up to.

Lisa Guidroz, for being Jason's Mom, and opening "Bryson's Angel's" gift shop. Your incentive to bring an awareness of the spiritual world to others because of your love for Jason has helped more people than you will ever know. I never dreamt that when I purchased your angel lamp, it would be the beginning of many wondrous experiences. I thank Terry, too, for being receptive and not being skeptical anymore.

Bobby Schultz, for never *not* being there for me. Your not hanging up on me while listening to my far-out escapades has been a true indicator of what a special friend you are to me. Sharing your personal heartaches with me is further proof that we have connected to be here for each other. I still plan on taking you up on your offer to "carry my bags." So stay in shape.

DeDee McDonald, for being a part of Kyle's life. Though we did not know one another before Kyle's death, I am blessed that you have become so involved in our lives. Your willingness to be open to connecting with Kyle's spirit has given me added strength. Kyle apparently knows *everything,* because you are still in that relationship. You are a beautiful soul, who Kyle is blessed to have known in this lifetime.

Shelly Tate, for being a part of Kyle's life. Your continued love and concern for Kyle and his family has meant more to me than you will ever know. Kyle was blessed to have you in his life, and we are blessed to have you in ours. When I see big lobsters I will always think of you and Kyle. And I hope you keep your windowsills clean. Thank you for being the very special person that you are.

CeCe Tye, for being there for me *so* many times. You've been like a sister to me. Your love for Kyle has touched me deeply, and your willingness to keep Kyle's spirit with us has comforted me immeasurably. And I want to apologize for Kyle's tearing off your fingernail.

Nell Meriwether, an accomplished authority of the English language. Your willingness to spend hours on my grade "F" manuscript pages and turn them to "A" pages is greatly appreciated. My reluctance to share with you *Quit Kissing My Ashes* for fear of what you would think of me was soon put to rest by your pleasant manner and encouraging words concerning the successful publication of my story.

DyAnne, Gail C., Emily, Nina, Carol, Bert, Jackie, Gail M., Cecil, Linda, Ruth, Megan, Lynn, Mary Pat, Pat, Kathleen, Dayle, and *Brenda,* all classmates in Mary Jo's Thursday night class. We brought to each other an unexplained desire to connect with one another on a spiritual level that enriched our lives in many ways. Mary Jo's teachings, and our ability to grasp them and share what we had learned, opened up a beautiful new world of hope, compassion, and peace. My ability to live with the death of my only son in an accepting way is largely attributed to these fellow classmates and what they taught me.

I want to thank Barbara Bryan, Lisa Musgrove, Debbie Percy, Deanna Falcon, Jean Adams, Donna Steib, Adrianne King, Joe Ann Guillory, Beverly Tully, Miss Norma, Michael Bester, Diana Drewett, Barbara Johnson, Debi Grymes, and Peggy Stewart for being there for me, for never questioning my search for answers, and for lending an ear when I needed to talk about my heart-ache. You have all contributed to my emergence into the light.

And I want to thank the many parents of deceased children who have shared their stories of love and pain with me, in an open and confiding way, that only a parent who has experienced such a loss can understand.

Last, but not least, thank *You* for reading my story and giving me another reason to have experienced so many blessings. I hope you, too, find comfort in what I have experienced by being able to think of the death of your loved ones in a different light, a much brighter light.

Foreword

Mary Jo McCabe

Author of *Learn to See* and *Come This Way*

When I met Judy two months after her son's death, she had no prior knowledge of my work. She had never been to a psychic or medium and had never read a book on spirituality or life after death, but that changed radically when Kyle died. Suddenly, she was thrown into a world of uncertainties. In her appointment with me, she desperately hoped Kyle would be able to reassure her he was still alive and that life did continue after death.

Quit Kissing My Ashes is truly a heart-wrenching story of Judy's search to prove that her only son is at peace after his death. This book not only *proves* that Kyle still exists, but more importantly, that he has succeeded in letting Judy *know* how happy he is in his continuous journey toward God's light.

This is a wonderful book for those who are in need of comfort and who want proof that life does continue after death.

This is the message I am most excited about—the reality of never-ending life. Kyle has put forth a great deal of effort in showing his mother he spends time with her and his family and friends every day. Kyle shows he still has his sense of humor, his play on words, and his love of animals, indicating that people don't change once they die. Kyle *proves* this continuously as you will see throughout this eye-opening story. He has also reassured his mother that, as a result of his death, he has found his purpose, which is to bring peace to all who have lost loved ones. He continues to touch people's lives after his death, just as he touched people's lives while here on earth. Kyle verifies that we are always connected to our loved ones, even though we may be in two different worlds for a time.

This is a marvelous book to share with others. Even if you have not lost someone close to you, it will open your eyes to the world around you. If you are open to the possibility of communication from the Other Side, it will give you a different meaning to your life. It will make you aware of messages being given to you every day from the heavens. I guarantee what you experience by reading this awe-inspiring story will allow you to feel closer not only to the loved ones you have lost, but also to yourself and to other people here on earth as well.

I thank you, Kyle, for making me a part of your effort to bring peace to those who have experienced loss.

Quit Kissing My Ashes is an extraordinary gift to anyone who reads it.

Preface

When my only son, Kyle, died as the result of an automobile accident in 1996, I wanted to die. I did not want to live without him. He was so very, very special to me, and my obsession with him and his happiness did not end with his death.

What has transpired these past five years is truly beyond belief. Kyle's unrelenting determination to bring comfort not only to his father and me, but to others who loved him as well, is a story that had to be told. Kyle's ability to manipulate the physical world from the spiritual world in hundreds of ways is a beautiful story of love and connection between the two worlds.

I had never heard of after-death communication before Kyle's death, and the amazing thing is that I never searched for it after his death. It came to me in the most unbelievable ways . . . from strangers I had never met and from the world-renowned psychic/mediums, John Edward, Mary Jo McCabe, and James Van Praagh.

When Kyle died, my first thoughts were of heaven, and if there were really such a place, and if Kyle were there. The never-ending episodes and "happenings" that occurred soon after his death are truly remarkable. He not only proved to me that there was an after-life, but also that it was a far better place than here on earth. When things happened, I would think, "This can't be true," but it *was* true, and they continued to happen over and over again.

Because of what Kyle has been able to do from his new home, we not only *know* he still lives, but more importantly we also know he is the *same* person now, with the same personality, the same sense of humor and the same interests. In addition, we also discovered that he is aware of everything in the physical world.

I never planned on writing a book. But the overwhelming evidence of life beyond death that kept coming my way brought me peace and comfort. I knew there had to be a reason God had given me so many blessings. I knew I had to share this story with you so that my blessing can become your blessing. I wanted you to understand that love never ends; it only grows. And more importantly, I wanted you to see that the death of a loved one can afford each of us the opportunity to grow in a way that can only strengthen our bond with the very special person we will love and be with forever. I *know* I will be with Kyle again. After reading *Quit Kissing My Ashes*, you too will know your loved ones will always be a part of your life, now and throughout eternity.

1

When Kyle's Door Closed, He Opened a Window

When I came out from under the grogginess of the anesthetic on March 12, 1970, my first words were, "What did I have?"

The attending nurse told me that I had a son.

"How much does he weigh?"

"Eight pounds, seven ounces," she answered.

Excitedly, I said, "Oh good! Then we can keep him."

Looking back, I guess the nurse must have thought I was crazy. But earlier that year, on February 10th, my husband, Jim who is an avid fisherman, had landed an eight pound three ounce largemouth bass. It was the largest bass he had ever caught. He sent it to a taxidermist and had it mounted. Later, a picture of him and his "prize" catch appeared in the local newspaper. At that time, Jim had jokingly said the baby I was carrying had better weigh more than his fish, or we'd have to throw it back.

Kyle was our third child and only son. His two sisters, Jill and Jamie, were nine and seven years older. When I saw my husband for the first time after giving birth, he was crying. I immediately thought something must be wrong with the baby because I had never seen my husband cry before. I kept questioning Jim, but he reassured me that all was fine, and they were only tears of joy.

The next time I saw my husband cry was on April 25, 1996, after I received the phone call no one wants to get.

When I picked up the phone at 10:30 that night, my life changed forever. Kyle, then twenty-six years of age, had been in an automobile accident. I knew it was serious when I asked how he was and was told that he was breathing.

Kyle had been driving fast and did not have on his seat belt. He apparently was reaching for a CD on the floorboard of his Bronco when he slid onto the shoulder of the road. In his attempt to regain control, he overcorrected, hit a bridge railing and was thrown eighty feet, landing between two bridges.

Hitting his head upon landing, Kyle suffered severe head trauma. When I saw him in intensive care, his body had no visual signs of any injury. He looked as if he were in a peaceful sleep; however, we were given no hope from the beginning. The doctor told us it was a mortal injury and even suggested we should consider organ donation.

Though we were given no hope for Kyle's survival, we prayed he could somehow live. After two days in intensive care and tests that showed there was no oxygen getting to his brain, we decided to take him off life-support and donate all of his organs.

The funeral and the days following all seemed like a blur. The pain that a parent endures upon the loss of a child is indescribable. I loved Kyle so much.

Jamie had gotten the name of a grief therapist while at the funeral. Sister Rita Coco is a nun who is the head of The Grief Recovery Center in Baton Rouge. About a week after Kyle's death, I made an appointment with her, grasping for anything that might help me. I felt as if I had no reason to get out of bed, no reason to exist. I did not want to live without Kyle.

For some reason, both Jim and I were obsessed with Kyle and his happiness. Often people were surprised that we had other children. It was always Kyle this and Kyle that. Before his death, people sometimes joked that when they died, they wanted to come back as our third child. It was evident we loved Kyle dearly and felt we could never give him enough love.

I have since learned from talking with many other parents of deceased children and receiving the gift of spirituality Kyle's death brought, that on a soul level I knew Kyle would not be with us for very long. Many other parents who have lost a child, upon reflection, have sensed the same feeling.

Sister Rita, more or less, listened to me talk about my heartache. She was a comfort in that she told me Kyle did live on, that he was in a much better place, and that I would one day be with him again. But for a person who has had little religious upbringing or knowledge of the spiritual realm, I was grasping at whatever hope I could find.

After three grief sessions with Sister Rita, she mentioned she had the name of someone who might be able to help me. It was then that she wrote down the name of Mary Jo McCabe on a piece of paper.

She told me Mary Jo founded the McCabe Institute in Baton Rouge, and she had comforted many people in the past. I don't really remember if I were told she could communicate with the dead or exactly what she did, but I do remember calling for an appointment as soon as I got home. I was in excruciating pain and grief, but more importantly, I was concerned about Kyle. I wanted to know he was okay. As any parent knows, love and concern for their child lasts for a lifetime. Trust me, it does not end with their death. The concern escalates to unimaginable heights.

I was totally unaware of any possibility of after-death communication. I had never heard of the term nor had I ever thought it existed. I had absolutely no knowledge of any paranormal activities. I knew there were psychics but thought it was all a scam. I had twice encountered a fortune teller at a carnival during my first two pregnancies and was told both times that the baby would be a boy. Since there was a fifty percent chance they would be correct and since I delivered a girl both times, I didn't have much faith in this so-called ability.

This skepticism on my part enables me to understand others' skepticism when I tell them of what I now know to be true. It's so frustrating because I know our lives never end. It is because of this frustration that I am writing this book to share my truth.

I had to wait three weeks before I could get an appointment with Mary Jo because of her growing recognition and popularity. Now it is a six month wait. When I walked into her office, I looked around at the surroundings, finding comfort in how "normal" the place looked and how tastefully it was decorated. Later, when I met Mary Jo, I was stunned at how attractive she was. She was also very compassionate. We sat down, and I told her that my son had died in a car accident. It was then she told me she had a son and could not imagine the pain of losing a child. In the past three years I have come to know Mary Jo personally, and I know how much her only child, Bhrett, means to her. So on some level, I believe she can imagine at least some of my pain.

After a few minutes, Mary Jo closed her eyes and went into a trance, something I had never seen before. She took a few deep breaths and began speaking with a different accent.

That's when my life changed.

The first thing Mary Jo said was that I was being presented with a bear, a brown bear. If it didn't have any meaning to me now, it would later. Little did she know how my heart jumped and began racing. I was overcome with excitement. It was my first taste of something beyond comprehension. It was my first confirmation that there might be more to life than the physical world. Mary Jo had no idea I collected bears and that over one hundred were scattered throughout my house. Kyle would often lie on the sofa watching TV surrounded by my bears. And when I used to drive to Arkansas to watch Kyle play college football, I often rode with a bear to keep me company.

Mary Jo then spent about five minutes giving me messages about my life and the particular years that had made the most impact on me. At the time, I didn't fully digest this information.

I was numb when I went for my reading with Mary Jo. It was June 27, 1996—exactly two months after the doctor had pronounced Kyle dead. Weeks before, when I made the appointment with Mary Jo, she had sent me a letter stating I should have a number of specific questions written down to ask during the reading. When it came time for me to ask the questions, I was nervous with anticipation.

I just wanted some verification that Kyle was "in a better place" and that he didn't simply die. So I asked how the accident happened, and she explained that Kyle had veered to the right, his wheel had gone off the pavement, and in trying to get back on the road, he over-corrected, hit a bridge and was thrown from the vehicle.

This was exactly what the policeman had told us.

She told me he did not suffer and his soul left his body immediately. She then said something that has comforted me beyond belief.

She said, "He thanks you for taking him off life-support after two days."

Since the accident, when I've read of someone's being in a coma for months and then recovering, I've always wondered if the doctor were correct in his diagnosis of no brain activity and if we had made the correct decision. But then, I always hear Mary Jo's words, "He thanks you . . ." and I feel at peace with our decision.

About a year and a half after Kyle's death, I asked Mary Jo if Kyle actually died on the 25th or the 27th of April. I didn't really know which day I should celebrate his "going home."

Without even hesitating, she said, "Thursday," which was the 25th. I had never mentioned the day of the week of the accident or the day he was declared dead, only the dates.

Because she told me his soul left on Thursday, Jim and I release balloons and light candles on a cake on the 25th in celebration of his graduation to a higher place. Kyle has since given me a message through Mary Jo thanking us for this tribute and saying he would blow out the candles if he could.

Some of the more profound things Mary Jo told me that I constantly tell people when mentioning my reading and Mary Jo's gift is that she could see my son. I asked her if he were still good looking. She immediately said, "Well, his head is shaved, and he has on a blue or green cap. Not a baseball cap, but a nicer cap."

We had an open casket at his funeral and because his head had been shaved, we put a blue Tommy Hilfiger cap on him. Before the funeral, my friend, Bunny, had bought two caps, one blue and one green, so I could decide which one would be better.

Then I got a little greedy and asked Mary Jo if she could see the logo, but she told me no, his head was turned sideways.

When she described how he looked in the casket, I started to cry. I knew she didn't know Kyle or attend his funeral, but I knew somehow he was there with us. I will

never be able to explain how this exact information overwhelmed me. It was the first time I had felt hope since Kyle
died.

Mary Jo then proceeded to tell me he was showing her
a little piggy bank. Two days before the funeral, Kyle's
three-and-a-half-year-old son, Cain, was given a little piggy
bank to play with while at our house. When money was put
in it, its head would spin around and say, "More money,
more money." This is the only time I can remember a little
bit of laughter and lightheartedness during those awful
days. A few days after the funeral and Kyle's son had
returned to Arkansas, I mailed the bank to him.

Mary Jo not only mentioned accurate things that took
place during the funeral, but her mention of the piggy bank
made me aware that Kyle knew everything that had happened elsewhere.

Probably the most comforting thing Mary Jo told me,
however, which I have read and heard many times since, is
that there are no accidents or victims. We, as souls, have
chosen our life's path and the way in which we leave this
earth, and the time we leave has already been determined.

Three of my friends have told me their children dreamt
of their deaths and told their parents about their dreams.
Then a few days later, their deaths occurred the exact way
they had dreamed.

"Why do children dream about their own deaths?" I
asked Mary Jo one time.

"Children are so open," she began. "It's when we get
older that we start coming down into the world. We get
heavy. That's why it's real hard for angels and higher spiritual beings to come into our world. Our energy here is so
dense, it's hard for us when we get older, because we get buried in the energy. It just gets deeper and deeper. Children
and teenagers still have that air of lightness about them;
therefore, they dream of their deaths more than someone of

our age. It's because they're still connected to the spiritual world. They may not know it on a conscious level, but they do on a subconscious level. Many of their souls actually begin the transition before they die." Mary Jo continued, "Children know and they look to you to say, 'Please tell me it's not true.'"

There is a story about the well-known seer, Edgar Cayce, that confirms this belief. He is said to have been waiting to get on an elevator. But when the door opened, he immediately saw that all the souls of the people on the elevator were gone. Only bodies were there. He chose not to get on the elevator. The elevator crashed and all the people died.

Though I miss Kyle more than words can express, I truly believe his death occurred exactly as his soul planned it.

During my reading with Mary Jo, she told me Kyle was getting in a race car. That would be like him. He loved to drive fast; having numerous speeding tickets verified this. She said she also saw him sitting on the floor surrounded by books. Ironically, one week before his death, Kyle told me he was going to start reading again.

Then Mary Jo asked as she relayed Kyle's message, "Do you know what it is like to be able to climb mountains without the fear of falling?"

Later, I learned that Kyle had climbed many mountains while in Arkansas, including Mount Pinnacle three times in one day.

Mary Jo also told me Kyle had a sense of humor (which was true) and for me to be happy for him. She said he was very happy.

For the last five years of Kyle's life, he had not been happy. He had battled clinical depression. He was seen by many doctors, put on many different anti-depressants, and even had ECT shock treatments. He would improve a little, get his smile back, and talk about his future. But, unfortunately, he would always succumb to the disease again, and it would break my heart.

Almost two years later, on May 21, 1998, Kyle gave me a message through Mary Jo. It was very comforting to hear. "There's no night here. It never gets dark."

Mary Jo explained that Kyle never liked the dark. Then she said, "Because it never gets dark there, that in itself is rejuvenating. He says he never wanted to sleep when he felt good, so he never has to sleep. How much more can he want?"

While Kyle suffered through bouts of deep depression, he often stayed in bed for days. Nothing I said could coax him out of bed. It hurt to see him so miserable. When the depression lifted a little, Kyle would be constantly on the go. It was almost as if there weren't enough hours in the day for him to do all he wanted.

I had never told Mary Jo about Kyle's depression. So what she told me in May of 1998 made complete sense and gives me added confirmation concerning his happiness. But I still wanted something tangible. Something to prove his existence.

2

Animal Sign Language

I never remember Kyle's not being interested in animals. He loved to hunt and fish. But it was much more than that. He always had pets. He had dogs that had many litters of puppies. He had cats, gerbils and hamsters. He and his daddy spent many hours trying to trap pigeons down by the Mississippi River levee.

On Kyle's eleventh birthday we bought him a pair of homing pigeons. Jim had built a very large, wire cage. The pair had babies and Jim let the adults loose so they could fly, thinking they would stay close to their young and return. What did Jim know about pigeons? Apparently not much. We had to cancel two short vacations that summer, and we became very adept at feeding baby pigeons through an eyedropper.

We lived a couple of streets from a ditch and about six blocks from Dawson's Creek. I don't think a day went by, weather permitting, that Kyle did not come home from school, change into his "ditch" clothes and boots, and bring home turtles, frogs or snakes. At one time, we had three snakes roaming around in our house. He had put them in an aquarium in his room and somehow the wire top came off. Needless to say, I wasn't very comfortable trying to sleep. Four days later, we found the last one curled up beneath my vacuum cleaner.

One time Kyle put a rather large salt and pepper king snake on the chain of our light fixture hanging in the den. We had to wait quite a few hours until the snake writhed from the chains. Often, on family outings, he would wander off and come back with a snake wrapped up in his T-shirt.

Kyle set a cage trap down by the creek and checked it daily. He always let the animal go. I guess it was a "boy" thing, seeing what he could catch. One time he brought home a possum and since it was late, he put it in a large cage in the backyard. He let it go early the next morning after realizing its pouch was full of baby possums. Even the Easter Bunny knew of Kyle's craze for animals. He didn't get Easter baskets. He got minnow buckets with grass and candy in them. And his love for animals never left him. In his apartment at college, he had a pet pig and an iguana. Then just one week before Kyle's death, while walking on property we had bought for him, he said, "Wait!" and quickly snatched up a small snake slithering by.

I've mentioned his love for animals for a particular reason. It is because I was told by Mary Jo during the reading that our loved ones on the Other Side could communicate with us through signs. She told me to look for odd birds and animals where they aren't usually seen and for birds hitting windows.

Our son was a baby when we brought him to our present home, and never during that time until his death did we see a crow, owl, raccoon or possum in our backyard unless Kyle brought it home. Granted, birds have hit my windows in the past, but only after his death did the birds hit the windows at specific times. Once, I asked God to help me get out of bed and into the shower because I was so overcome with grief. I did manage to shower but began sobbing while in there.

Just then, a bird hit the small window in the bathroom so hard I stopped crying, got out of the shower and went to see if the bird were injured. There were only a few scattered feathers on the ground, but the bird had flown away.

On another occasion, my daughter's friend, Wendi Haydel, and I were discussing Kyle's funeral. She told me during the funeral she knew Kyle was not in the casket. She heard him through some sort of telepathy saying, "I'm okay, I'm not in there." She heard that the entire time she was walking out of the funeral and even when she was getting into her car. When she first told me that, I was unaware of being able to communicate with him, so I assumed she was trying to comfort me in some way. But after my reading with Mary Jo, I asked Wendi about it again. She told me it was real and it did happen. I became emotional and began to cry. Suddenly, a bird hit the middle of the large kitchen window right where we were standing. Both of us were startled, looked at each other and agreed it was a confirmation from Kyle.

Kyle and his father often went crow hunting. One Christmas, Kyle received audio tapes of an owl and crow fight and also decoy crows. He and his dad would drive miles out into the country, open the truck doors and play the tape loudly over the speakers. They waited for hours with their fake crows to see if any live crows would show up. This appeared rather senseless to me, but then again, what did I know? They never shot any crows, just wanted to see them, I guess.

On June 28, 1996, the day after Mary Jo had told me to look for birds as a sign from Kyle, three crows flew to our large water oak tree, sat on the branches, and cawed over and over.

I ran out the back door and said, "Kyle, I know you are here. Stay here until I go and get the camera."

I took three pictures of the crows. They would fly off for a few seconds, then land on another branch. All the while, I kept talking to Kyle. I guess I know now why we had previously installed a high wooden fence around our backyard. Maybe subconsciously, on a soul level, I knew I would need some sort of shield to protect me from neighbors who might think me a little crazy for talking to crows.

Actually, this was not our first sighting of crows. A few weeks after Kyle's death, two crows were on our driveway, and Jim commented, "I think Kyle's here." At that time, we hadn't received Mary Jo's message, so I wasn't quite a believer.

By the time I saw the three crows, I was much more receptive to his message. Remember, we had never seen a crow in our backyard in over twenty-five years. That was why it meant so much to us.

Looking back, I think our being aware of accepting signs from Kyle actually escalated their appearances. I admit I sometimes go a little overboard in looking for signs, but I soon realized that wishing and hoping for them did not make them happen. Every sign we have received has been spontaneous and has caught us off guard.

Once, upon returning from a visit to family in Arkansas, we rounded our driveway and spotted two crows sitting in our dry birdbath. We had been gone for over a week, and no one had fed any birds during that time. So we thanked Kyle for welcoming us home.

Another crow sighting happened the following year when Jim and I checked into the Charles Hotel in Boston. We were unpacking our clothes in our ninth floor corner room that overlooked Harvard Square. It was a beautiful day, and we were looking forward to the wedding festivities of our daughter's sister-in-law, Lisa. This trip was very emotional for us because Kyle had been to Boston with us when Jamie, our daughter, had gotten married.

I was thinking of Kyle as I unpacked, and suddenly I heard, "Caw, caw, caw." I couldn't believe my eyes when I saw a crow perched on the railing outside our large plate glass window on the ninth floor. The crow just sat there and kept cawing endlessly. I grabbed my camera and began taking pictures of it. Jim asked me if I thought I'd taken enough pictures, but I just kept clicking away. I walked right up to the window and the crow still didn't fly away. I wish I would have timed how long it sat there cawing.

Both of us knew it was Kyle's doing. I knew he was letting us know he was with us.

It had been a little over a year after Kyle's death when I received a phone call from one of Kyle's girlfriends, DeDee. It was May 27, 1997, and DeDee was on a short vacation in Cancun. She'd looked forward to this getaway trip, but she was still grieving deeply. She was getting ready for an early evening social gathering that was going to be held out on the lawn overlooking the beautiful Caribbean waters. Though she tried to focus on the moment, she told me her mind kept wandering to thoughts of Kyle and what might have been.

DeDee said she was standing near the large banquet style table that was beautifully set with fragrant flowers and a spread of food that would definitely break anyone's diet. As she was biting into an hors d'oeuvre, she heard a fluttering. A large black crow landed right in front of her and was standing on the tablecloth. She immediately thought of Kyle and laughed at his impromptu appearance. It comforted her greatly. She phoned me to share that Kyle was in Cancun with her.

When Jamie returned home for a visit in June of 1996 to help us go through Kyle's things, more signs began appearing. One day while out in the carport, I heard a strange noise. I couldn't figure out what it was. I followed the sound to a garbage can placed out in the open in the carport. A very large possum was in the bottom of the can. I couldn't figure out how it got in there without tipping it over. The can was not placed next to anything that would have enabled the creature to jump or crawl in it. I was so excited and once again, ran for my camera. I shouted for Jamie and Jim to come and see. I knew it was another sign from Kyle. Because we live on an eighty-foot lot in an established subdivision with houses all around, seeing a possum was a rarity.

The remarkable thing is that two weeks later, Jill came for a visit and the day she arrived, I again heard a noise in the carport. This time there were two possums in the garbage can. I thanked Kyle and ran for my camera again. In reflection, I suppose the photo developers must have wondered about me with all the strange pictures I've taken in the last three years.

Eventually, Kyle brought another creature to our attention. This time it was an owl. It was very early in the wee hours of the morning on October 21, 1996. For some reason, both Jim and I were awake when we heard the owl hooting for the first time. Two nights later, we heard hooting again.

Remember, Kyle used to play crow and owl fighting tapes in hopes of enticing these feathered enemies. Before Kyle's death, no one in our family had heard or seen these animals in our yard. I definitely would have remembered if we had, and I would have told Kyle there was no need for him to drive miles away. He could just play the tapes in our driveway.

As I mentioned, Mary Jo had told me to look for signs from him, for unusual birds that we usually didn't see. She later reaffirmed to me that, yes, these were signs from Kyle.

In October, 1996, while visiting Lance Alworth, a friend and former All-Pro football player in Del Mar, California, we received another sign. We had spent the evening at

Lance and Laura's house, and they had driven us back to our room at the condominium style motel we had rented for the night. I had gotten out of the car and was talking with Laura through the rolled down window. Lance and Jim were standing outside the back of the car, also talking.

Laura said, in the middle of a sentence, "Look who is waiting for you at your door. A possum."

Immediately, I turned to look, called to Jim, and we both shook our heads and walked toward it. The possum was right at our doorstep and kept walking in circles. I didn't seem to scare it when I walked up to it. It kept walking around my feet.

Jim blurted out, "You better look out! It might bite you."

Of course, Laura and Lance didn't have any idea about what was going on. They'll only know why we were excited to see a possum if they read this book. At that time we had only told about our experiences to people who we knew believed in the possibility of signs from dead loved ones.

Later, we learned that possums were not common in the area where we stayed. Jill, our daughter, lived in Long Beach for two years and never once saw one.

Since DeDee is very aware of after-death communication, however, I could confide in her about the possums. She said once while working in a downtown Dallas office building, she heard a secretary scream. DeDee and everyone near looked to see what had happened. Standing directly outside the plate glass window, in downtown Dallas in the middle of the day, was a possum. No one could figure out what it was doing there. DeDee knew. She immediately called me.

While visiting Kyle's son, Cain, in Conway, Arkansas, after Kyle's death, another strange, but comforting incident happened. Cain and I were alone in his house, and I was feeding him breakfast as we sat at the bar in the kitchen. Across the large room, the television was on. We were talking about his friends at school, when suddenly Cain said, "I like possums." Then he returned to our discussion about his friends. It didn't make any sense to me why he said that. I asked him about it and whether or not he'd seen a possum on the television. He said no.

Right then I felt Kyle's presence letting me know he was aware I was with his son. I don't understand how it works, but I believe, somehow, Kyle got Cain to make that statement because it was irrelevant to what we were discussing. It was strange, to say the least.

While I don't share many of my thoughts and occurrences of signs from Kyle with Kyle's ex-wife, Angela, Cain, or her family for fear of their thinking me to be some sort of wacko, I did tell her about finding the possums in the garbage can. She then told me before she and Kyle were married, he called her around midnight one night and woke her up because he wanted to show her something. He wouldn't tell her what it was. Since they lived near one another, he wanted her to come downstairs and meet him outside. After much persuasion, she finally agreed to his coming over but asked him to be quiet so as not to wake anyone.

What did he want her to see? A possum in the bottom of his laundry basket.

Then still another animal began making its appearance. One night while looking through our glass windows onto our patio, I yelled to Jim, "There's a raccoon!" That was the beginning of hundreds of 18 lb. bags of Meow Mix, cooked chicken, Cheetos, marshmallows, and peanut butter and jelly sandwiches I gave them. Yes, raccoons love all of these. For the past two years, not a night has gone by that the food bowls haven't been emptied by the morning.

On one evening, I spotted a raccoon rounding the corner of the carport, and it walked right up to our glass back door. It was followed by raccoon number two, then number three, four, five and six. I yelled to Jim. We couldn't believe what we saw.

Let me remind you, we live in a very populated neighborhood. Our neighbors even own a big dog. I was so excited! I bought a perpetual feeder and got up enough nerve to ask our neighbors to replace the water when we were out of town.

One day I spotted another possum. This one was not in the garbage can. It was walking in our backyard. I quickly ran into the house, put some Meow Mix in a bowl and for some reason made a sign that read, "Welcome Raccoon and Possum." I stuck the eight-by-ten inch sign in the bowl, curving it so it would stay put. I went inside the house and within five minutes I looked back outside and could not believe my eyes. A large raccoon and a large possum were eating out of the same bowl and at the same time! I yelled to Jim, and he just shook his head. Granted, how many normal people make signs for possums and raccoons, but then again, something or someone made me do it.

Before Kyle's death, neither Jim nor I had ever seen a black squirrel on our property. Mind you, we have always had numerous gray squirrels and they can become a nuisance. They really have a voracious appetite. Even with the neighbor's pecan trees and all the sunflower seeds I've put in the many bird feeders we have, they still eat the metal off the vents on our roof. We've never killed any but have trapped a few and released them in the nearby woods. I used to get upset with Kyle because he'd put sunflower seeds on the kitchen windowsill and open the window, then put more seeds on the kitchen table. A squirrel never got loose in the house, at least not that I know of, but they did eat off my kitchen table.

A year after Kyle's death, both Jim and I were in the den. We had remodeled before Kyle's death, and the large plate glass window now went to the floor. We had always spent a lot of time looking out the window and into the backyard. Because of Kyle's ability to bring us so many signs, we spend even more time now enjoying the outside view, hoping he'll let us know he's around.

Once we were looking at the scenery when Jim exclaimed, "Look! A black squirrel. It's going into our carport."

I got a glimpse of the bushy black tail and jumped up to get the camera. Upon returning, my subject had vanished. Jim then told me about the time he and Kyle were deer hunting.

They had both been sitting on different deer stands. After getting off their stands, Jim told Kyle he had seen six black squirrels. Then Kyle commented he could top that. He'd counted eight black squirrels. This was the only time either had seen black squirrels while hunting.

What made them both see them and count them? Who knows?

One thing I've learned these past four years is there are no coincidences. Everything happens for a reason. God gives us many gifts or messages throughout our lives, but we don't always understand them until much later.

It was May 18, 1997. It was also Jim's birthday, his first birthday after we had become aware of Kyle's ability to communicate with us from his new home. I was silently wondering whether Kyle would do something for his father. I didn't want to say anything to Jim but hoped that Kyle would affirm his father in some way.

While walking through the den, I looked outside. Standing directly in the center of the hot concrete driveway were two wood ducks. What two wood ducks were doing during the middle of a hot, muggy day in our backyard may have been a mystery to someone else but not to me. Kyle was letting Jim know he was with him on his birthday. No one in our family and none of our neighbors have ever seen any ducks in our subdivision in over twenty-six years. I'm sure the wood ducks weren't too happy with Kyle, getting burnt feet most likely, for the length of time Kyle made them stand there to get our attention. Needless to say, Jim was deeply touched.

It is my ritual on Saturdays to hit garage sales very early in the morning. It was April 8, 2000, and I embarked on my "hunting" trip with much anticipation. I'd already hit about ten sales, and I was headed toward the next address on my list when I decided to make a detour. I drove by my house to see if Jim had heard the alarm that morning.

Looking down the side of our property from the street, I noticed the truck was gone. I turned into the driveway anyhow and drove to the back of the house. I was startled when I spotted two wood ducks standing where I had seen them nearly three years before on Jim's birthday in 1997. I knew Kyle had sent them as a present for his father back then, but I couldn't imagine what they were doing there now. April 8th had no special meaning to me. Why was Kyle giving me this sign, I wondered?

I got out of the car, said a few words to the ducks and asked Kyle, "Why did you bring them?" Walking into the boat port in search of the bag of Jim's deer corn, I didn't seem to scare them. They waddled into the carport and walked around in circles. They banged into the garbage cans, making a loud noise, and then they flew off, passing directly over my head.

I immediately phoned Jim and told him about the ducks. "Why would Kyle have brought them?" Jim responded he didn't have any idea. I told him there had to be a reason, but I couldn't figure it out.

Later, while standing at the kitchen counter chopping vegetables for a salad, I kept thinking about the ducks. Why did Kyle bring them? The question would not leave my mind.

About two hours later it finally registered. I *knew* why Kyle had brought the ducks. I could not believe it. April 8th was our wedding anniversary! Jim and I had not forgotten our anniversary in thirty-nine years, but we had both forgotten it this year. But Kyle didn't forget. And was I ever excited. I phoned Jim. "Happy Anniversary," I said.

"Who's this?" Jim questioned.

"It's me, your wife. Now I know why Kyle brought the ducks. Can you believe it?"

Jim and I have absolutely no doubt our son was responsible for reminding us of our wedding anniversary. And because of Kyle's escapade, I didn't spend that evening on the couch. Jim took me out to celebrate a day that will always be special, in more ways than one.

To me, this story is solid verification that our loved ones on the Other Side know *everything* that is going on, just as the next account verifies.

For the first three years after Kyle's death, Jim and I attended a Christmas Memorial Service at a local church. After the names of the children of The Compassionate Friends members were read, those in attendance would light a candle in memory of their child who had died. Kyle even acknowledged our doing this during a reading that I had with the world-renowned medium, John Edward, in New York. "He thanks you for lighting a candle in his memory," were John's exact words.

This past Christmas, things were different, though. Instead of having a memorial service at the church, a memorial service was scheduled during The Compassionate Friends meeting at the local library. December 12, 1999, was designated as the date of the second annual "National Memorial Children's Day." People around the world were asked to light a candle at 7:00 p.m. wherever they live, so candles would be lit somewhere in the world for twenty-four hours in memory of children who had died.

At first, I had planned on attending the ceremony at the library. But it was a rainy night, and I decided to stay at home with Jim, and we would both light a candle in Kyle's memory. I got two candles, placed them on a saucer and put them on the coffee table. Jim and I both lit a candle. Then I got a little carried away. I started lighting other candles, even those in the bathrooms. After I had lit thirteen candles, Jim said, "What are you doing?"

"Lighting one for each of Kyle's girlfriends," I answered.

I turned off the kitchen lights and sat down in a chair at the kitchen table. I was in a melancholy mood, thinking about Kyle and wondering what he must think of all the candles I had just lit. Before Kyle died, I had never lit a candle in our house except for those on a birthday cake. I had plenty of candles around, but they were for decoration. I remember once Kyle lit a candle in his bedroom, and I got upset with him, telling him he might burn the house down.

That night, the large glass windows that encircle our eating area in the kitchen were reflecting some of the candles. While looking at their reflection, I noticed a nose poking against the window pane not more than two feet from where I was seated. A raccoon was looking at me.

Jim and I had never seen a raccoon on the side of the house. We have always spotted them in the backyard or in our carport. There is a tall wooden fence surrounding the carport, so to get to the side of the house, the raccoon would have to go out of its way, around the fence.

I knew the raccoon's appearance was Kyle's letting me know he was aware of the candles.

At exactly 8:00 p.m., not one minute before nor one minute after, I heard a thud coming from the next room. It was the end of the candle lighting memorial. What was the thud I heard? A candle that was sitting on the top shelf of the bookcase in the den had fallen to the floor. I had not touched this candle in months, and I didn't attempt to light it because of its proximity to the ceiling. Why did it fall at exactly 8:00 p.m.? I believe it was Kyle's way of letting us know he was aware of what we were doing to honor him.

Since that time, I have read that those in the spirit world are drawn to the flames of candles and can easily see the candle light. So now I light candles all of the time and have become obsessed with burning them.

Bunny Purvis was the first person I met when I came to Baton Rouge for the very first time. Her husband, Scooter, was one of the assistant football coaches at L.S.U. when Jim accepted a coaching position there. Bunny greeted me when I walked into the airport terminal in 1965.

During our years together as coaches' wives, we had a lot of fun. What I remember most about Bunny was our traveling to bowl games and shopping for our kids. Her children, like mine, liked animals, and we were always hunting for something different and unique to bring home to them. Jeff, her son, had a boa constrictor that slept on the fireplace hearth.

Once, I sat on the front seat of the team bus, holding a stuffed iguana that I had just purchased in Juarez, Mexico, while we were at the Sun Bowl. Quite a few of the football players jumped when they boarded the bus and first saw it. Most of the other wives bought souvenirs that were more practical and likely still have them to this day.

But not me or Bunny. I always looked forward to getting home and giving Kyle the stuffed turtles, alligator, iguana and snakes.

Bunny and Scooter's youngest son, Jeff, died in an automobile accident nine years before Kyle's death. At that time, I had absolutely no concept of the grief they must have experienced. I remember watching them walk from

the gravesite and feeling so sorry for them. Bunny was rubbing Scooter's back trying to console him. It was painful to
watch. But no one can truly imagine the pain unless it is
through personal experience. Trust me, I know.

Bunny was one of the first to arrive at the hospital after
Kyle's accident. She will never know how much help she
was. I really don't know what I would have done without her.
She went with us to the funeral home, helped me write
the obituary, and helped with the funeral arrangements.
She even shopped for the cap for Kyle to wear, and she
brought Kyle's clothes that I had chosen for him to wear in
the casket. She gave me support during the time spent at
the viewing and during the funeral. I knew she understood
what I was experiencing.

Before Jeff's death, he had apparently forgotten to
order flowers for his mom for Mother's Day. At the very last
minute, he stopped and bought a rose bush and told Bunny
she would always have roses from him every year. This comment from Jeff eased his guilt. Little did Bunny know, at
that time, how special his rose bush would become to her. It
was the last Mother's Day that Jeff was alive.

While at the hospital, when we knew that Kyle had died,
Bunny handed me a pink rose bud. She told me the rose
bush had always bloomed around Mother's Day, and it
brought her a lot of consolation knowing it was from Jeff.
But that year for some reason the rose bush was late in
blooming. It had worried Bunny. She even asked Scooter if
he had fertilized the plant or done something different to it
that year. Scooter assured Bunny he hadn't done anything
different and the bush was waiting for something special to
happen, and then it would bloom.

With the rose bud in my hand, Bunny said the bush had
finally bloomed—the day of Kyle's death. There was only
one bud. Something very special had indeed happened.
She said she knew Jeff and Kyle were having a great time

together and have probably spent a lot of time with their snakes on the Other Side.

I freeze dried the pink rose bud. It is on the shelf with Kyle's ashes.

3

Kyle Stays in the Hearts of the Ladies

Kyle always seemed to have a way with girls. I must add, while writing this part, the tape deck came on all by itself and played, "I'll be seeing you in all familiar places." He always had a steady girlfriend from eighth grade on. He broke up with every girl he dated, breaking each girl's heart, or so I was told. I used to tell him one day someone would break his heart. That never happened.

Kyle gave his first jewelry gift when he was in the seventh grade. He had me buy a bracelet and have the girl's name, Maria, put on it. In the tenth grade, he dated a senior, Leigh Anne, for the entire year. He broke up with her when she went off to college, but I remember her coming home and seeing her at Kyle's high school football games. In his junior year, he dated another senior exclusively, Candi. Even though she married and had two children before Kyle's death, she was at the funeral home both days.

A few months later, I saw Candi with her husband and two children in a department store while shopping. She introduced me to her husband; then he wandered off with the children. Candi asked how I'd been doing and told me Kyle was often in her thoughts. She told me soon after Kyle's

funeral, she was driving on the interstate, sobbing because
his death tormented her so much. She said she asked Kyle
to give her a sign that he was okay. Just in that minute she
heard a loud horn honk, and an eighteen-wheeler passed
her with "Collier Industries" written on the side in large
letters. She had never seen a truck with that logo before. I
had no idea Candi was even aware of after-death communications. But she told me she had been to see Mary Jo many
times. Small world.

During Kyle's senior year, he went steady with Lauren,
a senior at St. Joseph's Academy in Baton Rouge. She
even went with us on a trip out of state when we checked
out various colleges for Kyle. Once she contacted him when
she was attending a college in another state, but Kyle had
apparently moved on.

I knew Kyle had a number of girl friends in high school.
Then when my husband and I attended his first college football game at Ouachita Baptist University in Arkadelphia,
Arkansas, I learned of his continued ability to charm the
girls. While we were signing in for "Parent's Day," a girl said,
"Oh! You're Kyle's parents. He dates my roommate, and
you should see the beautiful flowers he sent her."

Kyle could be serious with a girl, be with her exclusively,
and then abruptly end it. I remember when he dated Cindy
while in college, she drove all the way from Arkansas to Baton Rouge to be with him. He broke up with her while she
was at our house. I was concerned for her having to drive
eight hours back, because she left our house crying. She did
call me, though, to tell me she arrived home safely.

During the time that Kyle and Cindy were dating,
Cindy's fourteen-year-old brother, Andy, had gone riding
with Kyle on an all-terrain vehicle. Kyle always liked being
around children, which I think was because he himself was
always a kid at heart.

A few weeks after Kyle had been with Andy, Andy was killed while riding this vehicle. Apparently it flipped over, and one of the handle bars impacted Andy's young body. Kyle didn't talk to us about Andy's death, but I heard he was devastated. I know he attended the funeral.

During the reading with Mary Jo, she told me she saw Kyle with a fourteen-year-old. I immediately thought of Andy and was glad that Kyle was with someone he knew.

When Kyle died, my first thoughts were of heaven. I prayed there was a heaven and Kyle was there. But then I thought he wouldn't know anyone. Mary Jo's message that Andy and Kyle were together relieved me. She hadn't just told me he was with a younger person; she stressed fourteen years old.

Of course, over the past three years, I've become much more aware of the spiritual world. I know Kyle is with many souls he not only knows, but he enjoys being with. But, in the beginning, I was very concerned that he wouldn't know anyone and he would be lonely.

That is a common concern for many newly bereaved parents I've met. They not only want to know where their child is, but they also want to know whom they are with. Just like here on earth, we have to know where our children are, what they are doing, and the company they are keeping. That is exactly why parents seek mediums and psychics, hoping they can get an answer that will give them some sort of comfort.

Two of the girls Kyle dated while in college, Shelly Tate and DeDee McDonald, played a major role in his life, not only when he was here, but also now. They both speak of Kyle as the "love of my life." I have become very close to them.

Both DeDee and Shelly were devastated by Kyle's death. They came to his funeral and rode home with us in the back seat of our car the night of the visitation. I couldn't help but hear them saying, "Oh, he told you that, too." We sat up most of the night, sitting around the dining room table, talking and looking at pictures.

While at our house for the funeral, Shelly, DeDee, and Angela, his ex-wife, all asked me if they could go in Kyle's room, look through his closet and have one of his shirts. They did this separately, unaware of the other's wishes. Angela wanted the sweatshirt Kyle had bought on their honeymoon. DeDee and Shelly both wanted the shirt he had worn on their first date. Thank heavens, he wore a different shirt each time. I might have had a problem otherwise.

But their wanting his clothes touched me deeply then and does to this day. Knowing that Kyle was loved so much by others means a lot to me. I know he will always be in their hearts and in their prayers.

Six former girlfriends and his ex-wife were at the funeral. While I was standing next to the casket, Judy walked up to me and said something about Kyle's being so special. I said, "I know. Can you believe all his girlfriends are here?"

Judy then said, "You know I dated him for a while and I was also one of those girlfriends." She said it as if she were honored to be in that group. I had forgotten he had dated her.

By now you might think Kyle was girl crazy. In reality, he led a very full life. He participated in sports during high school and was on a football scholarship in college. He was active in a fraternity and always had many close male friends. Kyle seemed to get along with everyone. Never in my entire life did I hear him say anything bad about anyone. If he were confronted by someone or knew the situation might escalate beyond what he could handle, he walked away from it.

4

Strange Things Begin to Happen

On June 28, 1996, the day after my reading with Mary Jo, I went to Wal-Mart to buy a tape player to make copies of the tape I received of my reading. The tape Mary Jo had given me of Kyle's messages was invaluable to me. It was a connection to Kyle that I could not lose. I asked a salesman to help me. I wanted to get the best possible tape player and blank cassettes I could buy. I wanted to make sure this message from my son was not erased.

The salesman asked what I wanted to tape because of my concern that it had to be "perfect." I hesitated. Then I got up the gumption to say quickly that my son had died two months before, and I told him I had visited a psychic and wanted to make a copy of the tape I had received. It was very difficult for me to say that. I was embarrassed to tell a total stranger I had been to a psychic. But God manages to put people in our lives at the right time. The man didn't say anything.

Then I said, "I don't know if you believe in that or not."

The salesman responded quickly, "Oh, yes, I do. I'm psychic. I can dream of somebody like you coming in here. I can see what they're wearing, what they'll say, and the items they'll want. A couple of weeks later, that person will appear and do exactly what I dreamt."

I couldn't believe what I was hearing.

The man said he hadn't dreamt of me, but he had done it many, many other times. He told me he often shocked customers, handing them what they wanted to purchase before they could tell him. I asked him how long he had this psychic ability, and he said since he was five years old. He told me his dreams came true ninety-five percent of the time.

I had never seen this man before.

Upon my thanking him and starting to leave, he said, "Earth is just a training ground for eternity."

This astounded me. That man at Wal-Mart will never know how he made me feel. But then again, maybe he has dreamt it.

Later on, during the same day as the Wal-Mart episode, another strange thing happened. Jamie was due to arrive from Massachusetts. I was in Kyle's bedroom checking it out since Jamie would be sleeping there. I pulled out the bottom drawer of the built-in cabinet, and my eyes were drawn to an orange composition book. I opened it and saw it was Kyle's handwriting. The first two pages were of notes taken while he observed a student teacher at his college. It was the first time I'd seen or read his handwriting since he died, and I became very emotional. I put it back in the drawer and then drove to Albertsons' grocery store to get some food for Jamie's visit.

When I returned home and walked into the kitchen carrying my groceries, I was startled to see that same orange composition book lying on the counter by the phone. I picked it up, opened it, and noticed Kyle's handwritten notes were gone. I couldn't figure out what was going on. I actually even wondered if Kyle could have torn them out. I was on such a high from Mary Jo's reading I thought any-thing could be possible.

I was still wondering what could've happened when Jim returned home after picking up Jamie at the airport. When I queried him about the notebook, Jim told me he had gone into Kyle's room, opened the same drawer, found the book, read Kyle's notes, torn the two pages out, and put the pages with photographs of Kyle on the dining room table.

I had only been gone about an hour to the grocery store. In that time frame, Jim had come home from work, show-ered, dressed, and gone to the airport. What made us both look in the same drawer with all the commotion that was going on? I hadn't opened that drawer in months, and I don't know if Jim had ever opened it. I know he hasn't opened it since because I put a note in the drawer telling him to tell me he saw the note. He has commented as I write this book, over three years later, that he has never seen my note. Remember, there are no coincidences.

Three years after Kyle's death, Mary Jo McCabe called me one evening. She asked if Kyle had ever had a green and yellow parakeet. I wondered why she wanted to know. I told her I didn't think so, unless he had one when he was in college that I didn't know about. I told her I'd check and see. She told me he'd come to her and shown her a green and yellow parakeet. We talked a bit more, then hung up.

Since I'm an itinerant teacher, I travel from school to school throughout the day. The day following my phone conversation with Mary Jo, I had finished teaching my classes at one school and was driving to another school. I happened to drive down the street where Wendi's house was located. She's the friend who had heard Kyle's voice while at the funeral home telling her he wasn't in the casket.

I turned into Wendi's driveway. I had never been inside her house before, since I had just recently found out where she lived. She seemed surprised to see me. *I* was even surprised that I was there, having no idea why I had stopped. She invited me in, and I told her I could only stay a minute or two or I'd be late for my next class. I remarked how nice her house looked and asked her if I could take a quick "peek."

We entered the den and Wendi commented, "I feel like Kyle's here."

It was then I spotted a green parakeet sitting in the corner in a cage. Reminded of Mary Jo's call the previous night, I said, "Oh! You have a green parakeet!"

"Yes," Wendi said. "And there's a yellow one in the cage below."

I leaned down and couldn't believe my eyes. I told her about Mary Jo's call.

The next time I saw Mary Jo, I told her about Wendi's green and yellow parakeets. Mary Jo told me it was Kyle's way of letting me know he is aware of everything going on in my life.

5

Kyle Leaves a Forwarding Number

Anyone who knows me could easily decode the security system in our home. They would know to push 42-42 or something with the number 42 in it. If either Jim or I heat up something in the microwave, it's either for 42 seconds or 1 minute 42 seconds, or a similar number. Everything has to be 42. I even took a picture of my car odometer when it turned over to 42,000 miles.

Kyle's football jersey number was 42 throughout high school, at the high school all-star game, and throughout his four years of playing college ball. Jim had a gold pendant with the number 42 in diamonds made for me as a gift when Kyle was in high school. That pendant has meant much to me over the years and is often the beginning of a conversation. It is something I hold dear to my heart.

While I was attending a spiritual weekend in New Orleans, Jim received a sign from Kyle. Jim was in the kitchen preparing to cook chicken on the grill. All of a sudden, he heard a noise coming from the den. When he looked through the opening between the two rooms, he was amazed to see the TV had come on all by itself and it was on channel 42. Jim never watched channel 42. The remote to the TV was in the den, and there was no reason for the television to have popped on, other that Kyle's letting Jim know he was there.

A college friend of Kyle's, Bobby, had called me one day from his home in Arkadelphia, Arkansas. He said he had been in his kitchen, and his roommate yelled to him and asked whether or not he had paid the cable bill. Bobby asked why, and his roommate replied, "Well, the TV is all snowy and number 42 is flashing in the middle of the screen."

Bobby looked and saw the number 42 on the television. He knew it was Kyle's doing, but he didn't say anything for fear his roommate might think he was crazy. Also, Bobby might have had trouble finding another roommate.

I was visiting my daughter in the state of Washington two years after Kyle's death. When we approached Jill's car parked in the airport garage, I remarked, "Oh, you parked in number 420." She hadn't been aware of the space at the time. She knows my obsession with the number 42, so she just smiled.

Later on that week, my son-in-law, Bob, was coordinating a baseball tournament in their hometown of Anacortes, Washington. The family and I had driven up to Bellingham, Washington, to pick up boxes of game baseballs at a sporting goods store. Bob drove up to the curb, parked the van, and we were going to wait while he went inside. I sat in the parked van a few minutes engaged in conversation with Jill, when I happened to look up at the outside front of the building. I was dumbfounded to see a red number 42, at least two and a half feet tall painted on the white brick. I couldn't imagine why it was there. It wasn't the address. That was a four-digit number. There was no reason for it to be there. It even looked out of place.

I immediately got out of the van. I had to find out why it was there. My son-in-law was surprised to see me. I asked to speak to the owner of the store. When I asked him why the number 42 was on the outside, he acted as if he didn't know what I was talking about. He then walked outside with me. I looked up at the 42 and pointed it out to him, and he shook his head. He said he didn't have any idea why it was there and as a matter of fact had never noticed it before. This was a very large, bright red number 42 painted on white brick. And the owner of the building had never noticed it before? That is one of the times, among many, that I wished I'd had a camera.

People who were close to Kyle are very aware of the 42 phenomena. His former girlfriend, Shelly, told me she always sees the number 42. She travels a lot and it always pops up. While making airplane reservations, she was surprised when she learned she was booked on Flight 42. After boarding, she glanced at her ticket and located seat 42A. When she arrived at her hotel she was given room 242. Once she met a business associate for the first time and after spending the day together, she felt connected enough to open up to this person. She spoke about Kyle and even mentioned the number 42. The next day when they both went to order a meal, Shelly looked at her ticket number and showed it to her new friend. It was number 42.

Shelly had been looking through an old family album while visiting her grandmother. She was jolted when she came across a photograph of a gravestone. The date of the death on the tombstone was April 27th, the date of Kyle's death. When she turned the page, the photograph fell from the book onto the floor. She picked it up and noticed there was writing on the back of the picture. What was written? The number 42. Nothing else. She asked her grandmother what the number meant. Her grandmother didn't know.

Shelly knew. The next page in the album included a picture of a group of people. They were all wearing Ouachita Baptist University shirts. Kyle graduated from Ouachita Baptist University as did Shelly's grandmother.

Shelly knew these pictures were not a coincidence. She was so excited when she phoned me to share what had happened. Later, when I questioned Mary Jo about Shelly's experience, Mary Jo told me Kyle was indeed communicating with Shelly, letting her know he was around.

Another of Kyle's former girlfriends, DeDee, is also comforted by this number. While eating with her boyfriend in Houston, they each ordered a light lunch of soup and a sandwich. They enjoyed their meal, but when Toby received the bill, he was puzzled.

"There must be some mistake," he told DeDee. "The bill should be under twenty dollars."

DeDee grabbed the bill from his hand. She couldn't help but smile when she saw what they were being charged —an even $42.00.

Right before Kyle's accident, Jim and I had gone to the airport to pick up our fourteen-year-old granddaughter, Jaclyn. After picking her up, we passed Kyle in his own car. When I pointed him out to her, she remarked, "He'll probably be in an accident." She does not know why she said that, and it haunts her to this day.

Since then, Kyle has come to her in her dreams. He is in the casket, but he sits up, smiles, and says he is okay. This comforts her.

One day Jaclyn called me, all excited. She left a message on my answering machine. She said she was sitting on the sofa, about fifteen feet from the fireplace. Seven picture frames that held family pictures were on the mantel. All at once, for no apparent reason, all the picture frames fell off except the frame that held Kyle's picture. She thought it was very weird, and she told me she knew Kyle did it. She said even though all the others fell to the floor, none of them were broken.

Two years after Kyle's death, Jaclyn was visiting us. We were shopping at the local mall and having grandma-granddaughter quality time. We were at the check-out counter at the Gap store, and I was getting my wallet out of my purse.

"Look, Grandma. All of these caps have number 42 on them."

Sure enough, there was a wide array of different colored caps all with the number 42 on them. The clerk probably wondered why I bought so many.

Since I am an itinerant school teacher, each school year I'm assigned different schools. This past year I didn't teach at Howell Park Elementary, even though I taught there the previous year. Near the end of the year I was in north Baton Rouge. Jamie and her friend, Angela, had flown in from Boston the day before. I had many errands to run. I had to go to the grocery store, the post office, and pick up some cleaning. It was hot and I was tired.

Don't ask me why I did it, but I drove to Howell Park for the first time in eleven months. I had no reason to be going there. I remember I even thought to myself, why am I doing this?

I drove into the circular driveway in front of the school and parked behind the only other car that was there. It was a white Lincoln Towncar. I looked at the license plate. I couldn't believe what I saw. Number 42! Just plain 42, nothing else. This was another time I wished I'd had my camera.

I walked inside the school building, still not having a clue as to why I was there. I spotted the secretary. She looked surprised to see me. We talked for a little while, and then I walked outside toward my car. Another car had pulled up behind mine. It was a white 1988 Nissan Maxima, identical to the car I had bought for Kyle when he went away to college. I walked to the back of the car to check its license plate. I guess it would have been too overwhelming if it had been 142.

Sometimes we do things and wonder why we do it. I truly believe all of us need to listen to our intuition or inner being more often. I believe all of us have many guides, angels, and loved ones around us. There are many spiritual beings who are always with us, helping us throughout our lives. So many times when something wonderful happens, we think, "Boy, was I lucky." In reality, it was planned for us. For example, after returning home from a presentation by John Edward in New Orleans, I checked my answering machine. I had 42 messages.

I can't begin to tell you how many times I wake up during the night and look at the clock. It is 11:42, 3:42, or some hour with a 42 behind it.

You might say that it is only coincidence. Sometimes I catch myself thinking maybe that's so. But upon deep reflection, too many unusual occurrences have happened. Some with the number 42 are so strange that one cannot help but believe. John Edward and Mary Jo have told me many times there are no coincidences. Everything has a reason behind it. God is perfect.

6

Playing Games with Kyle

Bennie Payne, a casual acquaintance, called me two and a half months after Kyle's death. She and her husband own a successful business in town. We met through a business club of which both her husband and my husband are members. There is a weekly breakfast meeting for club members, and Jerry and Jim see each other every Thursday morning. Over the years we've sat at the same table at Christmas parties and other events, but I've never been to their house, nor they to mine. They are die-hard LSU fans, so I guess that was the initial thrust that put us together.

When Bennie called, she asked how I was doing. I cried and told her is was so difficult. She said many things that brought me comfort. She talked about how close she had been to her grandfather, what a wonderful person he was, and how sick, paralyzed and bedridden he'd become before his death. She said one night in a dream she saw herself sitting on the ground, knees pulled up to her chest and sobbing uncontrollably. She then heard someone from behind say, "Why are you crying?" and she replied her Paw-Paw had died. She then felt a tap on her shoulder and the voice again said, "Why are you crying, my darling?" and she again replied that her Paw-Paw died, and she continued crying. Then a hand touched her shoulder. She turned around and there stood her grandfather.

He said, "Bennie, be happy for me. I can walk and talk again. All my life I've worked for God to one day have this. Oh! If you could only see what I have." He looked completely real to her and perfectly healthy. He told her to be strong at the funeral because everyone would be looking to her for strength, since she had been the closest to him. She then told me she knew he was okay and was happy. She made it through the funeral without shedding a tear, knowing he was in a much better place.

Bennie told me other spiritual stories. Her daughter, Tisa, had been in a severe automobile accident in 1989. Because of the drastic damage to the vehicle and Tisa's condition, she should not have lived. A friend of Tisa's had died in an accident the year before. This girl had come to Bennie in a dream and told her she would be Tisa's guardian angel, and she would always protect her. Bennie knew she had done just that. Tisa is now happily married, and she moved back to Baton Rouge this summer. I saw her with her young son, Kyler, at a crawfish boil in the spring.

Bennie's call helped me greatly. It made me aware of the power of the spiritual world. But the best was yet to come.

The phone rang the next morning. I was lying in bed, having difficulty getting out of bed. I had prayed again, as I did every morning, that God would help me get up and get in the shower and He would help me get out of the shower. Then I got back in bed. I was in a fog. I didn't care to go on, much less do anything.

I was surprised to hear Bennie's voice again. She said she had to see me immediately; she had to tell me something. Of course, I thought it concerned Kyle, and I became excited. She said she'd come by my house, but since she was at work, I offered to meet her at her place of business instead.

When I walked into her office, she leaned over her desk, and grabbed both my hands. She told me when she went to bed the night before, she prayed to God if there were any way she could help me, Jim, or Kyle, to please help her do so.

She said she woke up around 1:30 a.m. and started receiving messages from Kyle. She said she didn't see his body, but he was connecting to her through some sort of telepathy. She said he talked on and on for at least three hours. She showed me notebook paper with notes scribbled on them. There were pages and pages of them.

To this day, one thing that I deeply regret is I never took those pages. I guess I was too awestruck at the time. And over the months, for some reason, I never asked for them. Only this summer (1999) did I see Bennie in a store and ask her about the notes. She said just the week before, she had cleaned out her desk and had thrown them out. It bothers me that I don't have them, but there must be a reason why I never asked for them. Maybe there was something that would have upset me or I would have misunderstood. Who knows? Again, we can't change the past.

The first thing Kyle told Bennie to tell me was that he was very happy where he was. He said if given a choice, he would not come back. He said my grief was holding him here, and it would continue to hold him if I didn't let him go.

At the time she was telling me this, I had mixed emotions. It felt good to hear he was happy. Every parent wants to hear that. But the part about my keeping him here upset me. I thought, how does she know what I'm going through? She's never lost a child. What am I supposed to be feeling? Just say, "Goodbye, Kyle," and be over it? No way.

I told her I missed him so much. I did want him to be happy, but I couldn't help my grief. It had only been two months.

The next words stunned me. She said, "He wants you to quit kissing his ashes. He's not in there." I knew she knew we'd had Kyle cremated, but how did she know I *was* kissing his ashes every night?

Before the funeral, Shelly told us Kyle had told her when he died he didn't want to be buried under the ground. He said he didn't want bugs eating him. The discussion of how our children wanted to be buried had never come up with any of our children before Kyle's death. Rest assured, it has now, heaven forbid anything should happen. There are so many things we put out of our minds, so many thoughts and words that go unspoken throughout life. Many of you know what I am talking about.

Bennie continued, "Kyle is not happy with where you put his ashes. And in time you should release them."

Since those words, Mary Jo has told me numerous times Kyle wants his ashes put back in the earth, that his ashes are not what brings him to us. Our love is what keeps us connected.

John Edward, the well-known medium, told me he was devastated over the death of his mother from cancer at the age of forty-eight. He was an only child and was extremely close to his mother. I will never forget when he told me the only time he visited his mother's grave was the day she was buried. He said he knows she is not there; she lives on elsewhere.

Bennie said Kyle knew I thought the sun rose and set on him, but he wanted me to know he wasn't the entire sun. In reality, he was only a sunbeam, and I had many other beams: Jim, the girls, my grandchildren, and my students. He said I should focus my attention on them instead of focusing only on him. When I tend to become obsessed with thinking of him, I remember Bennie's words, and what Kyle wants me to do. This does help me.

"He wants you to listen to this song," Bennie began, as she looked through her notes, "'Seasons in the Sun.'" She added, "He wants you to get a message from him." She wrote the title on a piece of paper and handed it to me. After giving me a few more messages, Bennie stressed that Kyle was happier than we could ever imagine.

I immediately drove to Blockbuster's audio store to look for "Seasons in the Sun." I came home and put it in the CD player. I was getting ready to play a game of "Can you get the message?" with my dead son. But I could not believe what happened.

"Good-bye to you, it's hard to die," were the first words that I heard. I couldn't hear anything else, because I began sobbing so loudly.

After gaining some sort of composure, I started the CD again but had to turn it off again. Many attempts later, I was finally able to listen to it all the way through. Except for just a few words, the entire song fit Kyle to a "T." It could have been written by him. The part about the starfish in the sea even fit. When he was thirteen years old, he and I caught a starfish that was over one foot in diameter while at Puget Sound. We took many pictures of Kyle with his starfish.

I tried to understand the message Kyle wanted me to get. I thought I had figured out the answer, so I called Bennie and told her. She said what I said might be true, but it was not the message Kyle had intended for me. She said Kyle told her he didn't want her to tell me until I figured it out myself. So the game went on.

I can't describe the close connection I felt toward Kyle at this time. I felt as if this game really brought us closer and bonded us in some way. I called DeDee, Shelly, Jill, Jamie, and a few others I could confide in about the message from Kyle. I told them about "Seasons in the Sun" and asked if they could help me. I realize now I was cheating a little, asking others for the message that Kyle wanted *me* to get.

I did come up with the correct message by myself, though. I felt as if I had won the big contest when Bennie affirmed what Kyle wanted me to know.

Kyle's message was that he had lived his life as God had planned it. He said there was a time for everything, and he left the earth at the right time. His birth represented the spring of his life. His adolescence was summer. His maturity was autumn, and his clinical depression, which he suffered from for the last years of his life, was winter. The most important part of the message was he had completed what he came to do. He graduated. He told me I was in the fall of my life and I had not completed my work here and I had to go on.

Bennie shared with me later her gift of connecting to the spiritual world is something she has had most of her life. She said she's always considered it as a gift, and when she should know something, it is sent her way. She's never explored or tried in any way to enhance this special gift of hers and has never used it for anyone other than family members. Bennie's grandmother also had this ability.

This was the first and only time Bennie had ever actually asked for the gift. She prayed that God would let her help Jim and me because, "I came so close to losing Tisa, I almost knew how you felt."

I've often read that it's not the quantity of life that is important. It's the quality of one's life. It's possible for an eighteen-year-old to live more fully and touch more lives than a person who has lived to his eighties. That in itself brings some consolation. What comforts me most, though, is knowing there are no accidents or victims. Knowing that nothing we could have said or done would have changed the outcome helps me to accept Kyle's death to some degree. I'm certain when I die and reach the Other Side, and can see the whole picture, I'll understand completely why things happened throughout my life on earth.

Another unusual happening occurred one September evening. "I don't know why, but Kyle locked all the car doors," Jim said, as he entered the house. He had been working with other deer club members, demolishing an old house to get wood and materials to use at the deer camp.

Jim had gone directly to the demolition site after a day's work at our muffler shop. He had left the day's receipts, along with his car keys, on the front seat of his Honda Accord. Without thinking, he left the doors unlocked and helped with the demolition.

After a few hours, he offered to drive to a nearby convenience store to get some iced drinks. When he approached the car, he heard a click, and the front door lock went down. He then heard in sequential order another click, click, click. All the doors locked with his keys still sitting on the front seat.

Jim called to the guys. They came over and couldn't believe it. Now, mind you, this vehicle does not have any electrical locks and the only way you can lock the doors is with the key unless you are in the car.

Jim had one of the guys drive him back to the muffler shop so he could pick up the truck he always kept there to run errands and pick up parts during the work day. He drove the truck home. It was about nine o'clock at night when he got home and told me Kyle had locked all the car doors.

We immediately got another set of keys and drove back to the demolition site to get our locked car. I remember very vividly Jim's saying over and over, "Why did Kyle do that?"

When we reached the car, I unlocked the car door, got in and followed Jim to our business, so we could park the truck back there. As soon as we arrived at the muffler shop, we *knew* why Kyle did it.

Jim caught his manager "moonlighting" on a vehicle without his knowledge or permission. The manager was shocked to see us drive up at 9:45 at night, especially since we live on the other side of the city.

Kyle used to work at the muffler shop during the summers, and sometimes he would tell Jim if someone pocketed a few bucks here or there. Nothing big, but Kyle was concerned. Even in death, he was continuing to look out for his father. We have never doubted he locked the car so we could find out what was happening after hours; there is no other explanation.

7

Gloria Gets a New Pair of Shoes

After Kyle's death, it was a struggle to do anything. Many people phoned, encouraging me to go out with them, but it was too difficult.

Sherry, Gloria, and Evelyn taught school with me years ago, and we had managed to keep in touch. We'd meet over the summer months for lunch and try to catch up on all the news and gossip over the past year. On July 8, 1996, they coaxed me into meeting them at Mike Anderson's Seafood Restaurant. I was apprehensive about going, but they convinced me it would do me good.

We spent over three hours talking. Not about what had happened over the year, but about Kyle, Mary Jo, and after-death communication. They must have been intrigued because when I'd say, "Enough about Kyle, tell me about your families," they kept encouraging me to continue. This was eleven days after Mary Jo's reading.

Gloria Ballard told me an ex-boyfriend's father had a heart attack while at a camp. He was airlifted to a hospital and survived. He had a near-death experience (NDE). This boyfriend's mother told Gloria she got tired of her husband's continually talking about how beautiful and wonderful it is when you die. To this day, he tells everyone he wants to go back.

While at lunch, Gloria commented on how much she liked the shoes I was wearing. She even asked where I bought them. That night she called me, asking who else might carry them, because she couldn't find any. The next day she phoned again saying she looked everywhere in Baton Rouge and still couldn't find the shoes. I told her I would be going to Arkansas in a few weeks and I'd look for them there. She seemed obsessed with getting a pair, and told me she needed a size 8.

While blow drying my hair the next morning, I was thinking about the shoes. Suddenly, I remembered when I bought my size 8 ½ shoes months before, I had also bought a size 8 as well. Don't ask me why I would do such a thing, because at that time I didn't know anyone who wore that size. I looked in my closet, and there on the top shelf was the pair of shoes Gloria wanted in a size 8. I was so excited. I called her immediately and told her I was on my way to bring them to her.

After getting directions, I arrived in the town of Zachary, which is ten miles north of Baton Rouge. Gloria greeted me with a hug, put the shoes on, and we went inside her house. She introduced me to her two sisters who were sitting in the living room.

We spent hours talking about death and what we thought heaven was like. One of the sisters told me about her father-in-law who also had a NDE. She told me he would often go outside at night and cry because the afterlife was so beautiful, he wanted to go back.

On the drive home, I stopped at a Bible bookstore in Zachary. The lady who waited on me told me her brother was twenty-five years old when he died from cancer. We engaged in a very interesting conversation.

When I arrived home, Jim called me from work. He told me Rev. Larry Stockstill, senior pastor of the Bethany World Prayer Center, had been by his shop to get his car fixed. Jim and his workers immediately recognized Rev. Stockstill because of his television show which is broadcast each morning. Jim told Rev. Stockstill about Kyle, and while doing so he broke down and cried. Reverend Stockstill prayed for Jim and comforted him. He even phoned his secretary while at the shop and asked her to mail a book to me. I received *Intramuros: My Dream of Heaven*, by Rebecca R. Springer, in the mail the following day. It's a wonderful book. Reverend Stockstill mentioned Jim and Kyle during two of his radio shows that were broadcast after Jim's meeting him.

So, within three days, I was helped by many people who had shared their stories with me. The book that Rev. Stockstill sent me has been read by many grieving parents. And Gloria got a new pair of shoes.

Then DeDee called me from Dallas on July 12, 1996. I had last spoken with her on the 27th of June, the day of my reading with Mary Jo. DeDee spent the fourth of July supervising a number of children at an outing to watch a fireworks display. She was sitting on the grass, surrounded by many children and adults. All of a sudden, she smelled Perry Ellis cologne. She told me it was very potent. She even asked those around her if anyone had on that fragrance. When everyone said no, she knew Kyle was there.

Kyle only wore Perry Ellis. He even used Perry Ellis deodorant. I'd get a call from the local department store when a new shipment would come in. Apparently, I was their number one customer. Three years after his death, I still have four bottles of Perry Ellis in the bathroom cabinet. I really don't know why I have kept them. I've been able to get rid of most of his things, but somehow his fragrance is special.

DeDee has smelled Kyle's cologne other times since that first time. She immediately knows he is there. I feel so fortunate that DeDee and others are open to spiritual communication. Their sharing experiences with me is something for which I will forever be grateful.

A few weeks after Kyle's death, I received another phone call. "You don't know me, but I was a friend of Kyle's," is how Bobby Schultz greeted me when I picked up the phone. Bobby wanted my address. He wanted to send me something that Kyle had given him. Kyle had given it to Bobby when Bobby's grandfather had died. Bobby said for some reason, he kept the original box the gift came in. He said he never saves boxes, so it must have been meant for him to send it to me.

A couple of days later, I received a very sweet note and a framed "One Set of Footprints." It touched me deeply, and I have it hanging in my den.

This gift from Bobby let me know a side of Kyle that I was unaware of. After his death, I found out that Kyle attended three funerals in Arkansas, and that he was such a support and comfort to those who were grieving. People told me he was truly spiritual at these times. I also heard from college professors who shared with me how much Kyle had meant to them.

I realize this happens often when someone dies. All the good memories of this special soul rise to the top, and while we are comforted by the words, it makes us realize what a special person we have lost.

Since Kyle's death, Bobby has felt Kyle's presence in many ways. We have become very close these past three years. One time Bobby called and told me he bought a new car. He was excited because it had all kinds of gadgets on it, even electrical seats. Soon after he got it, while he was driving, the front seat moved back and forth. He knew he wasn't pushing any buttons. He commented to Kyle he knew he was doing it, but he drove it back to the dealership anyway. The salesman drove the car, with Bobby seated in the passenger seat, and all was fine. The salesman didn't see a problem. Then Bobby asked to let him drive. They changed places. The driver's seat began moving back and forth all by itself. Bobby's hands were on the steering wheel. The salesman couldn't figure it out, but Bobby knew the answer.

Bobby told me he often called Kyle, "Bubba." He told me they met when they were neighbors in an apartment complex in college. Kyle always played his stereo rather loudly. Bobby often heard the music, and one day they struck up a conversation. Though they were different in many ways, they had one thing in common that drew them together. Bobby also suffered from clinical depression. He told me they would drive for hours listening to music, and they frequently took long walks. He said they walked through a cemetery one evening, and Kyle told him, "I could stay here forever."

While in the cemetery, Bobby and Kyle had made a pact that whoever died first was to try and contact the other. Now, I want you to know these are two good-looking young men talking about their deaths. This, again, is a Kyle I did not know. Looking back, I have been so thankful for an awareness of this. I truly do believe on a soul level, Kyle was very spiritual and knew his time here was to be short.

This came to light another time. I used to worry about Kyle's many girl relationships and how he was always on the go and never still. Kyle gave me a message one time through Mary Jo that I will never forget. She told me he doesn't want you to think of him as being irresponsible. He knew he would be here for a short time, and he wanted to touch as many lives and do as much as possible. He succeeded in doing this.

Bobby and Kyle had gone their separate ways when the following incident happened. One day, Bobby was cutting grass at his home located on a wooded acreage just outside Arkadelphia, Arkansas. He still had Kyle's deer stand on his property. He said he kept thinking about Kyle even though he hadn't seen or heard from him in months. He'd take a break and get a glass of iced tea, but Kyle would not leave his thoughts. He drove to town later in the day with Kyle still on his mind. He even remarked to one of his friends, "I need to give Kyle a call. Something is going on." Something was going on.

The next morning, there was a write-up in the local Arkadelphia paper concerning Kyle's death in Louisiana. Bobby's friend read the paper. He drove to Bobby's house and told him, "You know how you kept talking about Kyle all day yesterday? Well, Kyle died."

Bobby couldn't believe it.

Later, Bobby's depression began getting the better of him. He had just ended a relationship, and he was torn apart by Kyle's death. His church minister was accompanying him to a treatment center in Hot Springs when Bobby said he got Kyle's sign from heaven.

The car radio was on. The disc jockey said, "I've had a request to play 'Desperado' by the Eagles from Bubba to Bobby." Bobby told me it was their favorite song, and they played it all the time. That was what Bobby was waiting for —confirmation from Bubba.

Sometime later, Bobby and I were talking over the phone, and he asked me the color scheme of my home. Shortly afterwards, I received a beautiful burgundy and hunter-green afghan made by an eighty-year-old friend of

Bobby's. Since Kyle's death, Bobby has remembered our birthdays and often has something made for us. He has told me he had never done anything like this before but somehow Kyle is making him do it.

One night Kyle came to him in a very vivid dream. He said it was unlike any dream he'd ever had. It was an actual "visit" from Kyle. I have learned these "visits" are possible because when we sleep our souls leave our physical bodies and can travel to the astral plane where our loved ones connect with us.

In the dream, Bobby was sitting on a blanket in a beautiful park. He looked up and saw Kyle standing there with a big smile on his face. Kyle had on jeans and a blue plaid shirt. He began walking up a hill. Bobby asked Kyle what he was doing there, since he was dead. Kyle kept walking up the hill and looked back at Bobby, smiling at him. Bobby said he kept trying to catch up with Kyle, but Kyle kept ahead of him. Kyle finally stopped, turned toward Bobby, and said to tell everyone that he was fine and that he was happy. He told Bobby that, in time, he would know how wonderful it is. Bobby often speaks of Kyle's "visit," and it makes me a little jealous.

It's been over three years and Kyle has never come to me in a "visit." Mary Jo and others have told me I am overly obsessed with it, and this helps to block it from occurring. Then, too, I remember reading about a mother who yearned desperately for a "visit" from her dead child. One time the child appeared in a very real "visit" and the mother never wanted to get out of bed again. She wanted to spend all of her time sleeping, hoping for a return "visit."

Evidently, Kyle doesn't want to tempt me, afraid that I, too, might never want to get out of bed. So, as much as I'd love to see Kyle's smiling face again, I know there is a reason for his not appearing to me. It's not that I haven't tried, though.

g happened a few months later that gave me
_____ about how to see Kyle. Jimmy Swaggart's ministry is
located in Baton Rouge. Actually, it's only a few miles from
our house. An Arts and Crafts show was scheduled at the
ministry for the week beginning Saturday, March 14th. I
grabbed my fabric samples, some cash, and headed out the
door. I'm always amazed at how many talented artistic people show their wares at these events. Never in my wildest
dreams could I imagine who I would meet and the effect the
show would have on me.

I was by myself, scanning each booth, when I came upon
a booth that contained homemade drums and Indian jewelry. It was there I struck up a conversation with Sharon
Perdasofpys. Sharon, a Comanche-Cherokee, has mastered
hand-sculpted wire jewelry, a 3000-year-old art form dating
back to the Phoenicians. Her husband Roger, a Kiowa
Apache-Comanche, creates handmade drums in Southern
Plains tradition. Many famous musicians own his drums.
Both Sharon and Roger have received numerous awards for
their work, and they exhibit in museums and galleries
around the world.

I don't know why I was drawn to Sharon, but we kept
talking and talking, and I ended up behind the counter,
sitting down with her. At first, she had no idea I had lost a
son, but her conversation with me was very spiritual. She
spoke of many of the Indian customs and beliefs about the
afterlife.

When I told her about Kyle's death and my inability to
dream about him, she said if I followed her directions,
I would definitely dream of him. I was skeptical but was
willing to try anything.

Sharon told me to get a full glass (about 8 oz.) of water
and put it next to my bed and say, "I'm going to have a
dream about Kyle. I will remember it and understand it."

Then she told me to drink half of the glass of water before going to sleep and say, "This is all I need to do to solve the situation." The next morning, upon awakening, I was to drink the other half of the glass of water.

That night I did as Sharon told me. Believe it or not, I had a dream and Kyle was in it! It wasn't a "visit," which people say is so real you can remember every bit of it, but it was a dream that I was able to remember.

Sunday afternoon, I went back to the Arts and Crafts show and told Sharon of my dream.

She said, "I knew you would dream of your son."

I shared this experience with Mary Jo's class, and later, over half of the class was successful in dreaming what they had asked for. Mary Jo even asked me to share this experience with a workshop she gave. I don't have any idea how it works. But if just one person is consoled by doing what Sharon told me to do, it's worth sharing.

On June 22nd, about three months after this experience, I received a typed two-page letter from Sharon who was in Oklahoma.

"Have you seen Kyle?" was how her third paragraph began, as if it were normal for him to just drop by and visit us. Sharon and her husband are very spiritual souls, and so much of what I've written about in this book parallels their beliefs. I keep waiting, however, for what she believes will happen.

Others have had experiences, though, in which they have encountered Kyle. It was around 10:00 a.m. on Thursday, July 25th, when I received a phone call from El Paso, Texas. DeDee was attending a convention. She said she had an unbelievable after-death communication from Kyle. She told me it was very real.

Kyle was wearing a red Polo shirt. He looked good and was with some fraternity brothers. I remembered that one of Kyle's frat brothers, Calvin Harniss, died as a result of an automobile accident when Kyle was in college.

After Kyle's death, DeDee had asked me some questions pertaining to Kyle, but I didn't know the answers. She told me he had answered all of her questions the night before when he "visited" her. He appeared happy and at peace. The only thing she couldn't figure out was that he walked into the woods with a person with long, curly hair who was wearing a white beanie type hat. She said it was like a Jewish skullcap, a yarmulke. She tried to follow Kyle and this person, but she lost contact with them in the woods. She stressed over and over that it was *real* and not like a dream. She was upset, though, wondering if he were with a girl with long hair. She was really bothered by this, not knowing who the person was. The memory of this meeting with Kyle will forever be with her, she told me.

I was in a Thursday night class taught by Mary Jo six weeks after DeDee's call from El Paso. Mary Jo was talking about her guides. I asked her when she saw her guides for the first time.

Mary Jo told me they appeared to her in 1981 in a field. She then said something that totally caught me off guard. She said, "They all had long, curly hair with little white beanies on their heads." I now knew who had accompanied Kyle into the woods.

I searched for DeDee's whereabouts and finally contacted her on her car phone. I told her there was no need for her to be jealous. Kyle was only with one of his guides in El Paso.

8

Flipping the Lights

On Monday, August 6th, a little over three months after Kyle's death, we saw Cain, Kyle's son, for the first time since the funeral. Needless to say, it was a very emotional visit. Kyle's former in-laws Elaine and Steve, his ex-wife Angela, her brother Paul, Cain, Jim and I went to a neighborhood restaurant for dinner.

We sat in a circular booth in the corner. It was early, around 5:15 p.m. and a clear day with the sun shining brightly. Cain, three years old and impatient, kept asking when he could say grace. When we all held hands and Cain said the blessing, the waiter remarked how impressed he was to see a family doing this, especially in public. Then, while waiting for our food, all the lights in the restaurant went off.

I looked at Elaine and quietly said, "Kyle."

She nodded, acknowledging my assumption.

Everyone in the place was wondering what had happened, but I knew this was Kyle's way of showing he was with us.

The ability of our loved ones to manipulate electrical things has been well documented. We are, after all, only energy. This energy continues with us when we enter the spiritual realm. John Edward, Mary Jo, and numerous books all mention the ability of those who have crossed over to make themselves known through this medium.

An occurrence that showed this ability happened once when Jim and I visited relatives in Hot Springs. We always check into a motel. Not that our family doesn't offer us their hospitality, but as we've gotten older, we enjoy the privacy and vacation atmosphere this affords us.

"Park under the light, park under the light," Jim kept telling me as we pulled into the Super 8 Motel on Central Avenue. I wanted to park the car closer to our room because our back seat was loaded with hang-up clothes. But Jim made such a big deal about the light that for one time I did as he said.

You may be wondering why I was driving. For many years I was always the back-seat driver. We finally learned the trip goes more smoothly if I drive. Besides, Jim likes to nap.

We carried in a few bags, flipped on the TV, and plopped on the beds to unwind. After a little while, around nine o'clock, I decided to call a friend. The phone number was in a book in our car. So I threw on some clothes and walked out to the car. It was completely dark as I walked toward the car parked "under the light." It was one of those one-by-two feet security lights.

While standing under the light, an overwhelming connection to Kyle came over me. It's peculiar how I'll be concentrating on something else and then the thought of Kyle just pops into my head, and I become very emotional. This was one of those times. I looked up at the light and said out loud, "Kyle, if you're here, let me know."

The light went off as I was looking at it! I couldn't believe it. I ran back inside the motel and told Jim. I was so excited, I didn't even get the book with the phone numbers in it. I was on a high.

Afterwards, I went back outside to get the book with the phone numbers. I had to share the news. I called Bobby, Kyle's college buddy. I told him I was sitting in the car, parked under a light that Kyle had just turned off.

I knew Bobby would understand my excitement. Looking back, I was so lucky to have such special friends with whom I could share this. And they, in turn, can share with me. I thank God every day for their being in my life on my journey.

Later that night, I had trouble falling asleep. I kept talking about the light over and over. Jim is so sweet. He lets me repeat the same thing and very rarely tells me it's the hundredth time I've said it. Because of our love for Kyle, we were always obsessed with him and his happiness. Both of us felt as if we could never do enough for him. Two different times we bought Kyle a car, without the other one's even knowing about the purchase. We often slipped Kyle a little extra money and did not find out until later we both had done the same thing.

In many ways, we are fortunate because to some degree we both feel the loss in the same way. It helps knowing that someone shares your feelings. I have great sympathy for some of my friends who have lost children without that support. Either their husband died before their child died or there was a divorce before the death. They don't have someone who will listen to their story over and over again.

The next morning, Jim and I got up early, around 5:00 a.m., to head back to Baton Rouge. It was pitch dark outside. We carried our bags to the car parked under the light that was now off. Jim told me to get in the car and he'd be right back after he went to the office to checkout.

I looked up at the non-illuminated light and thanked Kyle for the sign that he had given me. I then said, "Kyle, if you're still here, let me know."

The light popped back on while I was looking at it. Jim walked toward the car, looking a little startled as he noticed that the light was burning brightly.

"Kyle's still here!" I said, excitedly.

The neat thing about this story is that two years later, another unbelievable light story occurred. I was attending one of Mary Jo's seminars at the Best Western Richmond Suites Hotel in Baton Rouge. Darlene Clement and her daughter-in-law, Danielle, were also attending. Darlene's two sons had died in an automobile accident thirteen years before. I met her at a Sylvia Browne seminar in New Orleans the previous November.

We were in the parking lot talking. It was around 10:30 p.m., and we were standing under a similar security light. I was talking about our loved ones' abilities to give us signs. I had just made the comment that often people might think it is just a coincidence, but I *know* that Kyle is able to give me signs. Just then, the light went off! Darlene shook her head.

Danielle said, "I can't believe it. Those lights never go off."

I couldn't wait to get home to tell Jim over and over again.

I recall another similar incident occurred on Monday, April 7, 1997. The motion light located on the boat port stayed on all that day. I noticed it was on when I left for school, and when I drove in later that afternoon, I saw it was still on. It had not gone off for the last couple of days and nights. Normally, the light burns only when there is someone or something moving in the area.

Around six o'clock that evening, I asked Jim if there were any way he could turn the light off. Jim asked, "Why?"

"It keeps me awake at night and bothers me when I'm lying on the couch," I told him. I'd had difficulty sleeping the previous week and had discovered I could fall asleep easier while watching television in the den.

"Maybe Kyle wants you to sleep in the bed with me," Jim responded. At the exact moment Jim said that, I was looking directly at the light, and the light went off!

So I thanked Kyle for enabling me to stay on the couch.

Another incident involving lights flipping on and off occurred unexpectedly sometime later. Mary Jo McCabe had given me Kathy Hayes' name and phone number on October 7, 1996. Kathy had been to see Mary Jo after the murder of her only child, her seventeen-year-old son, Barlow. Mary Jo knew of my growing spiritual awareness and the comfort it was bringing me. I had lost my only son, so in some way I could relate to Kathy's pain. Apparently, Mary Jo thought I might be able to help Kathy.

I had not heard from Kathy for a few months until she phoned me concerning an upcoming "Evening Lecture with Mary Jo McCabe." Mary Jo often has these meetings in which the class size is limited to ensure personal attention to each person in attendance. The focus of the evening is usually devoted to her answering as many questions and performing spot readings as time allows. I encourage many people I meet who are in pain over the loss of a loved one to attend one of these meetings with Mary Jo. I know their experiences will open them up to the spiritual world and give them hope and comfort concerning their loved ones.

Mary Jo always asks at the beginning of each of these presentations how many in attendance have never seen her work before. It always seems to amaze her and comfort me that, for the majority, this is their first personal interaction with Mary Jo. Many become aware of her by the increased popularity of her radio show, but it's mostly by word of mouth, mine included, that people connect to her.

Kathy wanted to know if I could help make a reservation for the October 28, 1999, evening with Mary Jo for her and her friend. Mary Jo's classes and seminars always fill up, but

I phoned the next day and got them on the cancellation list. Later, two people were unable to attend, so Kathy was able to bring Marlene.

I was already seated and looking toward the doorway for Kathy. I wondered where they were. Mary Jo had just started speaking when they walked in. I no longer had two seats saved for them, because as the room filled up, others occupied the seats next to me. I gave Kathy a puzzled look as to why she was late.

"I got lost," Kathy mouthed to me.

I was happy they had made it.

Kathy told me she met Marlene at a meeting for Parents of Murdered Children. Marlene's only child, Allison, who was sixteen, had been murdered two years before. Her devastating loss had taken away her will to live. Kathy thought Mary Jo might be able to help her.

Marlene found a seat in the first row, right in front of Mary Jo. Kathy sat on the opposite side of the room, also in the first row. I sent Kathy a note, saying it was good to see them.

When it came time for Marlene to ask a question, she asked about her daughter. She was crying and very emotional, and was having difficulty speaking. I could feel her pain. I silently prayed that Mary Jo could connect with Allison. I knew nothing about Marlene or the circumstances concerning Allison's death, only that she had been murdered. I didn't find out until later, when we were eating a late snack at Chili's, how much of what Mary Jo had said made sense to Marlene.

Mary Jo told Marlene her daughter was there, and she could see her. She said Allison was not afraid of death and her journey to the spirit world. Allison then told Mary Jo the only job she ever had was working at a grocery store. Marlene acknowledged this was true. Allison's only job had been working in the family grocery store.

Messages that say our loved one is happy and at peace are, in truth, messages that can be considered very general and what we would want to hear. But when these messages are given with very specific information, the kind that there is no way the messenger (Mary Jo) could know the specific facts, it adds credibility. You *know* your loved one *is* happy and at peace. The generalizations become specific.

While eating french fries at Chili's, I shared some of my stories concerning Kyle's ability to give me signs. I mentioned the times that he turned the light off and on when I asked if he were there. I could tell Marlene was beginning to understand and have hopes concerning the whereabouts of Allison.

We had walked outside and stood near my parked car. Marlene pinned a pink ribbon on the lapel of my blazer, saying it was something she and others wore in memory of their deceased child. She wanted me to have one. When she pinned the pin on me, the security light above our heads went off. We all looked at each other and smiled.

"Can you believe?" Kathy asked in amazement.

Then as we talked about the light, another light turned off, then on. Then a third light went off, then came on. Then a fourth light started turning off and on.

"Kyle's taught Barlow and Allison how to turn the lights off and on!" Kathy joked.

It was a very moving experience.

Kathy and I have become special friends over the past few years. We often talk on the phone even though we don't spend a lot of time together, since we live in different towns. For some reason, and I believe I know the reason, we feel very connected to one another.

Kathy had dreams of Kyle and Barlow's being together. Also, Shelly, Kyle's girlfriend, has dreamt of Kyle and Barlow, even though she never knew Barlow.

During my third reading with John Edward, Barlow showed up, asking us to give his mother messages. "Barlow hogged our reading," Jim said to Kathy when we called her to deliver the messages from her son.

Bobby called me one time to share the following experience. He was driving home from work, leaving Benton, Arkansas. He was thinking of Kyle and talking out loud to him. He said he also included Barlow's name, just in case he was hanging out with Kyle. Previously, I had shared some of the Kyle/Barlow stories with Bobby.

Just as Bobby mentioned Barlow's name, a car came up real close behind Bobby's car and began to tailgate him. Bobby said he felt uncomfortable being followed so closely. He finally became so upset he slowed down, and drove really slow, so the car would pass him and get off his tail.

The driver honked his horn as he passed Bobby. Bobby read the personalized license plate on the car. It read *Barlow*. Coincidence? No way. Bobby immediately called me when he arrived home. I phoned Kathy.

9

An Incredible Journey

I was talking on the telephone with Kyle's girlfriend, DeDee. She mentioned her mom had seen a psychic on television. She told me his name was James Van Praagh. Apparently, her mother had commented, "I wonder if Mrs. Collier would be open to this." This was just four weeks after Kyle's death. I scribbled the name down, not even knowing how to spell it and put it away.

After my reading with Mary Jo, on June 27th, I asked Mary Jo when I could come and see her again. I had been moved and comforted by what had just taken place. She said a reading didn't have to be scheduled then, but later on I would know when it was time for another reading. For some reason, when I was getting ready to leave Mary Jo's office, I brought up the name James Van Praagh. I asked her if she had ever heard of him. She told me she not only knew of him, but she had also worked with him. She walked over to her computer, pushed a few keys and wrote down James's name and phone number in California on the back of her business card. That card is a possession I highly value. It was the catalyst for an unbelievable journey.

I called and found out that James would be appearing in North Hollywood on September 29, 1996. He would not be giving private readings but a rather new, young psychic, John Edward, would schedule some readings. I asked Cammy, James's secretary, what she knew about John. She told me he must be good because James would not risk his reputation having John appear with him. I scheduled a reading with John.

A few weeks before my reading with Mary Jo, Jim and I had discussed getting away. We thought maybe taking a trip might be good for us. We noticed an airline was advertising a great promotion. So fate was beckoning us. We purchased two round trip tickets to Los Angeles for one hundred dollars each. We had no idea our "getaway" trip would become the most important trip in our lives. You have to realize I made these reservations because Jim and I had never been to California together. I never knew about James Van Praagh's being there nor had I heard of John Edward when I made the reservations. To this day, I marvel at how perfectly things fell into place.

Before our day of departure from Baton Rouge, I had spoken with Cammy a few times over the phone. I needed to schedule a time for our reading with John and ask a few questions. She knew I'd found out about James through Mary Jo, so I had an inside track.

It was a hot, muggy afternoon in North Hollywood. The program "Spirit Communication," with James and John was to begin at 6:00 p.m. at the Beverly Garland Holiday Inn. They had told us they would begin letting people in at 5:00 p.m. We arrived at 3:00. I wanted a good seat. I was apprehensive and yet really didn't know what to expect. I had only had a thirty-minute reading with Mary Jo. I wasn't in tune with this psychic stuff. But I was in tune with my grief.

I struck up a conversation with a man who also arrived rather early. He told me unbelievable stories. He, himself, was a psychic and apparently was rather well known in that part of the country. He said he often went to Hollywood parties, and he mentioned famous people and movie stars for whom he had done readings. I wondered why he was there. He told me you can always learn from watching other psychics. I wish I'd written his name down.

A lady spotted Jim and me standing in line. She approached us and asked if I were Judy. I told her yes, and she told me she was Cammy. She motioned me aside and said Jim and I could come in early and get out of the heat. I felt wonderful. I knew I'd get a good seat.

The room was large. Chairs were arranged in a semicircle. Two bar stools were placed in the front of the room with a tall table between them. There were flowers on the table and two empty water goblets. We sat down, right in front, and waited. When they opened the doors, I spotted the psychic I'd met while in line. I motioned I'd saved him a seat next to me.

I had never seen a picture of either James or John, so I really didn't know what to expect. When they both walked out and sat on their chairs, I was surprised at how young John looked. Before the evening was over, I remember leaning over to Jim and whispering, "John's just as good as James, if not better." John never waivered with his messages, and his presence was without any stage mannerisms. He just seemed so natural.

Many people in the audience were deeply affected by the messages James and John were bringing them from their loved ones who had died. There was a man sitting directly behind us who had been in a Nazi prison camp during WW II. He even showed us the number on his arm. Most of his family had died in the Holocaust, and many of them came through and gave him messages. It was a very emotional evening, and I was more excited than ever for the following morning's reading with John.

John had switched hotels for some reason, and we were informed of this the night before by Cammy. It was only a short walk from the hotel where we were staying, but we made sure we got there plenty early. Our reading was scheduled for 10:00 a.m. We were told at the front desk to go up to the third floor and were given the room number. When we located the room, we sat down on the carpeted hallway, leaned up against the wall and waited. Jim and I assumed that John was giving another reading, so we didn't knock on the door. Ten o'clock came and went, and we were still sitting on the floor. I was a nervous wreck by this time. We decided maybe we had better knock and check because he had scheduled a number of readings in various time slots, and our slot was gradually disappearing.

John opened the door. My first impression was that for some reason he wasn't expecting us. He was dressed in blue jeans, a T-shirt with some logo on it and was in stocking feet. He said he'd been waiting for us and was wondering if we'd received the information on his change of hotels.

John sat behind a desk with a window behind him. He was curled up with one foot under him. He had never met me, knew nothing about us, and didn't have a clue as to why Jim and I were there.

The first thing he said was, "James is here and wants to tell Jim that he is fine." Kyle's first name is James. We never called him that, but ironically, only two weeks before, I had talked with two people about when Kyle had been in the first grade. I shared this story with them. The principal had called out the names of students during the first day of school and told them which class to report to. Kyle was sitting in the auditorium all by himself after all the names had been called. He didn't know who James Collier was.

I commented to John that we didn't call our son James. John said sometimes he is given the person's first name so we will know he is not reading our minds. When we entered

John's room, Jim made a point not to introduce himself, and John had never heard the name "Jim" from either of us.

John commented that someone who died young in the Persian Gulf was with Kyle. He then looked to Jim and said that a grandma on his side of the family was with our son. Grandma Hink, Jim's maternal grandmother, has since come through various other readings with Kyle. She more or less helped raise Jim, living next door to him all of his growing-up years. She was a loving, caring person. I know she would be trying to help Kyle.

Kyle told John he died from an impact, like one-two-three. It happened fast and there was no pain. He was speeding in his car, and he was irresponsible. He lost control and was not wearing his seat belt. He said there was major impact to his head, but there was no suffering. He said it was a very quick thing. His soul left immediately. He was fine.

Everything John was saying was one hundred percent correct. It only got better.

"It happened less than one year ago. I see April," John said, "and Kyle says, 'Dad, I'm fine.'" Kyle then told John I had reached out to him and Michael was with him. "Your son is telling me you are in a group of some kind, a grief group, where you sit in a circle. You met Michael's mother there. Michael died in a car accident, and he is with your son."

I had joined The Compassionate Friends, a support group of parents who have lost children. We meet once a month and sit in a circle. I had become friends with Michael Chadwick's mother, Kris. Michael died at twenty-one years of age in an auto accident. I also met Michael Wood's mother, Nancy. Both Michaels died in the same accident. To this day, I don't know which Michael is with Kyle. I assume, though, that all three of them are together.

John then said our son told him he was okay. At least six times during the reading, Kyle said he was fine. He said he knew I missed him and he was aware we would be going away for the holidays. We had already purchased airplane tickets to fly to Washington for Christmas. He said he'd be with us when we were there.

When he said I picked out his favorite shirt for his viewing in the casket, I knew Kyle was present. It had been a green and beige, large horizontal stripe, long sleeve Polo rugby style shirt with a collar. I remember Kyle's wearing it to the LSU vs. Arkansas football game and his commenting to me how much he liked it, that it was his favorite.

"He's telling me he lived at home, but didn't spend much time there." This could not have been truer. Kyle had moved back home with us and was working with Jim. He'd come home from work, take off his boots in the back hallway, take a shower, dress and pick up the meal I'd prepared as he walked out the door. I'd give him enough food for both him and Doug, a close friend who also worked at our business. Kyle spent many nights at Doug's apartment, and Jim would often bring work clothes for Kyle the next day. Kyle didn't even wait for us to return from the airport the day of his accident. Our cars passed each other on our way home, the last time I saw him.

I remember Jim's telling Kyle one time to sit down and talk with us for five minutes. We talked and when five minutes were up, Kyle stood up and left. So John's message about Kyle's not spending any time at our home could not have been more accurate.

John then told us our son was a "looker," that he was into his build, that he worked out, but was not cocky. This description of Kyle is also correct. Kyle was extremely handsome (Mothers aren't prejudiced, of course.) and was always working out at the health club or jogging. He'd flex his muscles in front of me, laughing, but no one ever thought of Kyle as being conceited. He was very aware of his appearance and would often change shirts two or three times before going out. He'd even ask for my opinion. But you would never have known this side of Kyle when he was in public or with friends.

"He's telling me you have a beautiful backyard." We no longer have any grass to cut in our backyard. It's all decking, with different levels, fountains, a stone creek bed with a bridge and lush green plants and hanging baskets. When I had a garage sale recently, two people asked how much I was asking for my backyard. One lady commented it was the prettiest yard she'd ever seen.

Kyle often went out there and sat on a wooden swing that hung from a wooden lattice frame under the trees. Every time someone comments on our backyard, I think of Kyle's telling John he thought it was beautiful. But how did John know anything about where we lived? We could have lived in an apartment with no yard at all.

These specific messages were overwhelming to me. There was no way a person who I had never known and who never knew anything about us could be giving us such "on target" information. As I tell people, none of this information is on a computer.

"He's twenty-six years old," was John's next statement.

Jim and I both looked at each other, tears welling up in our eyes. I would have been happy with "he's in his twenties," but John said his exact age. This floored us.

"He had a belief system, an open mind. He could adapt on the Other Side."

Granted, this could be a generalization, but the preceding information was so specific and correct that this message greatly comforts Jim and me.

Shortly before Kyle's death, he said something to me I relive over and over. "It's hell on earth; there has to be a better place." It hurt to look at Kyle as he said this. Tears were streaming down his face. "I look normal, but I'm not."

An episode of severe clinical depression was setting in. The peace that Kyle has now found is a comfort to me. But I still miss him.

John continued, "He had a son. Is there a birthday coming soon? He's showing me an eight." Cain's birthday was in ten days on November 8th.

"He said he's sorry he didn't get to play the role of Dad."

Kyle and Angela separated when Cain was a baby. They divorced soon afterwards.

"His son will look a lot like him, and you're to be happy about having Cain. You will be a part of Cain's life. Kyle will live on through Cain. One of his purposes was to bring Cain into the world," John said.

Fortunately, Jim and I are a part of Cain's life. We're Ms. Judy and Mr. Jim. I treasure the moments I get to be with Cain. He is a very sweet and well-mannered boy. Angela has done a wonderful job. I know Kyle is proud of him.

"We live in a very short-lived world," Kyle told John.

The older I get, the more I realize the truth of this. If our lives here are like the mere blink of an eye in the spiritual world, then we know our loved ones don't have to endure the loss and grief in the same way we do.

When something bad happens to us, it is natural to try and find some good, something that will help ease the pain. I am often comforted to know Kyle will never have to endure the pain of such a tremendous loss as the death of his child (at least not in this lifetime). I know he is playing a bigger role in Cain's life, being able to guide him from the spiritual world. I truly believe this.

"He's telling me you took him off life-support after two days. He thanks you for this."

Mary Jo's message from Kyle had been *exactly* the same. How would two people, who knew nothing about Kyle's condition, know he was kept on life-support for two days? It could only be because Kyle told them. This message from Kyle probably encourages me more than any other.

"He's telling me you let a plant die in his apartment."

Kyle's apartment was attractive, well decorated and furnished mostly with the help of Pier I. He liked the masculine, darker wicker. He could never have enough plants. He had a lot of silk plants, but he preferred the live ones. He had a hanging basket, an ivy plant, hanging in the corner of his living room. I remember his calling me one time after he had neglected taking care of this plant. He had thought he might lose it, but he was all excited when he phoned me. It had grown a new leaf.

Kyle had come home for an extended stay. I was visiting family in Arkansas. I went by his apartment to check on things. All was well. Even the plant hanging in the corner. But I rationalized that the plant would have a better chance if I'd move it outside on his fence by the patio. I hoped it would get the right amount of rain and light. I even remember trying out different places to hang it so his plant would stay green and healthy.

"I can't believe Mom killed my plant," is what Kyle said to Jim when they visited the apartment a few weeks later. Never again would that plant grow another leaf.

I have often heard John say, whether during his appearances on *Larry King Live* or on other highly rated television programs, that people wonder why our loved ones come through with such trivial and mundane information. Well, take it from me, this trivial, mundane information is very comforting and offers additional proof that our loved ones are indeed conscious and are quite aware of everything that is going on. Our loved ones aren't dead. They are just at a higher level where they no longer need their physical bodies to function. This trivial information lets you know there is not any mind reading going on.

My only son had died five months before. I was in such grief I could barely function. I had hoped for some assurance that he was okay. I wanted to know he did live on. And here I was thinking about a plant that died? A plant that died two years earlier? No way.

Another thing John revealed that showed insight happened next.

"He and his sister were at odds the last time they were together. He wants to try to resolve this. His sister has not unpacked this, but he is going to help her unpack it. Tell her he knows they had their differences, but he wants you to let her know he loves her."

Though Jamie and Kyle were seven years apart, they had an extremely close and unique relationship. She always showed concern for him and spent a lot of time with him. One of the most touching gifts I ever received was the picture Jamie had taken of both of them and had put on a calendar for me. Then, one Christmas, she and Kyle went to a professional photographer and had photographs of the two of them made. My other daughter, Jill, still lived at home, but I never thought of her not being included as that unusual. It was always "Jamie and Kyle" when they were growing up. When they were on a neighborhood swim team, Kyle's shirt read "Jamie's brother." Jamie's shirt read, "Kyle's sister." There was a very special bond between them.

The last time Kyle and Jamie had been together was when they attended the Sugar Bowl football game in the Superdome in New Orleans, the year before Kyle's death. Jamie and her family had flown in from Massachusetts for the holidays and the game.

A policeman actually called our home at halftime from the Superdome telling me my two adult children were causing a big stir with a verbal fight that was disruptive to others. Jamie left the very next day for Massachusetts, and she and

Kyle never spoke again. This is the girl who wore "Kyle's sister" on her shirt.

Kyle's death never let her reconcile with him. Kyle was able to, though, even in death. You'll read about that later.

I had not told Jamie about our going to California for a meeting with psychics and a reading with John Edward. When she heard about my visit with Mary Jo, she made some kind of cynical remark concerning my becoming obsessed with contacting Kyle. I remember Jim's telling her I could do whatever I wanted if it would comfort me. Until she lost a child, heaven forbid, she had no right to criticize what I was doing.

But, after this message from Kyle specifically for her, I called her from our hotel room immediately after the reading. I gave her Kyle's message. She was speechless. I asked her if she were still there because the phone was silent. She said yes, she was still there and would I tell her everything he said. Kyle had gotten her attention.

John then looked at Jim and kind of laughed. He said, "I hate to tell you this, but your son says that you are wearing his socks."

Jim acknowledged he was. I didn't even know it.

I would buy Jim and Kyle the same brand of socks, but would get them different styles so I could tell them apart. Kyle's had dark blue on the toes and heels. Jim's had gold on them. When Jim took his shoes off later in the hotel room, I noticed he had on the dark blue ones.

Then Kyle told John I stuttered when I was younger. Many people are flabbergasted now when they hear this, but I guess I'm making up for lost time. I didn't even know Kyle knew I stuttered when I was younger, but John said they know everything where they are. "Our loved one's knowledge on the Other Side far exceeds our awareness here."

"He's telling me you have his jewelry."

I had put his 14K bracelet and two necklaces in his "Cheers" mug. It's placed where we keep his ashes, a few pictures and other momentos. One thing that is also placed on that shelf is the little wristband he wore in the hospital when he was born. Believe it or not, when Jill visited us in July, after Kyle's death, she found it in the top drawer of Kyle's dresser with his underwear. What it was doing in there, I have no idea. It had been twenty-six years since he wore it, and I know I had put it away with his baby things. I hadn't looked at it in years. How it got in his drawer is unknown to me.

Jim then asked John if we could ask Kyle a question. John told us yes, that Kyle was still there. Jim told John the TAG Heuer watch Kyle loved dearly was not recovered after the accident. Did Kyle know what happened to it?

"They put it aside in the ambulance and someone picked it up," John said, repeating Kyle's words. John then said Kyle was stepping back, he was losing his connection with him.

Some people have commented to me that isn't it ironic the connection made between two worlds only lasts for thirty minutes, the time you pay for? My answer to them, as well as to you who may be wondering the same thing, is what I've heard from Mary Jo, John, James, Sylvia Browne, Rosemary Altea, and numerous other gifted psychic/mediums. We are all energy. We on the earth plane have a slow vibration rate, and we are inhibited while we are in our physical bodies. All kinds of limitations are put on us.

When our physical body dies and we are free of it, our vibration increases, and this opens up to us a new dimension that affords us abilities we are unaware of while on earth. The medium's vibration has to increase some, and our loved one now in the spiritual world has to slow his vibration down in order for them both to connect on a specific wave length. This takes a tremendous amount of energy and determination on both parties. It is difficult to maintain this connection between the two worlds for an extended period of time. John compares it to holding your breath while attempting to stay on the bottom of the deep end of a pool.

Apparently, some souls on the Other Side are more efficient at being able to do this, and there are some people on the earth plane who also are able to do this. That's why I believe this is a gift. If we all were able to make this contact between worlds, then we would not be able to learn the lessons we came here to learn. We'd just want to go on to the Other Side now.

Some connections, though, do last longer than others. One of my readings with John lasted an hour or so. On the other hand, some people have gone to either Mary Jo or John hoping for a connection with a certain loved one and that specific person hasn't even shown up.

Many times I have thanked John for the comfort he has brought us. He always tells me it's not he. I should thank Kyle because he is the one who is doing it.

"Kyle sends his love. He is fine."

That was the end of a connection with Kyle that both Jim and I know has reassured us beyond belief and beyond words. There is no way to express the euphoria we felt hearing from Kyle. We could not believe how accurate John was with Kyle's messages. Not one thing did not make sense.

The day before the reading with John, Jim and I had elected to go on a Hollywood tour. I've always been a movie star fan, and we wanted to take advantage of our being there for the first time. We wanted to do all of the tourist stuff. We were so nervous about John and James' seminar that night and our meeting with John the following day, we wanted to unwind a little, if that were possible.

At the end of our informative trip that included where John F. Kennedy met Marilyn Monroe, where Hugh Grant was caught with a prostitute in a car, where Elizabeth Taylor lives, and the home that Natalie Wood and Robert Wagner shared, I asked our tour guide about O.J. Simpson's house on Rockingham.

You have to remember this was right after the criminal trial had ended and O.J. had been acquitted. The previous year had been inundated with the "Trial of the Century." All you had to do was turn on your TV. Almost every channel was talking about it. Jim had even bought Kyle a white Bronco without my knowledge. This was after the infamous "Bronco Chase."

The guide told us that O.J.'s house was no longer included on the tours. Too many people were disrupting life for others on Rockingham and a high, bamboo fence had been installed around O.J.'s house. You could not even see O.J.'s house now.

That didn't stop me, though. We rented a car and were headed to the famous restaurant Gladstone's, which was on the beach. I thought, "Why not?" I got out the Movie Stars map I had purchased on one of the street corners and gave the directions to Jim who I'd asked to drive so I could "look."

As we rounded the corner and I saw the Rockingham Street sign, I couldn't believe I was actually at such a famous place. Somehow or another, when you see something on TV so many times, you get a mental picture about what it looks like and where it is. Well, it looked entirely different than I had pictured it. The homes were large and attractive, but somehow it seemed like just any other neighborhood. Of course, it was, but it had become bigger than life in most people's minds. Mine included.

When we turned onto Rockingham, from the picture I'd formed in my head, I said to Jim, "It's on the left." We kept looking on the left as Jim drove slowly. I kept looking for the playground out front or the brick driveway. Then I remembered I had to look for a bamboo fence our tour guide had told us about. We kept looking on the left, but when we reached the end of the street, Jim and I both commented it must be on the right.

We turned around and headed back down Rockingham looking on the other side of the street. Halfway back I yelled, "There's a bamboo fence!" I couldn't believe this was *the* place, the place where the limousine driver had waited for O.J., where the Bronco had been parked crooked, and where the police jumped over the fence without a warrant. I couldn't believe I was actually there.

Jim parked our rented car next to the driveway. It was Sunday morning, around 10:30 and the street was quiet. No one else was around, not even another car. Just then, a large dark blue Suburban drove up and turned to enter the driveway. My first thought was that it was a delivery truck.

Jim said, "That looks like O.J. driving." The windows were darkly tinted, and I thought it was just wishful thinking on Jim's part.

The electronic bamboo covered gate opened, and the vehicle drove in. We watched. As the gate was closing, we got a glimpse of O.J. stepping from the vehicle. He had on beige shorts and a yellow Polo shirt. My first thought was, why didn't I bring a camera. I could have taken a picture of O.J.

I yelled through our open car window, "O.J., my daughter took a picture of you when you were in Baton Rouge doing the commentary for the NCAA track meet."

I was shocked when O.J. responded, "That was a long time ago."

"My husband played for the Giants when you played for the Bills," I quickly added, not even knowing if he were still there since he'd parked right next to the door of his house.

"I've been watching the Giants play on TV this morning," he said.

I couldn't believe I was carrying on a conversation with O.J. over a fence.

The gate began to open and O.J. walked toward our car. He leaned in, shook both our hands as we introduced ourselves. His arms were resting on my open car window, and his face must have been a few inches from mine. I commented I had not planned on seeing him, that I didn't even have a camera. He just laughed.

He and Jim carried on a conversation about football. He mentioned our daughter must be in her thirties, since I told him she was only nine when she took his picture in Baton Rouge. Jim had that photo blown up to an 8 by 10 and sent it to Buffalo. O.J. autographed it and sent it back to Jamie.

O.J. talked about his mother who lived in the Shreveport area, and the conversation kept going. I thought, at that time, he was getting ready to invite us inside, but another car drove up.

"Oh no! They've spotted me." O.J. thanked us for our visit with him and turned to go back through the open gate.

A couple from Salt Lake City jumped out of their car with a camera, yelling, "O.J., O.J.!"

I immediately jumped out of our car. Jim was still seated, wondering what in the heck I was doing. "I have an idea," I said, "I'll take a picture of you with O.J. if you'll take a picture of me with him."

O.J. hesitated, then turned around and gladly posed for the pictures. He even suggested we stand in a different area for the pictures, that the lighting was better there. You could tell he was used to this.

I gave my address to the lady from Utah, and asked for their name and address. Thank heavens, I did. Weeks went by and no pictures arrived. After a couple of phone calls, I finally received not only some pictures, but the negatives as well. I had told my students I met O.J. and they didn't believe me. I needed the proof.

Back to our reading with John Edward. After he said our son had stepped back and left, I became emotional. I made a little small talk, for whatever reason I don't know. I told John the day before, we were looking for O.J.'s house.

John interrupted, "You were looking on the left side of the street, and it was on the right."

I was stunned. "How do you know that?"

"Your son is still here and he is telling me. He wants you to know he has been with you the entire trip, and he knows everything you are doing."

After our reading with John Edward in California, both Jim and I were no longer the same people. The *knowing* that both of us had concerning Kyle's continued existence gave us an indescribable peace. We *knew* there was a heaven and that Kyle was there.

We decided to travel down the coast and stop in Del Mar, near San Diego and visit with Lance Alworth who had played football with Jim while at the University of Arkansas.

Every time we stopped along the route, a crow landed overhead near our car. We stopped at a mall and while pulling into our parking space we heard, "caw, caw," and a crow landed on the light above our car. Then when Jim pumped gas at a corner gas station, another one landed on the wire directly above us. When we drove into the motel for the night, Jim parked the front of the car directly next to a pine tree, even hitting the tree branches when he came to a stop. When we opened our car doors, a crow landed in the tree. Since we had grown accustomed to Kyle's animal sign language, we knew this was Kyle's accompanying us.

While sitting on bar stools, reminiscing about college days, the subject of Kyle's death and cremation came up.

Lance looked at Laura and laughed. Apparently, I was sitting in the spot that was his mother's favorite chair, hence her ashes usually sat there. He pointed to a vase set on the floor in the adjoining room. They'd removed them before our arrival.

We dropped by Lance and Laura's house for breakfast before our drive back to Los Angeles. We were saying our good-byes. Jim had already walked outside to our car when Lance asked me to wait a minute, he wanted to give me something. He ran up the stairs, and I wondered what he was up to.

"These books might give you some comfort," Lance said as he handed me two small paperback publications. "They have helped me concerning my mother's death."

I thanked Lance and headed toward our rented car where Jim was already seated behind the wheel. We waved to Laura and Lance as we drove off, and I immediately began skimming through the books Lance had given me.

Both booklets, *Dying Grace* and *Victory Over Death* were written by R.B. Thieme, Jr. Lance told me he had become friends with Colonel Thieme when he was living in Dallas and playing football with the Dallas Cowboys. Colonel Thieme attended the Dallas Theological Seminary, which eventually led him to Houston where his teaching the Word of God has become a worldwide ministry.

Victory Over Death, a small publication of thirteen pages has brought me much comfort. I keep this booklet handy and have looked through it many, many times during the past four years. Lance probably had no idea how much his running up those stairs to retrieve these two books would help me.

10

Kyle Celebrates with Us

People often say that holidays and special days are the hardest. I honestly can't say that has been true with us. I guess knowing Kyle *is* in a better place and that we will be with him again has been a contributing factor in our ability to get through these times.

John Edward once remarked, "Do you know what it's like to be at a party and no one acknowledges you or speaks to you? Well, your loved ones will be attending all the special occasions and you need to know they are there. Talk to them and include them in your celebration."

We have done that. We've had birthday cakes made for Kyle's 27th, 28th, 29th and 30th birthdays. We sing "Happy Birthday" to him and take pictures of the cake. We've released 27, 28, 29, and 30 white helium balloons to celebrate Kyle's years with us. We also celebrate Kyle's graduation. We've had 1st year, 2nd year, 3rd year and 4th year "In a Better Place" cakes. We also take pictures and release balloons for those occasions as well.

The Baton Rouge Chapter of The Compassionate Friends, Inc. publishes a monthly newsletter which is mailed to bereaved parents and siblings in our community. Included in this newsletter are dedications written by parents in memory of their children. Pictures are often included. It's strange in a way. I'll read about an accident in the newspaper concerning the death of a young person. Then not many months later, I'll be able to put a face with that particular accident. The child's picture will appear in the newsletter.

In the March, 1998, edition of the newsletter, I wished Kyle a Happy 28th Birthday. I would like to share it with you.

HAPPY 28th BIRTHDAY, KYLE!

3-12-70   4-27-96

The ache in our hearts goes on
We know it will always be
The love we shared together
Is eternal — that we see
March 12th won't be forgotten
God brought you into our life
28 years we've known you
Have been filled with love and strife
We know that we're truly blessed
For the life we have in Cain
He's brought joy into our hearts
But it doesn't ease the pain
We often feel your presence
We talk to you every day
We believe you're very aware
Of everything that we say
We'll celebrate your birthday
And the life we have with you
We know we'll be together
When Heaven is our home too
We'll have 28 candles

That will brighten up your cake
We'll thank God you are with us
We're certain, there's no mistake
You will always be with us
Though we miss your smiling face
We truly believe that you've found
That you're in a "better place!"

We love you,
Mom and Dad

While we celebrate special days in memory of Kyle, he has made it clear he is also a part of the party. One night Mary Jo told me Kyle said he was at a birthday celebration at our house the previous week. He told Mary Jo there was only one candle on the cake. It had been Jim's birthday the week before, and because of Jim's mounting years and the exorbitant cost of so many candles, I had put only *one* candle on his birthday cake. It was the only time I put just one candle on a cake, other than when the children were one.

Not only does Kyle let us know he is in attendance at birthday parties, he also doesn't miss weddings. DeDee's sister, Kortnee, was getting married in Hope, Arkansas. They had a beautiful white floral arrangement made and placed in the lobby entering the church in memory of Kyle. They had thought about singing something in memory of him, but upon reflection, decided it inappropriate. Their love for Kyle has truly impressed me. The wedding was beautiful. DeDee was a bridesmaid and was in attendance with her boyfriend. She cried during the ceremony, telling me later she'd wished it could have been Kyle and her getting married.

At the reception, I couldn't find Jim. I found him later on the porch crying. He missed Kyle. I told Jim, "Kyle's here with us."

Everyone was waiting for the bride and groom to make their grand exit to their decorated car for the beginning of their honeymoon. We all had rice bags and those small bubble blowing things. They had to run right by everyone, along a long, covered, well-lit breezeway. DeDee ran by one time to check if the getaway car were ready and waiting.

We kept looking for the bride and groom. Then "pop!" —all the lights along the exit route went off. Someone yelled, "Turn the lights back on!" Then someone else asked who turned them off, and we all heard, "No one turned them off. No one is even near the light switch."

DeDee ran back by us again and laughed, "Don't you just love it? Kyle is here!"

Kyle's presence was unmistakable another day, on October 12th, the day before my first birthday without Kyle. I wasn't looking forward to the next day when I would become fifty-five years old. It was one of those days that everyone said I would dread, one of those days we are to "celebrate." Like most things in life, it's the anticipation of the event that is so highly profiled. It's not the day itself, which is usually a letdown.

It was around 5:30 in the morning. I was in the bathroom, the one we used to call Kyle's bathroom, because he used it exclusively when he was at home. I was putting some make-up on in order to go to a few garage sales. I'd become addicted to garage sales since the birth of my first grandchild. I remember one time when I gave my grandson, Dane, something I'd bought at a store, he kept saying, "You mean you really bought this, like at a real store?" He was so used to getting bargains I'd bought while on "the hunt."

I didn't really feel like going, but I was getting ready anyhow. I felt very emotional when all of a sudden, the eight lights on the mirror began going off and on. It wasn't just a flicker. They went completely off and then turned on again, as if someone were actually turning the switch off and on. This kept on and on, like thirty or more times. When it didn't stop, I yelled to Jim who was in the kitchen reading the paper. I told him to hurry.

As Jim slowly walked down the dark hallway, he could see the lights going off and on. When he walked into the bathroom, he flipped the switch.

I asked, "Why did you do that?"

"I don't want Kyle to burn down the house," he said.

I was actually a little mad at Jim for making it stop. I said Kyle might have been doing it fifty-five times for my birthday. It actually lasted that many times.

When I got home from looking for bargains, there was a message on my answering machine. Jim wanted me to call him at work as soon as I got the message. When I called him, he told me when he got out of his shower and began drying off, the eight lights above his mirror began doing the same thing, going off and on.

You have to understand these two bathrooms are in different parts of the house, are not on the same electrical circuit and none of the light bulbs were bad. They all were still working over a year later. It had been four years since we remodeled and installed these lights, and it had never happened before. Believe it or not, Kyle's blinking the lights to let me know he was celebrating with me was the *best* birthday present I ever received.

Kyle has made himself known to others in the same way. I had never met CeCe Tye, DeDee's mother, who lived in Hope, Arkansas. She told me she saw me at one of Kyle's college football games, but I don't remember being introduced to her. She and DeDee were coming to Baton Rouge for a visit six months after Kyle's death. CeCe told me later she was very apprehensive about being with us so soon after the funeral. She even thought it best to check into a motel to play it safe.

From the moment they drove in our driveway and got out of their car, though, we have been like one. CeCe looked so young. I thought DeDee's sister must have come instead. She is truly a blessing God put into my life, I'm sure, to ease the path of my journey. When they entered our house, Jim laughed at something one of them said. CeCe immediately commented, "Oh, you laugh just like Kyle. Kyle had such a special laugh."

At least five or six more times that night, CeCe remarked how much she loved Kyle's laugh. She said his laugh was unique and beautiful. I had never really paid any extra attention to Kyle's laugh. I kept thinking to myself, "Why does CeCe keep mentioning his laugh? Was Kyle's laugh really that unusual?"

CeCe had a scheduled reading with Mary Jo the next day. That was one of the reasons they had come to Baton Rouge. Mary Jo knew nothing about who was coming for the reading. I had scheduled two consecutive time slots for them, but told her nothing about whom they were for.

CeCe went in for her reading first. Mary Jo told her she had to become grown up when she was nine years old. CeCe's mother had died when she was nine. The messages given were unbelievable. When CeCe returned to the waiting room, she was in tears. She was very emotional and has become Mary Jo's number two fan. I'm number one.

During the reading, Kyle came through and delivered to CeCe some very meaningful messages. The one that stands out most to me is Mary Jo's saying, "This is really funny. I don't know why, but he's just laughing and laughing."

DeDee spent the first night sleeping in Kyle's bed. I felt sorry for her the next morning. She was so emotional she was sick to her stomach and was crying. I didn't know how to comfort her, but Kyle did.

DeDee was in the bathroom washing her face when the lights started going off and on, the same lights that went off and on for my birthday. Of course, I'd told her about the first occurrence. She yelled to me, and sure enough, Kyle was at it again. To this day, over two a half years later, she'll often ask me if the lights have done that again. When I tell her those were the only two times, it comforts her. She feels she was special that Kyle made himself known to her in that way.

The second night of their visit, we took CeCe and DeDee to Al Copeland's, a Cajun restaurant with delicious food. Afterwards we went to a local casino and donated some money, then came home. We didn't want the night to end. At about two o'clock in the morning, CeCe, DeDee, and I were sitting on a bed in the guest room talking. Jim was in our bedroom. "Look!" Jim yelled. We could see the lights in his bathroom going off and on. Kyle was letting us know he'd been with us the entire time.

We finally called it a night and went to bed, but something else happened that let us know Kyle was still with us.

At 3:30 a.m., we were all awakened at the same time. "Love Will Keep Us Together" was blaring loudly over our speaker system. The CD player in the kitchen had come on by itself, and all four of us heard those exact words. We all got out of bed, walked into the kitchen, and knew that Kyle had done it. Everyone was tired the next morning, and Kyle got blamed for it.

11

Kyle Uses AT&T

The first anniversary of Kyle's death was approaching. It had been five months since our trip to California, and Jamie was still struggling with Kyle's death. Jim kept saying that Jamie needed to see John Edward. But I had to be cautious; I didn't want to strain our relationship over this psychic thing.

Jamie had always joked about having ESP. She called me ten days after Kyle's funeral, telling me she had seen Kyle's face on the TV screen while putting in a VCR tape. She said it was in black and white spots. The next night while she was in bed with her husband, her son Jared, crawled into bed with them. She said Kyle grabbed her shoulders while she was in bed, and she heard him say, "I'm okay." Then she and Kyle walked down the hall together. A few days later while feeding Jared and Josh at the bar in the kitchen, she felt a presence of someone behind her. It was 5:30 in the evening and thinking her husband had come home early from work, she turned around and screamed.

Jared, her three-year-old asked, "What's wrong?"

Jamie said, "It's Kyle!" She said he was like a gray mist, but she knew it was Kyle.

Poor Jared. He couldn't figure out what was happening.

I knew it was time for Jamie to talk with John. There was only one way to get a private reading with him. He had call-in dates scheduled in which he assigns appointments. The call-in time occurs only one time a month. At that time, it was for two days: between 9:00 and 3:00 on Saturday and from 9:00 until 1:00 on Sunday. Presently, it is the first Wednesday of each month.

After reading many messages on John's website "Guest Book," I realized most people trying to schedule an appointment with him become frustrated when they try to call-in because they only get a busy signal.

I decided to try to get a reading near the first anniversary of Kyle's death. I began dialing John's phone number ten minutes before the scheduled beginning time, but it was already busy. I pushed redial over and over again. I carried the phone with me everywhere I went, walking from room to room. I had a nervous, anxious feeling because I wanted to get through so badly. I wanted to visit with Kyle again.

After my first couple of attempts to get through, a funny thing started happening. I would hang up after the busy signal, then my phone would ring. I'd answer it, but there would be a strange sound on the other end, a sound never heard before. We have two cordless phones in our house and a permanent phone. In addition, I had brought my car phone inside. After a while, I decided to try using the other phones, subconsciously hoping they would bring some luck in getting through, but the same thing happened. When I'd hang up with the other phones, my phone would ring, and I'd hear that strange sound. It happened even when I used my cellular phone. I'd push *69, which identifies the previous caller, and none of the rings were registering.

Then I remembered when Shelly had called me, soon after Kyle's death, telling me Kyle had called her. At that time, I thought she was just deeply depressed and searching to find some comfort. But she convinced me he really did call.

It seems sometimes after they'd been together and maybe had a small tiff, Kyle would call her in the early morning hours, like 3:00 a.m. When she'd pick up the phone, he wouldn't say anything. I guess he wanted to make contact, know she was there, but not really want her to know it was he who was calling her and bothering her at such an ungodly hour. Every time it happened, she said there was this same sound on the other end of the phone, and she knew it was Kyle. Kyle later admitted he did call her. Shelly told me the night Kyle broke up with her she was mad at him and was walking around the house "in a huff, yelling at him." The phone rang, and she got the same strange silence and no hang up.

After Kyle's death, the phone at Shelly's house rang at three o'clock one morning. When she picked up the phone, there was this same sound on the other end of the line, a tone she knew all too well. No one spoke, but no one hung up either. It happened as it had when Kyle was alive.

Shelly is very spiritual and has always been receptive to contact with the Other Side. The following night she said it happened again. She was *sure* it was Kyle. The next day while at work, she told the people in her office that Kyle had telephoned her. I'm assuming her employer has a very open mind for her to confess she had a call from a dead person.

After Shelly's story, I can't tell you how many times I've read or heard of our loved ones' ability to phone us. So I do accept this communication from Kyle. Now whenever the phone rings and there's no response on the other end, I always talk to Kyle just in case it is he.

With the phone ringing so many times after I'd try to get through to John, I began to believe Kyle was aware of what I was trying to do and in his way, was encouraging me to keep trying. It made sense to me he would do this so I could make contact with him through John Edward.

After about four and a half hours of trying to get through, using different phones, saying prayers, and pacing the rooms of my house, I phoned Jim at work because I was completely frustrated and upset.

Jim asked for John's phone number in New York and said he'd call from work and maybe our luck at getting though would change.

Well, guess what? When Jim would call and hang up after getting a busy signal, his business phone would also ring. When a worker picked it up, he'd hear that same dead tone with nobody on the other end of the line. This was their business phone, and the workers couldn't figure out what was happening. It had never happened before. When I told Jim it was also happening at home, we both agreed it was Kyle.

I continued trying to get through on Saturday until I got John's answering machine message saying calls were over for the day. John's call-in hours for the next day, Sunday, were given.

Needless to say, I had trouble sleeping that night. I was too uptight about the anticipation of calling in the next day. My anxiety bore up the adage that the more we want something and the harder it is to get, the greater our desire is to have it.

When I woke up Sunday morning, I thought Kyle might not know about John's taking calls on Sunday, so maybe he wouldn't keep phoning us. But I couldn't fool him. His calls began even before I started phoning New York! Kyle was very persistent. I realize now how important it was for him that I have another reading with John.

There was about one hour left of the call-in for an appointment time on Sunday. Our phone had been ringing all morning long, with that same strange sound and nobody on the other end. Then the unexpected happened.

"Hello, John Edward's office."

Luckily, I didn't faint. I couldn't believe I had gotten through. I said something like, "Is that really you?"

Ellen, John's secretary, laughed and said that most people are caught off guard when they finally do get an answer.

I scheduled my reading for April 19, 1997, at 11:30 a.m. It would be at John's house located in Huntington on Long Island. I can still remember the feeling I had when I hung up. I kept saying, "Thank you, God," over and over.

I had planned to fly into New York with Jim and sightsee a little, but mostly concentrate on the reading. Jim commented it would be wonderful if Jamie would go with us, but we didn't want to initiate it or push her. She still wasn't into this psychic stuff.

Before the scheduled date, however, Jamie called me one day just chit-chatting about the boys and what was going on in her life. I mentioned that Jim and I were flying to New York in April. She asked why. I told her we had scheduled a reading with John Edward. I was surprised but also ecstatic when she said, "Why don't you fly into Boston? You can stay with us a few days, and I'll go with you since it's only a four hour drive to New York."

I cannot tell you how happy I was that she invited herself to go to the reading. It was too good to be true. Jim's wish had been granted. Ever since Jamie and Kyle had fought in New Orleans and then later Kyle's message to Jamie in California, Jim talked about Jamie's seeing John. It was now actually going to take place.

It was after nine o'clock at night when the phone rang on April 8th, just eleven days before our scheduled appointment. I picked up the phone and thought I recognized my friend, Kathy's voice.

"John Edward's office," was what I heard.

"Sure," I said. Then I made some stupid remarks, trying to be funny.

"This is John Edward's office."

Wondering whether Kathy was calling from New Orleans or Lafayette, I said, "Where are you calling from?"

"New York."

"Sure, you might as well make it a big lie, while you're lying," I said, rather upset with Kathy and the game she was playing with me.

Then I heard more comments on the other end of the line and realized it might not be Kathy after all.

I felt like a complete fool. Embarrassed beyond words, I gave some apologetic statements to Ellen, John's secretary.

Ellen had called to give me the directions to John's house for my scheduled reading on April 19, 1997.

12

A Brother Brings Solace to His Sister

I went by myself to Boston. Jim and I thought it best that Jamie and I be by ourselves. We could spend more quality time doing girl things without Jim's tagging along. Jamie had picked up her new car the day before our drive to New York. She asked me to drive, because she was nervous about the trip, as if I weren't. I don't like driving in a strange city in heavy traffic, and it didn't help that it was snowing on April 18th.

We made it safely, checked into our hotel and headed out for a walk along Broadway. Our only purchase while strolling the streets was a wool cap for each of us. Our ears were aching, it was so cold.

Jamie had gotten us tickets to see *Miss Saigon*. It was wonderful. I had never seen a Broadway play before. But the main reason we were there was in the back of my mind throughout our stay in the city. I silently prayed that Kyle would show up, and Jamie would have no doubts about our ability to connect with him.

We drove by John's house, located at the end of a cul-de-sac, about an hour and a half before our appointment. I wanted to be sure we knew where we were going. We found a coffee shop located nearby. Jamie and I ordered a cup of coffee and a roll and waited. I kept checking my watch while making small talk with the owner of the coffee shop. I was praying silently, and my stomach was in knots. I couldn't eat my roll. I can still feel a little of that feeling as I'm typing this and reliving that moment. I so badly wanted the reading to go well. I wanted Jamie's pain over the confrontation with her beloved brother to be eased.

John answered the door. He told us to make ourselves at home in his living room. He said he was giving a reading upstairs and would be with us in a little while. He ran back up the stairs and I could hear talking, but not any words.

Jamie had worn boots. John had hardwood floors. I sat on the sofa, full of anticipation, but I was so scared and nervous that I couldn't move. Jamie stood up and began walking around John's room, looking at his knickknacks, making a clunking sound with her boots.

I whispered for her to sit down, that she was making too much noise and John could probably hear her. She wasn't concerned with my concern. She even started to walk into John's kitchen. When I said something, she reminded me he said to make ourselves at home. She was only in the kitchen for a few seconds. I couldn't believe she went in there. When she came out, she said she saw some of the pages of the book that John was writing, *One Last Time.* I could not believe this daughter of mine was walking around John's house. It made me more apprehensive and more nervous than ever.

Just as she came back into the room, two people followed by John walked down the stairway. They thanked John and exited his house. John then asked us to come upstairs. At the time, I wondered if John remembered me from California. I didn't say anything to him about it, nor did he to me.

Jamie and I sat in two chairs opposite John who was seated behind his desk. There was a big computer and phone machine sitting on a large table in the corner of the room. There were two windows—one overlooked the side yard, the rear window overlooked the backyard. We were too far from the backyard window to see through it, but I very clearly remember hearing a crow. I hoped it was a sign.

John asked if either one of us had been to a psychic. Jamie said no. I commented that I had seen him in California. I still didn't know if he remembered me. I made a point not to introduce Jamie, nor tell him anything about her.

He proceeded to tell us to be skeptical of what was going to take place. The reason is the more skeptical one is, the harder our loved ones or whoever comes through from the Other Side try to convince us it is they. He said to keep an open mind, and not to interrupt or offer any unsolicited information. Just say yes or no when he says something, and not to elaborate on anything.

"The grandparents on your husband's side of the family are here," he said, looking at Jamie.

I was prepared to take notes but didn't even write this down. I wasn't looking for them. I was only there for Kyle.

John proceeded to say who they were, what they died from, and gave their names. I was actually mortified when this was happening. Jamie didn't even know them, since they had all died before she had met David. The only one she knew a little about was her mother-in-law's mother, who had died from breast cancer. Jamie was taking notes, but I didn't see any need to. None of this information from her husband's dead grandparents was of any importance to me.

"A friend of yours from high school who died in a car accident is here." John was still looking at Jamie. I was beginning to wonder what I was doing there.

"She says you didn't stay in touch much after gradua-tion, but the last time you saw her was at some type of group celebration (high school reunion). Jamie apparently knew who this was. I didn't have a clue, and I really didn't care. I could not believe what I was hearing. I decided just about anyone can show up, that our strong love for someone may not be that important.

Then John turned to me and said, "Your son is here and he is so excited that you brought his sister. He's actually jumping up and down. He's so excited she is here. He's telling me he died as the result of an auto accident. He says his dad knows he came through in California and there will be a birthday coming up in May (Jim's is the 18th)."

Looking at Jamie again he said, "Your brother tells me you were away when the accident happened. He says you both used to tease each other a lot. (They would throw bugs on each other and put animals in each other's dresser drawers.) You used to poke fun at each other. He doesn't want you to feel bad about him. He's stressing that an occurrence has happened three times (Jamie's three sightings of Kyle after his death) and you were aware of it."

Kyle then congratulated Jamie on what she was doing and what was going on in her life. Jamie was preparing for the Mrs. Massachusetts pageant to be held later that summer. She had been on a strict diet, was working out regularly at a health club and was in the best shape I had ever seen her.

Then Kyle brought up his vehicular accident again and said something had not been repaired at the place where his accident occurred. I had not been able to drive by the scene of his accident, but Jim had to drive by it often because of his business. When I asked Jim about Kyle's statement, he said Kyle was right. Apparently the guardrail on the bridge had not been replaced.

"You wore his sweatshirt, a long sleeved sweatshirt, the week before," John said. This was also correct. I had worn Kyle's navy blue Polo sweatshirt the previous week when I taught at school. Jim had even commented the morning I wore it, that it was Kyle's. It was big on me, but I wore it anyway.

Then Kyle told Jamie she had moved a picture of him recently.

"No," Jamie said.

"He says, yes, you did," John responded.

"No," Jamie repeated.

John was emphatic when he said, "Your brother says you did move it."

That's one thing I admire about John and the information he receives and then gives. As I've mentioned before, he never waivers with his messages. I've never heard him change a message. He always sticks with what he says the first time.

On our drive home, Jamie suddenly said, "Oh yeah! I remember now. I did move Kyle's picture. As a matter of fact, I moved two of them. I rearranged things on the cabinet in the front room, and I moved his two pictures closer to the front of the shelf." When we were at her home later, you could even see the dust marks that were left from where the pictures had been.

John says this happens often. We are bombarded with so many messages, and, needless to say, we're usually not in a calm state. Most people are in deep grief and very emotional. It is difficult to relate to some of the information. Often we have to check with someone else to verify what is being told. He always stresses to write everything down, and with some deep thought later on, it may make sense.

As an example of being brain dead during a reading, I'll use my own experience. Jamie had commented during the reading that she had all of Kyle's furniture. I looked at her in disbelief. Had she forgotten that John asked us not to give any unsolicited information? Apparently so. I could not believe she had offered this information to John. This would have been a good message for Kyle to have brought up. Jamie had Mayflower Moving Lines transport all of Kyle's furniture from Louisiana to Massachusetts.

When I was looking at Jamie, with a look of "why did you say that?" John quickly looked at me and said, "But he's telling me that you have one piece of his furniture." I couldn't think of any piece of Kyle's furniture I had. Was he calling a bulletin board with pictures on it a piece of furniture? That's the only thing I could think of.

Again, on the drive back to Boston, a light went off in my head. Kyle's dining room table and four chairs from Pier I were sitting in my carport. I couldn't even pull my car all the way in. And I had forgotten. This is proof that John doesn't read minds. He told me, and I still didn't remember what he was talking about.

A little side note about Kyle's table and chairs. Bobby has them in his house now. I know Kyle knows he has them and is happy he is able to use them. Kyle probably sits in one of his own chairs when he visits Bobby.

Another brain dead episode happened with Janice Hurst. Her seventeen-year-old son, Cory, had died. During her reading with John, Cory mentioned she had a large religious statue. Janice told John she didn't have one. On our drive home, it came to her.

"Oh, my God! I can't believe I forgot about the big concrete statue of Mother Mary I have in the backyard. I even go out and pray to it every day."

John mentioned Jamie had Kyle's bed, (this was before the unsolicited information had been given) and her cat sleeps on top of it. The day I arrived at Jamie's house, she directed me to where I would sleep. I gasped when I walked into the bedroom. Everything in that room had been Kyle's. The Pier I dark wicker, the bedspread, pillows, flower arrangements, lamps and pictures on the wall. The only thing that wasn't familiar was the cat sleeping on the bed.

"Do you have another cat?" John asked.

Jamie said she did.

"Your brother says for you to take it to the vet. Something is wrong with it. Also, he is telling me about the accident the cat will have on his bed."

Jamie took her other cat to the vet because of Kyle's urging, and sure enough, it needed medical assistance. It was full of worms.

About one month after I returned home from Boston, Jamie called. It was very early in the morning, and I knew it must be important for her to phone before I headed off to school. It *was* very important. Her cat had poo-pooed all over Kyle's bed. Relating it to Kyle's warning, I yelled, "Good!"

Jamie laughed and I overheard her telling her family, "Mom's laughing about it." I told her I couldn't have received better news. I was so happy the cat had an accident on Kyle's bed. The cat had never poo-pooed anywhere but the litter box. I did offer to pay the cleaning bill, though.

Kyle had never been to Jamie's house before his death nor had he even seen a picture of it. He had never heard me talk about it, because I had not been there either. I had only seen a picture of the outside of the house that Jamie had mailed to me after they bought it.

Kyle began to describe the inside layout of Jamie's house. John was motioning with his hands as to where the rooms were located in relationship to each other.

"He's telling me there are three rooms, all connected and open into each other. Your brother stands in the middle room and watches you and your family," John said, looking at Jamie.

"That's exactly where I saw him one time when I was feeding the boys," she told John.

"He grabs your attention there. He keeps saying to you, 'Hey! I'm here.'"

Kyle then mentioned that Jamie's house was being re-modeled, and he liked all of the work they had been doing.

"No," Jamie responded after this message.

I shook my head. I couldn't believe it. When I had arrived at their home, they had proudly taken me on a grand tour. David had completely renovated the concrete slab basement, converting it to a children's playroom with carpet on the floors and built-in cabinets lining the walls for Jared's and Josh's toys. He'd even left a non-carpeted place in the middle area of one room for the pool table they hoped to get. The entire backyard and side yard were now decked, with wooden swings and a play yard for the boys. I had commented that it should be in *Better Homes and Gardens.*

I remembered we were only told to say yes and no, but I had to chime in here.

"What do you mean, you haven't remodeled?" I asked Jamie.

"Well, we're not doing anything right now."

Give me a break. Here Kyle was commenting on how much he liked what they had done with their house and because he didn't put it in the past tense, he wasn't right? Jamie was definitely fulfilling John's words to be skeptical.

Then these grandparents who I didn't know or care anything about popped back in again. I couldn't figure out what was happening. They gave out additional information, and Jamie began taking notes again. At the time this was happening, I was *really* upset. Any information from these dead grandparents that neither of us knew or cared about would in no way bring me comfort. Or so I thought.

Finally Kyle showed up again. John said he was jumping up and down, because he was so excited we were there. Kyle mentioned he had another sister and my birthday was in October. He talked about the cat again, and then John said Kyle was laughing.

Kyle talked about an endangered species collection Jamie had in her safari decorated room. He mentioned that one of her walls was darker than the others because she ran out of paint while painting, and the new paint didn't match the old paint. Kyle mentioned the futon chair in the basement. He said he sat there and watched the boys. He also said there were two bathrooms upstairs on the second floor.

I knew Jamie's den was decorated in a wildlife motif. I had even sent her a wild animal rug, but Kyle was unaware of this. Her throws and pillows were animal prints. Also the covers of the bar stools. Even her picture frames were done in tiger and zebra patterns.

What I didn't know until we came home from New York was that the three shelves that were hanging on the wall in the den had ceramic animals sitting on them. They were all part of an "Endangered Species" collection that Jamie had acquired. To be honest, I hadn't even noticed this collection until after Kyle brought it up.

Jamie and I walked into the living room. She pointed out the wall that was darker, the wall that didn't match the other three. I had seen the futon downstairs in the playroom, and I knew there were two bathrooms upstairs.

"Your brother tells me he will be on the white sand with you in the Caribbean later this year. He also says November 11th will be an important date." Undoubtedly, Jamie didn't think this was important and didn't jot this down in her note taking.

During the fall, Jamie and I were talking on the phone. She said they decided to get away, and had gotten a good deal on a cruise ship. It was then I reminded her Kyle told her he would be with her. Jamie was snorkeling off the white sands of Cancun on November 11th!

Then Kyle mentioned I'd received something spiritual, a cross. That is another time when I went blank. I mentioned a guardian angel pendant and a guardian angel pin I'd been given.

John said, "No, he's telling me it's a cross."

A bell rang. Kathy Hayes, whose only son, Barlow, was murdered, had given me my first rosary, one from Lourdes. Kyle acknowledged this was what he was referring to.

Then something unbelievable happened.

John said, while looking at Jamie, "Your brother wants you to know that he, Kyle, is responsible for bringing these grandparents you don't know and your friend from high school to the reading."

John then stood up, put his hands on his hips and said, "He's going, 'Huh! I brought them through. Now what do you think of that?'"

This had no meaning to me at the time, but I knew it touched Jamie. When we left John's house to head back to Massachusetts, Jamie told me she *knew* Kyle was okay. I asked her how she knew that. It was only then she told me how she had tested Kyle the weeks prior to our reading.

After she decided to go to the reading with me, she would talk to Kyle throughout the day. Sort of testing him, I guess. She'd tell him, "If this is really true, that you are aware of everything and you still exist somewhere, bring with you David's grandparents, whom I don't know, and Tracy, a friend from high school who died."

Kyle not only brought them, but seemed rather proud that he was able to fulfill Jamie's test. Jamie has never been the same since. She is on a spiritual path, and I know Kyle is responsible for it. I know how happy they both are that their estrangement before his death has been repaired.

"Stay positive," were the last words John gave me from my son. Too many things were happening to brighten up my life. Kyle was doing so much to help me. How could I not stay positive with all the many blessings I had received?

On our drive back to Massachusetts, the time flew by. Both Jamie and I were ecstatic. We had received a miracle. A large part of the wound that had created such a big scar was miraculously healed for Jamie. Kyle was able to bring solace to his sister.

We were immediately greeted by skepticism, though, upon our arrival back at Jamie's home. Upon sharing all of the information Kyle had relayed to us through John, David, Jamie's husband, said, "John probably came up here and looked through the windows."

Jamie and I laughed.

Sure, John drove four hours, eight hours round-trip, to Jamie's house, not even knowing who she was, much less that she was coming to the reading with me. He found time in his busy schedule to peek through Jamie's windows with binoculars so he could detect the paint that didn't quite match on one of the walls. He then climbed up a ladder he had brought with him, so he could see there were two bathrooms upstairs, and the cat was sleeping on Kyle's bed that Jamie now has in a bedroom. How John was able to know about the futon downstairs in the basement is still a problem. Maybe John was able to ask a groundhog.

There is no possible way for John to have known beforehand the information that was given, other than receiving messages from Kyle.

I would have been happy with one reading with the best medium in the world. But why was I honored with this second one, and why would it continue? I only hope these stories of true happenings in my life will give you added proof that *your* loved ones live on. They are still a very big part of your life, and one day you will be reunited. Mary Jo told me one time Kyle told her he would greet me on the Other Side with a wreath of red roses. I look forward to that meeting, more than anyone can imagine.

Knowing all I know now, I'm often amazed our society rarely speaks about death. It is, after all, the one thing all of us will do. We treat it as something bad. Kyle has taught me we should be happy for those who have gone on before us, that they are in a much better place.

I picture Kyle living in some sort of log cabin type home on his wooded property near a lake with his beagle dogs. He's able to fish, hunt, and enjoy the nature he so loved while here. He doesn't even have to worry about my yelling at him to take off his muddy boots. He can be with whomever he wants and do whatever he desires.

I *know* he is no longer depressed. He's happy *all* of the time. It's almost as if he's on a vacation doing everything he loves, and one day I'll be able to travel there.

13

Kyle Meets Us in Dallas

Twelve days after Jamie's and my reading with John at his home in New York, John was scheduled to appear in Dallas, Texas. I could not pass up this opportunity. He was going to have a two-and-a-half hour presentation on Friday night and then would conduct an all-day spiritual workshop on Saturday. Private readings would be held on Sunday. He would be appearing with Judy Guggenheim, co-author of *Hello from Heaven*, a bestseller. This book contains many incidents of after-death communication. It was one of the earliest books I bought and describes in detail the various ways our loved ones can contact us. I even bought a few extras to give to others who were in grief. I sent one to Jamie letting her know she wasn't crazy "seeing Kyle." This book validated the different ways she had seen him.

Hello from Heaven has a picture of a butterfly on the cover. After the reading with John in New York, I told him I was planning to see him in Dallas. He then told Jamie and me this story. He was sitting in his backyard reading *Hello from Heaven* so he would be familiar with Judy's book when they appeared together in Dallas. He said there were never any butterflies in his backyard, but while reading the book with the butterfly on the cover, a butterfly landed on the book. He saw numerous other butterflies that day. This is just another example of the signs we get. I'm hoping you will become aware of signs from your loved ones after reading this book. Just think how excited they'll be. Maybe they'll even jump up and down like Kyle.

I picked up Kathy Hayes in Lafayette, Louisiana, on April 25, 1997. It was the one-year anniversary of Kyle's automobile accident. I had convinced Kathy to go with me to Dallas and had scheduled a private reading for her with John. When I made the appointment over the phone with Ellen in New York, all I gave was the name "Kathy."

DeDee was working in Houston at that time, and she flew up to join Kathy and me in Dallas. She'd heard so much about John and his wonderful gift, she wanted to see for herself. I also scheduled a private reading for her.

As I write now about scheduling these private readings for others, I'm actually in awe that I was afforded these opportunities.

DeDee's plane had to be rerouted due to bad weather. Kathy and I drove through a monsoon for most of our trip. A car directly in from of me hydroplaned as I was driving on the interstate. I called 911 to report the accident as others stopped to help. We were also rerouted in Dallas because of an accident involving a police fatality. I was completely lost. And I was beginning to wonder about all these signs. I had bought a Texas map with a detailed outline of Dallas before I embarked on the trip. I had highlighted our designated route, because I was driving in a big city about which I knew nothing. Above all else, I could not be late for this major event with John Edward.

Kathy and I finally arrived at the hotel where John would be appearing, or so we thought. When we checked in at the desk, we were informed the event had been changed to another location, a location that was not highlighted on my map. Apparently there had been such a huge response to his appearance they needed a bigger room to accommodate more people.

We made it to the right place, though. We spotted DeDee, hugged, and hurriedly told our stories of frustration trying to get there. The room was full of people. I was so excited that Kathy and DeDee were going to see John.

Because of the change in hotels, the program started late, at around 8:30 p.m. After giving very accurate and emotional spot readings to others in the audience, John headed in our direction, and he said, "I have a son here who died recently in an automobile accident. There's an April (Kyle's death and DeDee's birthday) and Libra (my birthday) connection." I raised my hand up, thinking at the time, "Oh, no. He'll see it is me again." But I was excited.

"Your son has a son who is around three years old."

I told John four. Cain was three years old when Kyle died.

John then looked at DeDee, never having seen or heard about her before, and said, "But you're not the mother, you're the girlfriend."

Kyle said DeDee was now in a committed relationship and DeDee responded she was thinking of breaking up with this person.

"No, you're not," Kyle said.

To this day, two years later, DeDee is still in that relationship. (An update—DeDee became engaged to this person, Toby, five years after Kyle's death.)

There were many specific bits of information given out by John from loved ones that evening. You can tell by watching people's expressions and reactions when the message is making sense. As usual, John was "hot."

Some of the on target tidbits that John gave out were "a person is named 'Tootsie,' a man's best friend is now dating *his* girlfriend, a man is here who bought a new set of tires the day before, and a man is dyeing his hair blonder." It was a wonderful evening. Kyle had even acknowledged DeDee.

DeDee, Kathy, and I were staying at the Solana, a beautiful hotel located on the outskirts of Dallas. The eight-hour workshop was just down the street. DeDee and I awoke early and got a bite to eat. Kathy said she'd join us later.

We didn't really know what to expect, whether John or Judy would appear together or what. There were fifty people in attendance. We were seated in cushioned chairs, facing the front of the room. There was some type of stage in the background with curtains pulled shut. John came into the room and sat down on the floor of the stage. He talked from 8:00 a.m. until noon. It was awesome.

Some of the specifics mentioned were that he explained the vibration levels of our energy and how they meet and that souls come to you; you can't call them. He told us how to create our private place, our psychic center where our loved ones can join us. He began a meditation and took us to a cabin in the woods to meet our guides. I didn't see anyone, as usual, but DeDee met Abraham and four others. He told us that loved ones could come through the mist. Again, I didn't see anyone. DeDee said she saw her grandparents and then Kyle jumped through with thumbs up like "Tah dah! Here I am."

John asked others in the audience who they saw. Some people saw people they weren't wanting or weren't expecting.

When I attend an event like that, I always look around the room and take a survey of who are attending. My first thought usually is how normal everyone looks. Somehow it makes me feel good to know that so many people who are well-groomed, nicely dressed, and have pleasant smiles and engaging personalities are also into this psychic stuff. Looking at each person, I always wonder why they are there and who they have lost. I've met some of the most wonderful, compassionate souls at these events.

After sitting up on the stage very relaxed and talking about how we can be receptive for communication, John began giving spot readings. Now, I thought, I would be able to find out something about who these people are.

While outside, waiting to get in, I had struck up a conversation with a couple from New York. Their son had died of leukemia at ten years of age, less than two years before. They told me they had been unable to get a reading with John in New York, so they got one in Dallas which was scheduled for the next day. I remember the father's telling me he was Catholic and very skeptical of all of this. But during the workshop, their son showed up. He commented, through John, the music that had been played the night before was the music from a Casper movie his family had seen together shortly before he died. The mother began crying and the father shook his head.

Kathy saw this father in the lobby of the hotel right after their private reading with John on Sunday. He was very emotional. He told Kathy there was no way he could be skeptical anymore. He knew his son was okay.

One of the spot readings was very unusual as well as specific. John called out the exact name of a man who had died, saying it was not a common death by any means. It was the husband of the lady sitting right behind me and to my left. He even mentioned the family name of Barlow, which got my attention because it was Kathy's son's name, but the message was for the other lady.

When John said her husband's death was caused by a helicopter blade's decapitating him, she knew this was proof her husband was there. His body hit the ground before the helicopter crashed, as was evidenced by his body's being found quite a distance from the wreckage. He said there had been five men in the helicopter at first, and only two were in it when it crashed. He acknowledged the necklace he'd been wearing when the accident occurred had been damaged. He was aware his wife had taken the damaged necklace to a jeweler and had the usable part of it made into a necklace for her.

He brought up the two mastectomies his wife had and was aware that she had taken up smoking again after his death. The woman told John she didn't worry about the effects that smoking might cause.

"But he does," John said.

The ability of our loved ones to manipulate physical matter was also presented during the reading. John mentioned at this woman's house, the door going into her house was found open four different times.

"That's exactly what happened," she said. "I even called the police and reported these instances, thinking it was a burglar."

"You don't have to worry," John said, "It's your husband doing it."

I could go on and on about how accurate John was. When I was in the restroom during a break, I spoke with the woman whose husband had been decapitated by a four-day-old helicopter. She said she was in shock. Everything John said had been correct. She had even been concerned when John was giving the messages. Apparently there was litigation going on and some information was not to be discussed.

I vividly remember telling John about Mary Jo for the first time. It was near the end of his Saturday workshop in Dallas, and everyone was more or less standing around talking. No one really wanted to leave because the day had been so wonderful. DeDee was partially behind me and to the side. We didn't want John to know anything about her, because she was scheduled for a private reading the next day.

"Have you ever heard of Mary Jo McCabe?" I asked John.

When he told me no, I told him she was a psychic/intuitive who lives in Baton Rouge. I said both of them would work well together. I told him I didn't mean to criticize Judy Guggenheim, but both he and Mary Jo's personalities were very much alike. They were both natural, upbeat and had a sense of humor, not to mention the unbelievable gifts they both had.

John was going to appear in New Orleans in October. Mary Jo had been impressed with all my stories about John's accuracy, so she offered to do a mail-out to her client list and help promote John's upcoming appearance. I told John about her offer, and he seemed pleased she would do this. Especially since they didn't know each other.

The following day, Kathy was having her private reading with John, and I prayed that it was going well. The death of her only child had been terribly devastating to her. Not only had she had to grieve over her loss, but she also was having to deal with the circumstances of Barlow's death. The evidence supported that he had been murdered, but when the case became entangled in snags, the authorities reversed their opinion and ruled Barlow's death a suicide. Kathy knew he had been murdered. She was hoping John could shed some light on what actually happened.

DeDee was scheduled for her private reading immediately following Kathy's. The time slots were forty-five minutes apart. The readings were taking place on an upper floor, the eleventh floor, as I remember. The hotel was beautiful. DeDee and I were killing time in the lobby. Both of us were nervous. We kept talking about Kyle, wondering if he'd show up. He had been so accurate with me. I wanted DeDee to feel some of the solace that a reading could afford.

There were some Thomas Kinkade prints displayed in the lobby, and we were admiring his artwork. DeDee spotted a brightly colored fish print hanging nearby and said,

"Kyle would have loved this. It would have looked good in his apartment, with all the matching colors." Kyle's bedroom motif was all bright primary colors: red, blue, yellow, orange, and green. You almost needed sunglasses to look at it. His accent pieces, even a small decorator lamp with fish were these colors. I agreed it would have matched perfectly.

Kathy walked out of the room. She was very emotional and obviously moved by what had taken place. John had known nothing about Kathy. We made sure nothing was mentioned while she had been in attendance on Friday night and Saturday. But John told her that her only child, a son, had died. He said he had been murdered by three people in an open field while in his truck. It was drug related and there had been a cover-up.

"They have labeled it a suicide, but it was definitely not suicide," he said.

Kathy now had her answer about how Barlow died. Though John could not identify the killers by name, Kathy has an idea who was involved. At the present time, the case is being looked into, but Kathy believes she will probably only find out the exact circumstances when she herself gets to the Other Side.

I know the most difficult death has to be the murder of your child. Not only do you have the pain of such a loss, but having to face those who did it, go through trials, and maybe still have no answer is something that I cannot even imagine.

After Kathy's reading, I was sitting on the window seat overlooking the city, praying that DeDee's reading was going well. It was exactly one year before that Kyle had been pronounced dead. Here I was in Dallas, Texas, hoping to make contact with him again. I'd been to Hollywood, California, and Huntington, New York, to connect with him. It was difficult to comprehend how radically my life had changed. What was important before didn't even matter anymore.

As I kept overlooking the Dallas skyline, I remember thinking to myself, "I hope I don't see a crow now. I hope Kyle is only concentrating on connecting with DeDee." It's odd what goes through our thoughts, the games our minds play.

Then when I saw DeDee as she rounded the corner, her first words were, "Kyle told me to tell you to quit worrying about his coming. He told John he knew we were admiring a picture in the lobby of the hotel, a picture he would like, right before the reading."

I couldn't believe what I was hearing.

"Oh, my gosh, I forgot to pay him," DeDee said. "I was so excited, I just thanked him and walked out."

I told her not to worry, we'd try to catch John between his next two appointments and she could pay him then.

"I know, without absolutely any doubt, that Kyle was there," she said. "He talked about our sex life and no one but he and I knew about that. Do you want me to tell you?"

"No!" I quickly jumped in. "There are some things about Kyle I don't need to know."

Kyle had told DeDee to quit comparing everyone to him, that she needed to get on with her life. The real shocker was Kyle's telling John he didn't like what DeDee put on her body after he died. DeDee had managed to hide it from me the two previous nights in the hotel. She then raised her shirt and exposed the ring she'd had pierced on her naval. DeDee was a former "Miss Arkansas World." I was even surprised to know she had done this. She had it removed soon afterwards because, "Kyle doesn't like it."

It had been a wonderful weekend. John, as usual, was unbelievable. There is no way you can be around John and watch him work with your loved ones on the Other Side and not believe you don't die. His accuracy, compassion, and honesty are evident throughout everything I have ever seen him do.

While driving back home to Louisiana, another car hydroplaned right in front of our car. It went back and forth across the interstate before ending up in the median, upside down. I called 911 on my car phone, again, and the cars behind me stopped to aid them. Never, in my entire life had a car hydroplaned in front of a car I was in. On this trip it happened two times. I tried to figure out what this meant, but I never got an answer. I did drive slower, though, so maybe that was it. Who knows? There are lots of things we'll never know, at least while we're here. Of course, once we cross over, we'll have *all* the answers.

14

A Club You Don't Want to Join

I was a "greeter" at The Compassionate Friends the first time I saw Janice Hurst. My job was to look for anyone new who might show up and welcome them. Trust me, this is a club that no one wants to be a member of. One thing all of us have in common—none of us ever wanted to meet the requirements of belonging to this group. You have to have a child to die to become a member.

When I handed Janice a form to fill out, my heart ached for her. She told me her youngest child, Cory, had been murdered. He was seventeen years old. Her husband, Jimmy, had died of cancer seven years earlier. She was having to face this unspeakable grief alone. Somehow, that night I felt a connection with Janice. I felt she needed me and I wanted to help her.

She told me she had been to see Mary Jo. I knew she was like me as well as all the other parents. She had an unrelenting need to find out all she could about Cory's whereabouts.

So many people don't understand this need we as parents have. I can relate, though, because before Kyle's death, none of this would have made any sense to me either. I remember my Dad remarked one time he couldn't understand why I was going all the way to New York to see John Edward again.

My only response had been, "Why do you visit Mom at the nursing home every day where she has lived for four years with Alzheimer's? Why not go just once?"

We, as parents, still have a need to keep in touch with our children. We want to know what they are doing and if they are happy. Our concern for them doesn't lessen because they have died. It only increases.

At one of John's workshops, I commented to a number of bereaved parents, "Why don't all of us move into a condominium together? We could hire John Edward to be our gardener. We could pay him whatever it takes. That way, we could be comforted all of the time." (An update as this book goes to press—Because of John's highly successful national TV show, *Crossing Over*, and his world-wide popularity, we'd probably have to hijack a number of Brinks trucks to entice him now.)

Sharing with others who have the same sorrow is the only way to make it through such grief. Knowing you aren't alone helps to some degree. You can always find someone who is worse off. There are people I know who have lost two of their children, even three. And I can't imagine having a child who is "missing." How do you ever sleep or get up? Life can truly be a struggle.

Some say we are rewarded in heaven for our suffering here. I always joke with Janice that she'll have the fancy house on the end of the street when we get there. I'll live in the poorer part of town.

Janice's name was added to John's list of people who wanted readings when he appeared in New Orleans in October. I also had DyAnne's name added to the list. DyAnne's oldest son had disappeared, and he had been missing for ten months. Two weeks after they found his murdered body, her second oldest son died in an automobile accident. I met her in Mary Jo's class. Her mother, who was also her business partner, had just died, and DyAnne was divorced. She definitely met the qualifications for being "worse off."

I spent most of Thursday in the hotel lobby either waiting for someone to go for a reading with John or waiting for their exit. As I've said before, no matter how many times I go through this, I am nervous and apprehensive. To this day, though, I've never been disappointed. Not even a little bit. It's always been beyond belief.

Not only did DyAnne's two sons come through, the son who was murdered told her the day he was murdered. No one had known the exact date of his death. DyAnne now knew. She could not believe how accurate the messages were. Both of her sons' distinct personalities showed up. She knew it was they. Even her mother came.

An interesting appearance from someone on the Other Side occurred during DyAnne's meeting with John. This is proof that we, as well as John, have no control over who will show up. Just wishing doesn't make it happen. Let me explain.

Hale Boggs, a United States Representative from Louisiana, had disappeared while over Alaska in an airplane in 1972. The wreckage has never been spotted nor has his body been recovered. His wife, Lindy Boggs, succeeded him, and represented the people of Louisiana from 1973 until 1990. In 1997, President Clinton appointed her as U.S. Ambassador to the Holy See (Vatican). Although DyAnne had never met Hale, DyAnne's sister married into the Boggs family shortly after Hale's disappearance.

"I don't know who this person is," John told DyAnne. "It's like Hale-Bopp (referring to the comet that had been in the news recently) or something. He's telling me he died in an airplane crash in Alaska, and he would like for you to give the following message to his wife. . . ."

DyAnne asked me later, "How do you call the Ambassador to the Vatican and tell her that her dead husband has a message for her?"

This attempt by Hale Boggs makes us aware of the concern of those on the Other Side to let us know they didn't quit existing. They're just in a different body, in a better place. I can imagine how frustrated they must be. This appearance shows that John, Mary Jo, and the other gifted psychic/mediums cannot only bring comfort to us, but to those who have died as well.

I recognized DyAnne's voice as a caller the other night on the *Mary Jo McCabe Radio Show*. DyAnne's brother had disappeared and Mary Jo's message was not reassuring. Poor DyAnne. She'll live in a mansion on an estate when she gets on the Other Side.

Janice's reading with John had been wonderful. Her husband Jimmy even showed up. He said he knew the main reason she was there was to make contact with their son, Cory. Jimmy told her that Cory was with him. Jimmy apologized for never thanking Janice for taking care of him while he was sick with cancer. He wanted her to know he did appreciate all that she had done for him.

Janice often spoke to me about how sick and helpless Jimmy had become near the end of his illness. She had bathed him, fed him, and changed him, all the while being a mother to their three children. She had commented to me how difficult those times were, and that she had never even gotten a thank you from Jimmy. She now knew her husband appreciated her caring for him. This is a comfort to her.

John told Janice her son had died and his name is Cory. I'm always amazed at John's ability to come up with specific names, even quite unusual ones.

"He's telling me he went by a nickname, though. He's saying something like Gumbo."

"Do you want me to tell you?" Janice said, trying to help John.

"No, I'll get it. He went by the name, Gumbo. Gumbo, no! Gumby, he's telling me."

The pallbearers at Cory's funeral had worn special ties in Cory's memory. They were black with a green Gumby painted on each of them. Gumby had tears coming from his eyes. Some of the floral sprays also contained "Gumbys." There are often Gumbys left at the burial site.

Janice was very moved after her reading. As usual, right after the reading, you are elated, because you feel closely connected to your loved one. You actually know they are there, and you are aware of their presence, their being close to you again.

We were jubilant on the drive home. I even commented that both Cory and Kyle were probably glad the reading was over, that we were likely keeping them from the John Denver concert that night. It was October 13th and John Denver had died in a plane crash the day before.

Just yesterday, Janice and I were driving to get a bite to eat and talk. I almost pulled out in front of a car.

Janice yelled, "Look out!" and then added, "Wouldn't it be something if we died at the same time?"

We have often talked about our own deaths, wondering how we'll die and who will die first. We even mention being jealous of the one who gets to be with her son first.

"Cory and Kyle would probably really be upset. There would be two of us with them telling them what to do," I responded.

Only two mothers in such deep grief can joke about such things. If not, we'd be depressed more of the time. Janice and I often talk about how much we want to talk about Cory and Kyle. This upsets our other relatives who think we are more obsessed with our sons now than when they were living. I guess that's why I'm drawn to other bereaved parents. That's why I enjoy going to events pertaining to communication with the dead. You can always find someone who is experiencing what you are.

15

My Turn to Comfort Bobby

Bobby's father, Bob, died unexpectedly at his home in Arkadelphia on September 6, 1996. Bobby, an only son, was devastated.

Because of my experiences, Bobby was aware of John Edward and his ability to connect with our deceased loved ones. When John's office called me in October, 1997, wanting to know the names of people who might want to schedule a private reading, I put Bobby's name on the list.

I had never met Mickey, Bobby's mother. Bobby told me she would be coming with him to see John. I found Mickey to be a very attractive, articulate woman in her late sixties. Her husband was a retired colonel in the military. They were upstanding members of the community, and since Bob's death they have held an annual golf tournament dedicated to Bob's memory. Bobby presents the trophy.

On the way to New Orleans, Bobby sat in the front seat, and Mickey was seated behind him in the back seat. She was so quiet, it almost made me feel uncomfortable. Bobby and I talked about what might happen during the reading and how it might affect them. Our discussion led us to talking about getting rid of Bob's and Kyle's possessions after their deaths.

Bobby commented that his father had given him his ring before his death, but he had felt uncomfortable wearing it after his father died. At that very moment, I thought to myself, "Please mention the ring that Bobby doesn't wear during the reading." I have so much faith in John's ability, that I felt good about what was going to take place at their reading with John.

Mickey continued to remain quiet throughout the hour and a half drive. I tried to break the silence by saying, "I bet you never would have thought you'd be going with a stranger to see a psychic in New Orleans."

She said definitely not. Her friends would think she'd gone crazy. Deep grief can let us do unusual things, though.

As I sat in the hotel lobby looking at my watch, the time moved on. When thirty minutes had passed, I felt as if the reading must be going well, that there was probably a connection being made. I was nervous, excited and scared all at the same time. As I've stated before, this happens every time someone I know is having a reading with John or Mary Jo. Not that I doubt their ability—no one could be better—but I still pray and worry.

Over an hour later when Bobby and his mom stepped from the elevator, I looked at their faces for an expression. They were ecstatic! Mickey sat next to me on the drive home and talked on and on about what her husband had said. She even used my car phone to share the happy news with others, saying it was wonderful.

You have to understand that John Edward is only given a name. I had told John's secretary, Ellen, I wanted certain time slots and had given her the name of "Bobby," nothing else.

Bob came through John and called to "Bobby G.," which is what he called Bobby. I had not known this. He brought up Mickey's name, the names of his other children and also

Mikal, the grandchild he had raised as a son. He mentioned many personal things, even that Mickey had not gone back to the country club after his death. Then Bob told Mickey to say hello to his best friend, Al, who lives in Philadelphia. I don't know if Mickey has had the courage to share the message with Al yet.

As I listened intently to all the messages they received from Bob, my excitement reached a pinnacle when Bobby said, "Oh, yeah, Dad asked me why I wasn't wearing his ring." Bobby now wears his father's ring daily.

16

Together at Last

Friday evening, John was to do his seminar. Over three hundred people had made reservations to listen to John talk about what he does and how he does it. If you've read *One Last Time*, a bestseller John has written, he explains everything about his gift. It's a must-read. I've read hundreds of books, but this book is one of my favorites. It's easy reading, and it helps to erase any skepticism you might have about reaching your loved ones. It's an eye opener.

As usual, we arrived early. Jim, Bobby, Mickey and I were seated in the lobby area just outside the room where the event would take place. I thought I recognized the voice of the lady sitting behind a table taking tickets. It was Ellen, John's secretary from New York. I was able at last to meet her and put a face with the voice I'd often heard over the phone.

Mary Jo was finally going to see John Edward. Though she had not seen him at work, she had done a mail-out to help promote the event. John had remarked to me how much he appreciated her doing this. He said it was very rare to have someone in the field helping to promote someone else, especially someone who doesn't even know you. Fate was beginning to work.

Almost everyone was seated. John was in the lobby area where we had been seated earlier. I could see him pacing back and forth, rubbing his hands together in a sort of meditative state. I've seen him do this before every event. I purposely kept watching Mary Jo. Jim and I were seated on the right of the aisle near the front. Mary Jo was mingling with friends and had seated herself across the aisle from us on the left side. People were still coming in. The show was due to start in about ten minutes.

Mary Jo stood up and walked out through the door. I thought I knew what she was going to do. I stood up and walked part way down the aisle so I would have a better view outside the door. There is no way of expressing how excited I was when I saw Mary Jo McCabe and John Edward introduce themselves and shake hands. I thought of the first time I met Mary Jo two months after Kyle's death. Then I thought of when I met John three months later. From that moment on, I always thought about how wonderful it would be if they worked together, never dreaming it would actually happen. But finally, John Edward from Huntington, New York, and Mary Jo McCabe from Baton Rouge, Louisiana, had met. Mary Jo seated herself with a friend at the very back of the room. She was going to see John's ability for herself.

Later, when Mary Jo and John were appearing together in New Orleans in February, 1998, Mary Jo acknowledged me and asked me to stand up. Then in April, 1999, when John was appearing in New Orleans by himself to a packed house, he asked if I'd get in front of the audience and talk about Mary Jo and give out her phone number since, "She is a gifted psychic located in the area." They complement each other and support what the other does.

About an hour and a half before this event began, I spotted Janice with her friend, Siri. Janice was still exuberant from her reading the day before. She commented that she wished Cory's friends could be there. She said they had been very close to Cory and were really having a tough time dealing with his death.

"Why not call and tell them to come down?" I asked.

Janice hesitated.

"Why not? It's a little over an hour's drive. They might get here a little late, but they'd get to see most of it."

Janice found a phone and told me three of them were on their way. At the time for John to begin his presentation, I was not only watching Mary Jo but was also looking for the three teenage boys. They walked in just as John was being introduced and seated themselves near the back of the room next to Janice and in front of Mary Jo.

John was preparing for a documentary. A video, *After Death Communication*, was in the planning stages, and his appearance that night was being filmed for possible use on the tape he hoped to release in the near future. John prefers the audience not to tape his readings or his appearances. He says it interferes with his energy connection. He said he didn't like having to tape the show, but it needed to be done for a video he was making. At that time, I wondered if the taping would affect John's performance, but I soon learned it made no difference.

In the back of my mind I was hoping Cory would be one of the souls on the Other Side to come through. But that would be asking for too much, or would it? No, it wasn't too much. There is on record a film of when Cory showed up. You can even see Mary Jo shaking her head in disbelief on the video.

Cory directed his messages to his three friends. He thanked them for being the pallbearers at his funeral, and he mentioned the Gumby key chains that each of them carried. Cory reminded them also they had chickened out about getting the Gumby tattoos they had talked about getting. He talked about the class trip to Cancun they had all planned to go on and that he had purchased a ticket for before his death.

"Don't worry," Cory said, "I got to go anyway. I was there." He proceeded to mention some of the things that took place during the boys' trip to Cancun. You could tell his friends were shocked. They kept smiling while shaking their heads.

Cory then brought up the episode when the four of them had camped in the woods behind Janice's house. He talked about how they had gotten scared and ended up camping in his backyard. He brought up different things that had happened while in high school, and the boys acknowledged they were all true. Janice was not aware of some of the information from Cory.

Janice and one of the boys' mother appear on the John Edward video, *After Death Communication*. As Janice remarks on the video, "Yes, it does bring you comfort, but it also acts like a Band-Aid. The wound will always be there, and there will always be a scar."

As I write this, John is putting together some new videos. I hook onto his website every day, trying to keep up to date on the progress of this new endeavor.

This brings up something. John is responsible for my becoming somewhat computer literate. We have had a computer in our house for over two years. I am a schoolteacher, a college graduate and was an honor student. I believe I have at least average intelligence. But until I found out that John had a website, I had never even attempted to turn on our computer. I thought a "hard drive" was a trip over six hours, with no knowledge of how long a "soft drive" might take.

But I'm learning. My favorite sites are www.johnedward.net, www.mjmccabe.com, www.artbell.com (go to Albert Taylor's website, www.alberttaylor.com, from there) and the Beanie Baby site.

Albert Taylor was involved in NASA's International Space Station program and has performed development engineering on a top-secret program which has since become known as the F-117A Stealth Fighter. In 1992, he developed two prototype computers and started a company called Phoenix Computer Systems. After many paranormal events, including Out-of-Body Experiences, he left behind nearly two decades of work as an aeronautical engineer/ scientist to author and publish his book, *Soul Traveler*. This book and his appearances on the *Art Bell Radio Show* have made me even more spiritually aware of an existence beyond the present world. In a nutshell, his book explains how he is able to leave his body and travel to other places, then return to his body. More than any other, his work enables me to understand who we really are. We are not just our body if we are able to leave our body behind and go to other places. The fact that Dr. Taylor is more aware of things when he is out of his body adds credence to why Kyle seems to know *everything* now.

About the Beanie Baby site, since I got caught up in the buying frenzy of animal bean bags, I often check to see if, in the future, any of my investments might pay off and I can use my hot tub once again. Yes, the Beanie Babies are now stored in my dry hot tub. What we won't do for an addiction. I was one of those who stood in line at five o'clock in the morning in hopes of getting a "Princess" or an "Erin." And I bought hundreds of McDonald's Happy Meals in order to get the smaller versions. The raccoons probably couldn't figure out why they were getting so many hamburgers. Here again, this might be a "non-normal" part of me.

17

I'm a Student Again

While attending Mary Jo's lectures or appearances, people often ask me how many readings I've had with Mary Jo. They are surprised when I tell them only one. Then I explain how fortunate I am that she started the "Thursday night class" soon after my reading. I tell them how I have spent every Thursday night with her for over two years except for a couple of nights I missed because I was out of state. I'd have come back then if I'd only been out of town.

Often, upon finding out about this class, people want to know more about it and what they have to do to join. I jokingly say, "You have to hope that one of us dies or moves far away or you'll never have a chance of getting in." The class size is limited due to the number of seats in the room. Mary Jo feels comfortable with only so many, because she wants it to be a close group. And it is just that.

We first met in Mary Jo's office on Wrenwood Drive in Baton Rouge where she gives private readings. But when she was able to acquire a lease for an adjoining larger room that connects to her office, we moved there. We always sit in a circle, grabbing the same seat each night. If someone accidentally sits in another seat, we act as if someone has stolen something. We have to get it right before we begin. One night, the chairs were arranged in a semi-circle. As everyone walked into the room, you could see the same expression, like "No, this can't be." We moved the chairs back into our familiar circle.

I felt out of place the first couple of times we met. I walked in the first night very much in grief. Everyone was laughing, talking, and greeting each other as if they were having a big reunion. I felt a complete stranger until I met Ruth, who told me she didn't know anyone either. So I had found a comrade. One other thing that Ruth and I had in common . . . both her husband and Kyle had died as a result of an accident occurring at the same bridge, the Amite River Bridge.

But no one there had a child to die. Why were they even there, I thought?

Things changed as time went on. I soon felt as if I were joining family every Thursday night. Looking back, I see how special everyone in the class was. Each person was on his or her own soul's journey, experiencing very different paths along the way. But these very diverse paths taught us so much. I truly felt as if we were "one" when we were to-gether. But it was not only the closeness of the group that helped me, often Kyle would show up, and you can imagine how thrilled I was.

One night, Mary Jo told me Kyle was there, and I was to look for a one-legged blackbird as a sign from him. Jim and I hardly ever sit on the sofa together. He has "his" recliner chair, and I usually prop my feet on the coffee table and sit on the sofa. For some reason, three days after Mary Jo's message from Kyle, both Jim and I were seated on the sofa together, looking out the window over our patio and backyard.

"Look! A one-legged blackbird!" Jim yelled. I couldn't believe what I was seeing. Here was this blackbird with only one leg. No, one leg was not injured and being held up. It only had one leg, and it was right in front of us, just a few feet from the window. It extended its wings to help maintain balance and turned around two times, as if to make sure we would notice it. It hopped and fluttered onto the driveway, then flew off. Jim and I were astounded.

Shortly afterwards during another class, Kyle showed up again. Mary Jo said he wanted to know what we thought of the blackbird. He then commented about a frog. When I got home from class that night, Jim was waiting for me, as he usually did. He was always anxious to hear what had happened during the class. He'd often flick the carport lights when I drove in, jokingly saying, "Kyle did it."

I told Jim that Kyle had mentioned a frog. Jim looked surprised. He told me the previous day while at work he had spotted a frog on top of the dumpster. He couldn't figure out how it had gotten there. He said he thought it unusual at the time, because he had not seen a frog on his property in over twelve years. Jim told me he caught the frog and then let it go in the grass.

Megan was one of my classmates. She sat to my right a couple of seats over. I always admired how neatly she dressed, often wearing black, which complemented her dark black hair. She owns a business in town, is the co-author of a book, and has had her picture in the newspaper promoting book signings at various stores. One night while channel surfing, I spotted her doing a show on TV. I had been to her house the night of Mary Jo's first radio broadcast, when she and her husband were having a party to celebrate Mary Jo's new endeavor. When I saw Megan on TV, I quickly reached for a blank video and taped what was left of her segment.

Why did I tape her? It still amazes me that these very intelligent, upstanding citizens with families and "normal" lives are very aware of their spiritual beings and are playing a major role in my spiritual path. I guess who they are in some way gives added validity to what is going on in my life now. It helps to let me know what I am doing is "normal" and I am following the correct path.

I was absolutely shocked when one Thursday night, Megan looked at me and asked, "Did Kyle have a birthmark on his chin?"

I told her, "No, but he had a scar there from an earlier automobile accident. Why do you want to know?"

"He's standing right next to you! He has such a big grin. His smile is a lot bigger than yours."

Other classmates became caught up in this conversation.

"He's got on a plaid shirt and blue jeans. He's putting his hands in his pockets. He's got thick hair and is smiling."

I couldn't believe what I was hearing. Of course, you can only imagine how excited I was. "Have you ever seen a picture of Kyle?" I asked.

When she told me no, I reached for my purse and pulled out a picture of Kyle and handed it to Megan.

She gasped and said, "It is Kyle!"

That night when I arrived home, Jim didn't have to ask me what happened during the class. I shouted when I walked in the back door, "Kyle was there tonight! Megan saw him."

Later on, I asked Megan about the vision she had of Kyle. She told me she usually doesn't share what goes on in the classes with her husband, but she did tell him about seeing Kyle. She told him she could feel Kyle's excitement of her being able to see him.

Another time when Megan brought up that she had seen Kyle standing next to me, we were in the lobby of a hotel in New Orleans. We were having a conversation with some people she had just met when she told them about the experience. Megan had no inhibitions about sharing this spiritual part of herself. Because of this, she will never know the good feelings her experiences have brought to me.

18

Kyle Wishes Me a Happy Birthday

When CeCe Tye found out John Edward would be appearing again in Dallas, Texas, I didn't have to twist her arm. She begged me to try and get her a private reading. She had been overwhelmed by both my daughter's experience and her own daughter's experience with John.

I called Ellen, John's secretary in New York, and she scheduled a time slot for CeCe. CeCe has often told me she wishes she had known what she knows now concerning the afterlife. She had struggled with the death of her mother at a very young age. Though she was raised by her loving Aunt Siso in a loving home, the loss of her mother when she was nine had left a void in her life.

I drove up to Hope, Arkansas, to pick up CeCe and DeDee. It's a good thing I'm not JayJay. This reminds me, though, of something I left out concerning the reading that Jamie and I had with John at his home in New York. John had said, "Your son is saying, 'JJ.'" I jumped in and said that both our names started with the letter "J." He then said, "No, he's saying JJ together, like it's one name." Suddenly it clicked. Jamie and I both remembered that Kyle often called her JJ when he was younger.

We were all excited about our trip to Dallas. I stayed with CeCe and DeDee the night before our trip so we could get an early start the next morning. I thought it was very early when I heard CeCe outside the bedroom door where I was sleeping.

"I can't stand the pain. What can I do?"

Sitting up in bed, I asked, "What time is it?"

"Two-thirty," I heard CeCe say. No wonder it was still dark outside.

CeCe is like me in so many ways. There are usually three or more Diet Coke cans sitting on various tables throughout my house. I open a drink, take a few sips, and put it down. When I'm thirsty again, I've forgotten where I put the first one, so I get another one out of the fridge. I know it's wasteful, but it's a bad habit I have. I laughed when I visited CeCe's house for the first time. I noticed Diet Coke cans placed everywhere. She even has the same two prints framed and hanging in her kitchen that I have in my kitchen. We often buy the same outfit, not knowing the other one has purchased it.

Apparently CeCe was having trouble sleeping as I often do. She decided to tidy up her house at 2:30 in the morning. While straightening out the recliner, one of her fingernails tore completely off. She was moaning in pain.

"Put it under cold running water," I said.

I remember her asking, "Why?"

"I don't have any idea," I said. I was only trying to help her. It was all bloody and she couldn't stand the pain.

DeDee awakened during the commotion and the three of us headed to the emergency room. Me, with my pj's on, covered by a coat.

She had the finger cleaned up, got it medicated and the doctor covered it with some type of gauze wrap. Her hand was put in a splint. They'd given her a pain killer, but gave her a prescription to be filled later to counteract the pain.

That morning, we three very tired women headed for our rendezvous with John Edward. We stopped at the first drug store we saw to get CeCe's prescription filled. It was closed. Her pain increased. We even stopped at one drug store and they didn't have what was needed to fill the prescription. So on we traveled. The reading was scheduled at noon at a hotel we were unfamiliar with and didn't know the location of. CeCe kept telling me to drive on, that we couldn't be late.

CeCe had planned on this trip to see John by herself. DeDee had already had a reading alone, and we all decided it better that this reading be for CeCe only. But CeCe's hand was all bandaged up and her handwriting hand, at that. There was no way she could take notes. I remember her joking that Kyle had caused the injury and was responsible for its happening. There was no alternative; CeCe had to have someone with her. DeDee volunteered to be the note taker.

What I was afraid would happen, happened. Who was the first person to show up from the Other Side? Kyle, of course.

John Edward began, "There is a son-like figure, a younger male, who is with your parents. He is a son-in-law type, but he is not your son-in-law. You're not here to connect with him, but he's sneaking up. You used to make this apple dessert he liked (apple crisp). He's funny. He's your favorite."

CeCe had often told me how much she loved Kyle. She said he was special. I remember when DeDee and Kyle were dating, I talked with CeCe over the phone, for what reason, I don't remember. I didn't even know her, but I remember her telling me what a cute couple they were and what beautiful children they would have. Honestly, at the time, I thought this a little strange coming from the mother of the girl Kyle was dating. Now, I don't question her statement at all. The special bond that CeCe had with Kyle has become very evident since his death. CeCe's continued concern for Kyle and us, his parents, has meant the world to Jim and me.

John Edward continued, "He was outspoken and sometimes you thought disrespectful. But he had this 'little boy' feeling. Even if he did something bad, you had to laugh and you loved him."

Once CeCe had bought a new bedspread and apparently after she'd made the bed, Kyle jumped on it and rolled around with her yelling at him to stop. Kyle liked to play pranks on everyone, especially CeCe.

Kyle's high school football coach Willis Stelly and his wife Connie were at the hospital after Kyle's accident. They were in the room with us when the doctor came in and told us that no oxygen was getting to Kyle's brain, that he was brain dead.

I'll always remember the story Willis told us about Kyle. Coach Stelly had come into the dressing room after football practice one day. His young son, Will, was in the garbage can all tied up with jock straps. Willis told us sometimes he got mad at some of the pranks Kyle pulled, but they were always so funny, he had to laugh and love him.

Everyone who knew Kyle knew this side of him, especially his mother. I used to worry about Kyle when he was driving his car. Like most parents, I was always concerned for his safety. I constantly said, "Put your seat belt on, drive slowly, stop and rest," along with all of the other parental advice.

It was at least a seven-hour trip from Kyle's college to our home. He called one time at about nine o'clock at night. He said he was leaving Arkadelphia then and would see us later.

"No, Kyle! It's too late. Get a good night's sleep and leave early in the morning," I tried to convince him.

"I'll be okay. I'll be safe."

"Kyle, please, please, don't leave now," I pleaded, "I'll worry all night."

Then I heard laughing and a horn honk. He was in his car in our carport.

Back to John Edward.

John then said, "I'm seeing the name KL, like Kal, no. It's Kyle. You have better memories of him than you do your mother."

DeDee then said, "I feel bad. It's not my reading. It's my mother's reading."

John replied, "He says he doesn't want you to miss the opportunity to connect with your parents. So *he's* here to validate that he is with your parents. The fourth month, he's telling me he passed in the month of April. I see the number 6, 16, or 26. Something with a 6." DeDee said he was 26, and John said that could be it.

"It was sudden. He is very rejuvenated. He is strong and has made a great transition. He has Peter Pan's freedom. Let his family know he is okay. He's telling me his family is okay. I mean, of course, it's a tragedy, but they're working really hard to get it. They are either very religious or have become very spiritual."

"Biscuits, who made the biscuits? It's like a really airy, spongy cake." Don, CeCe's husband used to make them and Kyle loved them.

John continued, "He died in a car accident. He's talking about his mom's birthday in October. Say 'Happy Birthday' to his mom. He has another name he went by. Not his first name, but another name." Paige, DeDee's sister called Kyle "Collyea" all the time. Kyle had even written "Collyea" on a big board.

CeCe's relatives did show up and gave very accurate information. Of course, I just copied DeDee's notes that pertained to Kyle's messages. Throughout the reading, John said, at least three times, "This funny kid keeps popping in," which showed Kyle still has a sense of humor.

I've heard and read so many times that just because we die, we don't automatically become a loving, caring and angelic being. We remain who we were. We keep our memories, our same personality, our same tastes, and our same interests. So if you're an uncaring, boring, pessimistic, lazy, criticizing, selfish person here, you most probably won't be real popular in the hereafter.

Kyle's interests continue on the Other Side. He's been seen with all kinds of animals, even holding a raccoon. He's been riding on an antelope, walking barefoot in a creek, chewing tobacco, at a race track, and with a beer in his hand. He did all of these when he was here, except for riding the antelope. But knowing Kyle, you never know.

"You need to call this guy's mom and tell her 'Happy Birthday.' He's persistent about it," were John's last words as CeCe and DeDee thanked John and got up to leave.

19

A Sellout for John

CeCe was apparently learning to live with her pain, because she didn't even bring up getting the prescription filled anymore. CeCe, DeDee and I drove by the Unity Church where John would be appearing that night.

"I wonder what's going on?" DeDee remarked. "Why would there be so many cars there at four o'clock in the afternoon?"

We turned down a few more streets driving through residential areas on the drive to the motel where we would be staying that night. It was three hours before John's scheduled appearance. I stressed that we just needed to freshen up at the motel because the fun part is talking with the people beforehand. They agreed to go early.

We quickly showered except for CeCe, because her hand was bandaged, and we put on fresh make-up. I started to put on my number 42 necklace, then said I'd wear something else. CeCe encouraged me to wear it. I made sure it was beneath my turtleneck. I didn't want John to be able to see it. I had worn it before, but always had made a point to keep it covered. We headed off for the big event.

"I can't believe all these cars are still here," DeDee said, as we rounded the curve and the church came into view. "Something else has to be going on here."

I drove around the big parking lot looking for a spot to park. I couldn't find any vacant places. I kept driving, but I still couldn't find anything.

"Drop me off at the entrance," CeCe told me, "I'll get us a front row seat."

DeDee and I kept looking. We were almost a block away from the church and still couldn't find a place to park. We passed some people walking who had apparently parked their car. DeDee rolled down her car window and asked, "What's going on here tonight? Why are all these cars here?"

We both looked at each other in disbelief when they responded, "Some psychic from New York. He was on the radio station this morning." We were stunned. All of the people for John Edward? No way. Not that he's not good, but John had even commented to CeCe during her reading that afternoon he expected maybe a hundred people or so.

Now we were really antsy. We still couldn't find a place to park. It occurred to both of us if all of these cars were for John, what must it be like inside? I panicked. I thought, hopefully, CeCe who is known for getting things done, had found a front row seat or at least one near the front.

DeDee and I spotted a vacant spot at the same time and yelled, "Yeah, at last."

It was a long walk to the entrance of the church. We walked fast. We passed lots of others who were scurrying to the door. Something else had to be going on tonight. There were just too many people.

"A psychic," a lady responded, as we passed her and asked why she was there.

"Can you believe all the seats are taken, even the balcony is full," was how CeCe greeted us. "I even walked up to the three tables in the lobby, asking which table was for John Edward, and they said, 'All of them.'"

The place was packed. I was concerned. CeCe and DeDee were concerned. Here I'd ordered the tickets to this event way in advance. They were numbered 003, 004, and 005. I commented to Jim, when the tickets arrived, "Can you believe two people got ahead of me?"

This was getting scary. I looked for Merrily, whom I'd talked with a few times over the phone when I was scheduling CeCe's reading. Merrily told me John's workshop for the next day had been canceled and when she could find time, she'd refund my money. That was the least of my worries.

"Where can we sit?" I asked her. "We drove all the way from Louisiana and Arkansas and bought tickets weeks ago." I was trying to get her sympathy. We were desperate.

"In a few minutes, they're going to get some chairs from another room and line them along the wall," Merrily tried to reassure us.

How big was this wall, anyway? The huge lobby was packed with people. I had peeked in the auditorium and every seat was taken. We didn't wait. We found a room with chairs and CeCe, DeDee and I picked up one. We didn't care what anyone said. We walked down the right aisle, each carrying a chair and put them down against the wall. Others followed and soon all the walls were lined with chairs.

The floors began filling up. There were four aisles. A woman appeared on stage saying the fire marshal said one of the aisles had to be cleared. No one moved. People began hollering they "sat on the floor first." Reluctantly, people cleared one aisle. I don't know where they went. Every space in that auditorium had a body on it, except for the cleared aisle.

DeDee told me the church seated 1200 people, so no telling how many were actually in attendance. John told me later this had been his largest turnout ever.

Talking with people seated around us before John came on stage, I found out that most were there as a result of hearing John over the radio that morning. One lady told me she became so emotional while driving she had to pull over, she was crying so hard. Most everyone I talked with was in deep grief over the loss of a loved one.

There was a man stationed in the balcony with a microphone and a man downstairs with one. You needed a microphone to hear any of the responses. John walked on stage. He explained what he did, how he did it, and again, as he always does, he told everyone to be happy for those who do come through. He said simply knowing your loved one does live on with proof through those who receive messages should be a comfort to everyone in attendance.

A husband showed up and talked about making love to his wife on a piano. This information embarrassed the lady because she'd brought their daughter to see John. Another soul from the Other Side spoke about a lady having a blue elephant in her purse. She pulled it out and showed us. I looked around the room. Everyone shook their heads in disbelief. The messages were very specific and the recipients acknowledged their accuracy. CeCe didn't even mention her hurting finger anymore. John was awesome.

John always says he is directed to the person for whom the message is intended. He usually begins walking in a certain direction and knows what area, or often what row, the intended person is sitting in. He is very accurate in locating the correct person.

He began walking over to the right of the stage in our direction. He said a young male who was thrown from a vehicle in April was there. His mother's birthday was in October. He thanks you for the birthday tribute you had for his birthday (cake and balloons).

"His father knows he's okay. He's telling me you are wearing a piece of jewelry related to him."

The microphone was in my face. I looked down at the frog pin that was on my blazer lapel. "I have this frog pin. Kyle liked frogs."

"No," John said. "He's telling me you have on a necklace with a number on it related to him."

The audience was stunned when I pulled out my number "42" and said, "This was his football number."

Before this trip to Dallas, CeCe kept urging me to get another reading with John. I'd already had two private readings and didn't really feel the need to have another one. I remembered back to October 13, though, when I was bringing others to New Orleans for their private readings with John. It was my birthday and I had wondered whether Kyle was upset with me for not having scheduled a reading. But I was receiving so much comfort from the others' messages from their deceased children I felt it was best for me not to push my luck. CeCe, however, was relentless, and I finally agreed if she could get me one, then it would be okay.

My phone rang at 9:25 p.m. on October 27, 1997. CeCe could hardly contain herself. Ellen had just called her from New York. Both CeCe and I had appointments with John in Dallas. We would see him individually on Friday, the 14th of November.

Ellen phoned me on Saturday, November 8th, from New York. She informed me that John's Saturday and Sunday workshops in Dallas had been canceled. She said, though, he was still doing my reading Friday and the seminar Friday night.

The very next day, I got another call from New York. Ellen said when John had seen my name on the reading list for Dallas, he had commented he didn't want my son to have to come up with new stuff and felt I should save my money.

When I questioned Ellen a little more, she said John apparently didn't want to put pressure on my son.

I was a little disappointed, but since I didn't really feel the need to connect with Kyle, I decided it was meant to be. I definitely didn't want to put any pressure on Kyle.

When John began directing messages to me from Kyle Friday night in Dallas, in a way, I felt guilty. But after I'd shown the audience my "42" necklace, John said, "He thanks you for taking the pressure off him. Do you understand what that means?"

I nodded my head and said, "Yes." None of the almost fourteen hundred people in the room had any idea what that message meant. But it made me happy, and DeDee, CeCe and I laughed. Though John hadn't wanted to bother Kyle, Kyle still managed to keep jumping in during CeCe's reading, and he came to me that night at the seminar. It is something I will never forget.

As John started to walk away from me, he said, "By the way, he wants you to know his coming tonight is his birthday present for you, for the birthday you had in October."

So Kyle let me know he was with me on my birthday, after all.

When we got back to our motel, I phoned Jim. I woke him up and told him over and over what had happened. CeCe fell asleep, never having had her prescription filled.

20

Is It Possible?

I have become obsessed with watching or listening to anyone psychic. I am drawn to anything having to do with the Other Side where my son is. One time Mary Jo was appearing on *The Edge of Reality*, a radio show broadcast from New York City. It was June 7, 1998. I spent the entire two hours she was on the air driving up and down my driveway very slowly trying to get a clear audio. I could only make out a few words, then it would fade, so I'd move the car some more. This happened over and over again.

When John appears on the *Rob and Robb* show in New Orleans, I sit in the car in my carport with the motor running taping it. I can't pick up the station as clearly inside my house. One time it was so cold outside, I had a blanket with me while I was drinking hot chocolate and taping through an open window in order to plug in my tape player outside the car.

So I do go to extremes not to miss anything. When I found out John would be appearing on the *Larry King Live* television show on the international channel, CNN, I was wild. I was so excited his name was on the TV screen, I took pictures for the promotion of his appearance later that night. I even mailed John one of the pictures with his name as it appeared on the TV screen. Maybe he thought I was a little odd, but I was excited about it.

I phoned everyone I knew who had lost a child and who was aware of my after-death journey. I wanted them all to watch "*The* John Edward," the guy I had been to who had brought Kyle and me together again. He was going to be on national TV. I taped his appearance as I tape all of his appearances if I know about them. I make tapes of the tapes and send them to people in grief. Mary Jo even supplies me with blank tapes now. She knows I also tape all of her appearances and make copies to give to others.

One time, Shannon, Mary Jo's secretary, phoned me. She asked if I'd taped Mary Jo's appearance of her being interviewed on television as a promotion for her upcoming radio show. Of course, I had taped it; she said Mary Jo knew I would have it. I've taped all of her radio shows except when I'm out of town, then I make sure someone tapes them for me.

Boy, I sure get sidetracked. But I did want you to know how obsessed I am about anything having to do with after-death communication. I'm assuming you get the point.

Anyway, what's really amazing is I get messages from Kyle through John's radio shows broadcast from New Orleans when he does short readings from call-ins. I even received messages during his first two appearances on *Larry King Live*, and his two appearances on the *Crier Report*. The messages apparently make no sense to the caller, but they make complete sense to me. After the first two times this happened, I commented to others about the possibility of Kyle's being responsible for these specific messages. Maybe it was just wishful thinking on my part, but they stood out and were very obvious.

Some of the messages were "Congratulations on the new vehicle." My husband had just bought me a Mercedes Benz.

Kyle would have been thrilled. We had never owned a luxury car, and I was upset when Jim bought it, because I didn't think we could afford it.

"Kyle will like driving in it with you, and it cost $42,000" were the exact words spoken. I never said another word.

John mentioned a green iguana in an aquarium. I remember the lady John was doing a reading for saying she had a dog. John remarked something to the effect, "Not unless you have a green dog in an aquarium."

I had bought Kyle "Iggy." We got the big aquarium, the heated rock and all. I never liked going into Kyle's room when he wasn't home. I never knew where I'd find Iggy. Kyle gave him the freedom to roam his room. Iggy's favorite place was the curtain rod.

Then one time John mentioned pigeons in a cage. This apparently meant nothing to the caller, but Jim and Kyle had constructed an unusually large pigeon cage. I even have pictures of Kyle's sitting in it reading the newspaper with his pigeons.

So maybe I'm looking for messages. But with all that has happened, I wouldn't put it past Kyle to pop in on other people's readings. Anything is possible from the spirit world.

21

There Are No Coincidences

The ability of our loved ones to send us signs is something I'd never even heard of or thought possible until after Kyle died. I've learned since, when we are ready to seek out this knowledge of after-death communication, we will become aware of it. There is a time for everything, the perfect time.

What has made me truly grateful is so many people who knew Kyle have been very open to his ability to give us signs. Sharing their special experiences with me has helped greatly in easing some of the pain.

On October 6, 1997, CeCe phoned. Kortnee had married a month earlier. She and her new husband, Denny, were watching the video of their wedding for the first time. Denny was holding a flashlight which had no batteries.

When a close-up of DeDee, Kyle's girlfriend, was shown as she walked down the aisle during the wedding procession, the flashlight went on and off.

Denny said, "Did you see that? How did that happen?"

"Yes, I saw it," Kortnee replied.

Later during the video, the camera again zoomed in on DeDee's face. The flashlight turned on and off again. Denny checked to make sure there were no batteries in the light. There weren't. It was then that Kortnee called CeCe saying she knew it was Kyle.

Another "sighting" of Kyle happened a little later. Kortnee was leaving from the hospital one night where she worked as a nurse when the light went off and on in the parking lot by her car. She took this as a signal of Kyle's presence. Kyle has come to her in dreams, very vivid dreams, she has told me. One time she and Kyle hugged in a dream, and she said she could actually feel him.

When Kyle was alive, he visited the Tye residence in Hope, Arkansas, one night very late. He knocked on Kortnee's bedroom window, but both DeDee and Kortnee were not at home that night. Don heard the knocking and thinking it might be a prowler, he grabbed his shotgun and went outside. Thank heavens, he recognized Kyle. Kyle spent the night on their sofa.

Don is a very religious and compassionate man. He's a hard worker, a family man, and I admire him greatly. After Kyle's death, Don told me this story. He and CeCe were in bed for the night when they both heard a "knock, knock, knock," on the bedroom door which was closed. They sat up in bed and asked who was there? There was no answer. Don and CeCe were uneasy. CeCe reached for the phone beside her bed and called the other wing of the house. Kortnee answered. Everyone was in their rooms and sound asleep. Don got his shotgun.

CeCe told Kortnee that everyone should lock their doors and stay in their rooms. Don searched the inside of the house, then went outside and searched. When he found no one, he *knew* who had done it. He told me he was sure Kyle was responsible. It was the exact "knock" that Kyle had done when Don had found him outside Kortnee's window. So the only two times Don has reached for his gun were when he heard Kyle's knocking—once in the physical and once in the spiritual.

One night, CeCe told me she awakened and saw Kyle and DeDee standing by the foot of her bed in Hawaiian luau skirts. Apparitions of Kyle and the awareness of his presence help me understand his whereabouts and know he is all right.

It was Tuesday, September 2, 1997. I received a phone call from CeCe. She told me that DeDee had been visiting in Miami over the past weekend. She was with her boyfriend, Toby and Toby' brother, Thomas and his girlfriend. Thomas plays professional tennis but had to withdraw from the U.S. Open in New York because of a fever. He was fifth in money winnings in 1999 on the professional circuit.

While staying at the Biltmore Hotel in Miami, DeDee was in the bathroom when the light turned off and on all by itself. Then when the bellhop brought food into the room, he walked toward the light switch and the light came on before he even touched the switch. He said, "Did you see that?"

DeDee said, "Yes, I saw that."

"We have ghosts in this hotel." The bellhop added, "They even open doors."

On another trip to Florida, DeDee and Toby were in Key West. They rented bicycles and were off for a tour of the city. They rode into a cemetery and DeDee laughed when she read one of the headstones, "I told you I was sick."

While in the cemetery, DeDee struck up a conversation with the caretaker, and he told her about a psychic who had an office nearby. Toby followed DeDee as they rode off.

DeDee went in to see the psychic by herself. Toby said he'd ride around a little, and come back later. Of course, DeDee's main reason for visiting the psychic was that she hoped to make contact with Kyle. Apparently Kyle did come through with some very specific information that brought relief to DeDee.

After the reading ended, DeDee and the psychic were talking, and the psychic questioned DeDee about having any other experiences with psychics. DeDee told her about John Edward and how I found out about John through James Van Praagh.

Guess who had been to see this psychic in Key West just before DeDee had walked in? James Van Praagh.

"No way!" DeDee said when she was told this.

The psychic showed her the sign-in book where James had just written his name. Remember, there are no coincidences.

It was only two weeks after Kyle's death. Janet Benson, the wife of Kyle's head football coach in college called me. During our conversation, she brought up something that had happened to an assistant coach and his wife.

Coach Murphree had a vivid dream of Kyle soon after the accident before Kyle was taken off life-support. The very same night, his wife Pat sat up in bed and felt a light of energy emitting from her head area. This energy was going to Kyle. She knew it was Kyle's letting them know he was okay. When I spoke with her later concerning this experience, she told me it had never happened before.

Then on Friday, October 24, 1997, I came home early from school, not feeling well. Jim came home later to check on me. When he parked his truck by the boat port, all was quiet. When he returned to his truck after seeing I was going to make it, he heard a loud noise coming from the minnow bucket hanging from the roof of the boat port. The aerator had turned on all by itself. Jim opened the lid of the minnow bucket and turned it off.

Another time when Jamie was visiting us, I parked the car in front of the boat port, and we both got out of the car. All of a sudden, a radio on the deck of the boat came on very loudly. We both looked at each other. She walked toward the radio and picked it up. She turned it off, but it kept playing. We couldn't believe it. She even went inside the house and got her camcorder. She recorded on the video, "The radio that Kyle turned on and wouldn't let us turn off." You can actually hear the radio playing after you see her turn the button to "OFF."

One day, I was very depressed and overly emotional. I was in the bathroom when all of a sudden, I heard music playing. I followed the sound and pulled out a drawer in the bedroom. I didn't even know a radio was in there and neither did Jim. We had not touched it. Kyle had to have turned it on. I immediately thanked him, and my depression lifted.

I hope by my telling you some of these episodes I believe to be signs, you will become more aware of signs from your loved ones. Imagine their flicking lights to let you know they're around and your thinking you just need to replace the light bulb. After awhile, I'm sure they get frustrated and give up. Trust me, noticing these messages will not only bring consolation to you but to them as well.

I was walking on our middle school campus one morning and the thought of Kyle came to my mind (as it often does). Just then, I spotted a penny on the sidewalk. I picked it up and said to myself, "Thank you, Kyle." Granted, sometimes Kyle might not be responsible, maybe a kid just dropped it, but I always acknowledge Kyle just in case he is there.

Anyway, thirty minutes later, while walking across the grass on the campus, I again thought of the penny I'd found, and just then I spotted another penny in the grass. Somehow before picking it up, I knew the date on the penny would be 1996, the year of Kyle's death. I was correct.

Later on that afternoon, I had to run a few errands and I drove to the mall. I actually was thinking of the two pennies I'd found that day as I stepped from my car. There at my feet was another penny on the ground.

When I came in from shopping, I flipped on the television and Sylvia Browne was on the *Montel Williams Show*. She was talking about the ability of our loved ones to put pennies in our path as a sign from them. One lady in the audience commented, "Why can't they put fifty cent pieces, or better yet, silver dollars?"

Coincidence? No way. Sylvia also said there are no coincidences.

Just this week, I was at a gas station filling up my car. I'd gone inside to pay. Yes, I was at one of those stations where you can pump your gas first. Don't you hate the ones where they don't trust you, and you have to pay first? How do we know how much gas our tank will hold? While I'm on my griping bandwagon, my pet peeve is when you return the nozzle to the pump and that noise keeps going off, to remind you to pay. I don't know why that bothers me so much, but it does every single time.

Back to my story. On my way out of the station, I recognized Alma, a lady I'd met at one of Mary Jo's seminars. We asked how each was doing and talked about an upcoming Mary Jo workshop. Alma then asked me if I were becoming more aware of the spirit world. I said that I was becoming more aware of signs. At the exact moment I told her this, I spotted a penny on the ground between us.

I said, "See, here's a sign."

She looked surprised. Somehow I knew it was a 1996 penny. I picked it up and showing it to Alma, said, "See, it's even dated 1996, the year Kyle died, the year he graduated and went home."

The ironic thing is when I left the house earlier, I had no intention of getting gas. I was going to the mall to return some items. I had put the items in my car after finally finding the receipts, which I always lose.

About six blocks from my house, I turned the car around and headed in the opposite direction. I even thought to myself, "Why am I doing this?" Then I pulled into the gas station two miles down the road, not realizing I would soon have another sign from Kyle.

Another incident that helps put perspective on the here and hereafter happened in Littleton, Colorado. The Columbine incident will forever be etched in our minds. The pictures that flashed across our TV screens of students running from their school with their arms up in the air, the unknowing of what drama was going on inside the building, and the pain of all those involved is something we will never forget. What made two teenage boys kill twelve fellow classmates and a teacher will never be fully understood. But the lessons learned from such a seemingly senseless tragedy can often be the catalyst for allowing us to grow spiritually.

In the copy of the June 18, 1999, *USA Today* newspaper, there was a rather long article entitled, "Surviving Columbine." Many of the surviving victims' individual stories were highlighted and their struggles in the aftermath of being caught up in such terrifying and life-altering circumstances were looked at more closely. The story put a name and a face (pictures were included) with the individuals who were involved.

One story stood out. Anne Marie Hochhalters was only seventeen years old when she was shot twice, in the chest and spine, paralyzing her permanently from her waist down. Her father was relaying what had taken place during Anne Marie's struggle to stay alive after the incident. He felt blessed that, with such severe injuries, the doctors were able to save her "although she went to heaven and came back."

This statement by Ted Hochhalter jumped out at me from the paper. When you have had a child die, any confirmation that there really is a heaven not only gives you encouragement concerning your loved one's whereabouts but also helps you in your journey. It gives confirmation you will be with them and see them again one day.

As I've said before, one thing I've learned because of Kyle's death is there definitely are no happenstances. Too many unbelievable things have occurred to give me proof of this. Bobby was visiting me in Baton Rouge soon after the Columbine incident. We were in my car, and I was taking Bobby on a sightseeing tour, trying to impress him with all that Baton Rouge has to offer. Though I've lived in Baton Rouge for over thirty years and the Rural Life Museum is only a few miles from my home, I got lost trying to find it. We were looking out the car windows at the Ollie Steele Burden Manor run by nuns and Bobby quipped, "I don't think this is it either."

I headed south on Essen Lane and drove right past a big sign on the side of the road with an arrow pointing in the direction of our intended destination. "I think you just passed it," Bobby said calmly.

I felt so dumb. I would have to drive a little farther so I could make a U-turn under the interstate. We started talking about the deaths of all the students in Colorado, now that I finally knew where we were going. For some reason, both of us could not recall the name of the school. You know how that happens so many times when it's right on the tip of your tongue, and you just can't get it. After I had made the turn and was headed to the museum, an eighteen-wheeler exiting the interstate passed directly in front of us. "Columbine" was the only thing written on the side of the truck in great big letters so we could not miss it. We both shook our heads. Kyle had done it again.

In the fall of 1999, Jim was seated at the kitchen table drinking his third morning cup of coffee, and I was searching for my car keys after picking up my paper work for school. I was standing in the den, right outside the opening between the two rooms. I had gotten up earlier than usual that morning and had spent a few minutes reading over some of the pages from this book.

"You know, it really is neat the way that Kyle is able to give us so many signs," I said, thinking about what I had just read.

"Yes, we are lucky," Jim responded.

At that exact moment, the wooden clock positioned on the opposite wall in the den came crashing down to the floor. It landed in a wicker basket which kept it from breaking.

"What was that?" Jim asked.

"Apparently another sign from Kyle. Can you believe? There is no reason for that clock to have fallen," I said as I walked toward the clock.

I checked the nail in the wall that held the clock up. It was not loose. It was still firmly nailed into the wall. No one had been near the clock, and I can't remember the last time I had put my hand on it to level it.

I knew it was another sign from Kyle, especially since I had just mentioned to Jim about Kyle's ability to do things to let us know he is around. When a sign like that appears, it lifts my spirit, connecting me to Kyle and the spirit world. It reminds me there is much going on that we here on earth are unaware of and know little about.

Later that evening, Jim and I were seated on the sofa together. We were talking about the clock I had put back up on the wall on the same solidly stuck nail. We heard a crash behind us. A candle I had not touched in months had fallen off the mantle.

Sometimes I wonder about all these signs. I don't want Kyle to be earthbound. I want him to be happy experiencing all the wonders of his new home. But I appreciate every single sign, and I know he understands they will be noticed.

22

Maybe Kyle Did It

I have to share this story with you. It may be a little crude, so I hope it doesn't offend anyone. Every time I think of it, I have to laugh.

CeCe, Don, and their six-year-old grandson, Kevin, were in the car driving to Fayetteville, Arkansas. CeCe and Don smelled something (gas) and Don asked Kevin if he had an upset stomach. Kevin told them no and asked both DeDon and BeBe (what he calls them) if one of them pooted? CeCe told Kevin that he shouldn't speak like that, and he must always tell the truth.

Kevin then said, "I didn't do it, DeDon didn't do it and BeBe didn't do it." Then out of the clear blue, he said, "Maybe Kyle did it."

This story is precious to me. Apparently Kevin is around CeCe and Don, and he's become used to their talking about Kyle and all that he is able to do. Why not blame this on Kyle? I'm smiling as I type this. Children are so uninhibited and special.

Now that I'm aware of it, I never cease to be amazed at how often people bring up after-death communication in one form or another. I often wonder if it's just that more people are open to the possibility of its actually taking place, and they don't feel they'll be ridiculed for sharing their story. Or if it has always happened and I had no need to be aware of it before now.

I was standing at the Wal-Mart check-out line when the cashier asked me, "Aren't you the one who just lost your mother?"

Thinking she might recognize me from one of the many spiritual workshops I've attended but had forgotten who died, I said, "No, my son died." Her next question was, "Have you seen him?" When I told this lady, whom I'd never seen before, "No," she immediately said, "Oh, you will in time." This experience lets me know others are aware of ADCs and the reality of their occurrences.

Soon after Kyle died, I called Linda Grabski, one of the leaders of the local chapter of The Compassionate Friends. I wanted information about when they met, what took place at the meetings, and who attended. She spoke about the death of her only daughter, Nicole, at twenty years of age. Linda had checked Nicole in at the hospital on a Friday because of a mild case of pneumonia. Nicole had improved by Saturday, and the doctor told her she would probably be able to go home on Monday or Tuesday so she could return to her classes at L.S.U. Linda visited with Nicole until six o'clock on Saturday night, then went home since Nicole seemed to be on the mend and in good spirits. They talked several times by phone that night before going to bed.

At 3:45 Sunday morning, Linda received a phone call from the hospital telling her that Nicole had taken a turn for the worse. When Linda arrived at the hospital, she was informed that Nicole had died; they had found her dead on a routine bed check.

Six weeks after Nicole's death, Linda was sitting on the sofa in the family room. She said, "Immediately I *knew* Nicole was standing there before me. I had never had any experiences with spirits or presences or anything of that nature. I had not read one book about the subject of after-death communication at the time. But I *knew* it was her."

Linda looked to her right where she felt Nicole's presence and right beyond that was a picture of Nicole on the mantle of the fireplace. "There were sparks emitting from the picture." Linda told me ordinarily she would have been frightened just thinking about something like this happening, but she was totally at peace and absolutely positive it had been Nicole.

Then one Sunday morning, CeCe, DeDee, and I were seated at their dining room table. Don, a very religious man, walked toward us. CeCe commented, "It's sermon time." But Don only wanted to relate to us a true story he'd seen on the TV the night before.

A lady and her son had disappeared while traveling to their destination in a car. There was no sign of them for two or three days. Along the route they'd taken, a woman appeared on the side of the road, lying down. A passer-by saw her and called the police. They scanned the reported area and saw no lady. But they did find tire tracks that went into the woods. They followed the tracks and found the car, way off the road. The woman who was in the car died on impact, but her son was still alive. The doctors reported he would only have lived another hour. The mother had become an apparition to save her son.

Another time my daughter, Jill, was on a bus headed to a fair in rural Washington. A casual acquaintance, Teresa, was seated in front of Jill on the bus. They hadn't seen each other in quite a while. Jill knew Teresa's younger sister had been murdered by her husband. She was only in her twenties when her life had been taken. Teresa's brother-in-law still has not been captured.

Jill asked Teresa how she was doing. She told Jill she knows her sister is okay because she often feels her presence. She said she could smell her and she came to her all the time in dreams. Teresa's sister told her it is beautiful over there and earth life is just a speck in time.

Teresa then told Jill about the time she was driving through a gorge, and her children were with her. She was very tired. She remembers looking at the clock and seeing it was 1:00 a.m. The next time she looked at the clock it was 4:00 a.m. She knew her dead sister had driven those three hours while she was asleep. It was only then, after these stories, that Jill told her Kyle had died four months earlier.

Because both of my daughters have been exposed to many after-death communication stories, it gives some validation to them about my experiences. They're not as apt to think of their mother as being "nuts" since people they respect have initiated talking about their own ADCs.

One of my sixteen-year-old students, Joshua, asked me one day how I was doing concerning my son. New in my grief, I told him I cried often, and it was really tough. He immediately said he knew my son was okay. He said the grandma he was very close to died the year before. After her death, he and his grandfather were sitting in a pew in church and both of them saw her standing up front near the communion table. He said she looked pretty and appeared much younger than when she died. He said his grandmother smiled when she saw them looking at her.

Nancy Wood, another friend, told me of the time she saw her son Michael, who had died in an auto accident. She was attending Michael's best friend's wedding. She, along with three others, saw Michael standing up by the wedding party. Apparently, the best man was having difficulty getting the ring to the groom because of the strong energy coming from Michael, who was standing between them. That incident is much like what Mary Jo told the Thursday night class one time. She said some of her clients have not been able to get through the door after a reading because of the energy from the deceased.

During the Christmas holidays, I was next door visiting our neighbors. Fred and Barbara's two sons, Chris and Bruce, were home. Kyle was between the boys in age, but he often hung around both of them while growing up. The Bryans built their home when we were building ours. We were talking about general things, such as how long the boys would be home, when the conversation turned to John Edward and Mary Jo and what had happened in my life.

Lady, (yes, that's her name) Chris's wife, asked Barbara, "Did you tell her about my dream?" When she said no, she had not, Lady proceeded to tell me the following. She said she had only met Kyle one time. The last time she visited Baton Rouge she became very, very sick and was almost unconscious. When she was "out," she saw Kyle very clearly. He didn't say anything. He just smiled. She immediately woke Chris because it seemed so real.

Now that we were in the ADC mode, Barbara told all of us about seeing her dead sister-in-law in her bathroom just recently. It had been years since she had even thought of her. Her sister-in-law smiled really big and looked very happy. Barbara immediately called home to Kentucky. She found out her wayward nephew, her sister-in-law's son, had called home from some country overseas that very day and said he had just married. No one in the family had heard from him in years and did not even know where he was. Barbara believes her sister-in-law was letting her know how happy she was for her son.

Soon after Kyle's death, Barbara became aware of my visits to Mary Jo, but she never questioned any of what I was doing. She even told me she knew of other people who had gone to Mary Jo. She told me she believed in what I was doing. She said one time her dead uncle came to her cousin, and they had a regular conversation while seated outside in their yard. It helps tremendously to have people understand and support what I know to be true. But I still speak softly when I'm in my backyard talking to the crows and butterflies.

While watching television and the biography of Andy Gibb, another ADC dream was brought to light. Victoria Principal and Andy had been deeply in love at one time. From what Victoria said, Andy's addiction to drugs was his primary need, and this ended their affair. She said they parted, never having the final conversation that would bring some sort of closure to their relationship. Andy died, and Victoria was unable to fulfill this wish of hers to tell Andy how she really felt. During the biography, Victoria said something to the effect that Andy was so special he made sure they had this meeting. He came to her in a vivid dream, and they were both able to be comforted by it.

Victoria said, "We never got to say good-bye and talk after our breakup. He came to me in a dream, and we had the talk we needed to have. It was so like Andy to find a way to give me solace."

In June, 1998, there was a special on television about Carol Burnett, the comedic actress. She said Joe Hamilton, her ex-husband, who died seven years before, comes to her in dreams. They had been married for twenty years. She knows she is in bed, but she and Joe have a conversation.

During a senate hearing concerning the ValuJet Airline crash in the Everglades in 1996 which killed 110 people, a man whose wife and daughter died in the accident was being questioned. The bereaved husband and father was telling the committee what "not to do" after such a tragedy. He said they shouldn't say body parts when referring to their loved ones, and lawyers should have a specified time period before contacting the survivors.

The man then said, "But I know they are both all right. My wife has already come to me twice and my daughter once. They are okay."

Then Michael Landon's daughter was on television a few weeks ago. I believe she was on the *Larry King Live* show. Her father was a famous actor, probably best known for his role on *Little House on the Prairie*. Michael died of cancer on July 1, 1991. Cheryl Landon Wilson said she communicates with her father's spirit. She wrote a book about her father entitled, *I Promised My Dad: An Intimate Portrait of Michael Landon*. During one of these after-death communications with her father, he told her he would come to her after her first book appearance and give her a red rose. Apparently, he came to her in another "visit" and told her to go to the Central Park fountain. She went to the fountain and a red rose was lying there.

On two different occasions, while Kyle's son Cain and I were at Playworld in Conway, Arkansas, I felt Kyle's presence. There is no other explanation for what happened. Let me share one of them with you.

Playworld is the kind of amusement place where you spend oodles of money to play various games to win tickets. The tickets enable you to purchase some trinket that will never be kept or played with for more than a few minutes, at best. Of course, I know it's a place to have fun and excitement. Most children love going to these places, and I wanted to go there with Cain.

I had spent I don't know how many dollars for tokens for Cain to play lots of games. He had amassed quite a few tickets, and Miss Judy was keeping them in her pockets until it was cash-in time.

In one game you shoot your token with a gun type apparatus, and the token lands on moving conveyer belts with a possibility of falling into various containers. Each container has a different number on it indicating its ticket value. A lot of the tokens land on a basket-shaped contraption at the very top and back of the game station. If you happen to hit three small teeth within a designated number of shots, the basket is tipped over and all of the tokens dump onto the moving conveyor belts. This gives you a greater chance of racking up lots of tickets.

Cain and I had decided the tokens he was now using were his last. Then we'd head to McDonald's. Jim had become bored with this ticket-winning escapade and had dozed off on a nearby bench.

Cain had played the game numerous times and I believe only once had hit one of the teeth. He had three tokens left. "Ping," he hit a tooth. When he hit the second tooth with his next to last token, I began thinking maybe I should quickly buy some other tokens because he was so close. He shot his last token and, I swear, it did not even go near the last tooth, but the tooth light came on and the bucket dumped. Right then, I felt Kyle's presence. Cain was so excited, he ran to Mr. Jim and told him to come and look. Hundreds of tickets kept coming out of the machine. You'd have thought we had won the national lottery, we were so excited.

I was visiting Jill and her family during the summer of 1999. Luckily, a quiet, quaint motel, The Marina Inn, is located only a few blocks from Jill's house in Anacortes, Washington. I usually make reservations there when I visit. It not only affords me a place to escape and unwind, but it also enables me to have one or two of my grandchildren spend each night with me. That way, I get to know them a little better, on a one-to-one basis.

Dane and Cole agreed to be my roommates one evening. After a dip in the indoor pool, and free snacking provided by our hosts, we retreated to my room. While playing cards on the table located in the corner of the room, Dane spotted John Edward's book, *One Last Time*, lying on top of my suitcase. He asked about the book.

I picked up the book, opened it, and showed Dane my name listed in John's acknowledgments. Dane was impressed.

He asked what the book was about. It was then I told my grandsons about their Uncle Kyle's ability to connect to me through John. They were very intrigued by what I was telling them, and I began sharing a few of the things Kyle has been able to do to let me know he is okay. Cole and Dane asked me to keep talking. They wanted to hear more stories.

An hour of stories later, I told them it was bedtime. After crawling into our beds, they asked me to keep telling them stories about Kyle. I said, "Only one more story, and then it's lights out and sleep time."

"Just tell us one more story," Dane would beg.

After another story I'd hear, "Just one more," from Cole.

Then Dane would beg again, "Just one more."

After I don't know how many "just one more" stories were shared, I said, "That's it! I'm not talking any more. It's lights out time."

Dane then popped in, "If Kyle's so good at doing all this stuff . . . Kyle, you turn out the light."

I laughed as I got up to turn off the light.

During the same summer, my granddaughter, Jaclyn, and I were driving from Bellingham, Washington, back to Burlington, Washington. We had spent a few hours at a mall looking for some clothes for her. We had dropped her fifteen-year-old brother, Cole, off at the Avalon Golf Course and were on our way to pick him up. The scenery was God's country. The ocean on our right, seen through picturesque mountains we were driving through, was a breathtaking sight. We were chatting about her school year, her plans for college and just making small talk, when all of a sudden she said, "You know, there are black bears in these mountains."

I said, "Really? Have you ever seen any?"

She told me no. Then we went on to another subject.

We drove in the driveway of the country club and spotted Cole on the putting green near the club house. He picked up his ball and walked toward our car. I rolled the window down.

"Guess what?" Cole said, "I saw a black bear on the golf course."

Jaclyn and I looked at each other. Coincidence? We didn't think so.

When things happen in your life that cause you to hesitate, and maybe cause you to think twice, know that it is possible for our loved ones to be with us, give us messages, and comfort us. Whether Kyle had anything to do with the bear, I don't know. But I do know it *is* possible that he did. That is what is important.

23

"Don't Be Surprised If He Doesn't Show Up"

Jim phoned me from Meineke, his business, on Saturday morning, January 24, 1998. He was busy, he told me, but a man who had been to John Edward's seminar in New Orleans had come into his shop. Jim handed Carl Harper the phone.

Carl's wife, Debbie, had died two and a half years earlier when her car was hit head on, just one hundred yards from their driveway. She'd left work early to get a dress hemmed for her 25th high school reunion that was to be held the following day. An out-of-control, speeding driver crossed the center line and struck Debbie's car. Debbie died at the scene. Travis, Debbie and Carl's son, was at home when the wreck occurred. He walked to the scene to see what was going on. In a matter of seconds, Travis discovered his mother had been killed. A few minutes later, Debbie and Carl's daughter, Krysté drove up on the accident and she, too, found out her mother had died.

Carl was still heartbroken over the loss of his wife. He desperately wanted a private reading with John. Jim had told him maybe I could help him.

I had stopped by Mary Jo's office on Friday, six days after having spoken with Carl. Just as I walked through the door, I heard, "Judy, hurry. Ellen, John's secretary, is on the phone and wants to talk with you."

It was then that Ellen told me she had two openings for readings with John when he would be in New Orleans. I mentioned Carl, and she told me he could have one of the spots and I could have the other if I wanted it. I was beside myself with excitement. I asked Ellen if I could call Carl to tell him and she told me, "Yes, when you speak with him, tell him I will call later to schedule the time for the appointment."

I could hardly wait to phone Carl with the news. Because I know how much comfort John can bring to someone in deep grief, I can't begin to describe the wonderful feeling I have when I know I am able to help someone else. My reading was scheduled for 6:45 p.m. on Thursday, February 5, 1998. Carl's was immediately afterward.

On our way to New Orleans for our reading with John Edward, I had mixed emotions. I was excited. I was worried. My stomach was churning. Only a mother whose child has died could know my feelings. Would Kyle show up? I wanted so badly to connect with him again. I missed him terribly. The past two years, though, I'd learned that just because we want someone to come doesn't necessarily mean he will. Was I pushing my luck? Kyle had been so clever and comforting the other times. During both of my private readings and the three other times during large group meetings when Kyle came to me, he was able to give me a peace and happiness beyond words. Until the day I die, I will relive these moments over and over again.

"Don't be surprised if he doesn't show up," John had told me one time. "He has a life over there and he is busy. Just because we die here on earth doesn't mean we have nothing to do on the Other Side. There will be a time when your son will move on. Not that he doesn't love you or have concern for you, but there is a world out there beyond our ability to know or understand, and your son will be busy experiencing it." It concerned me that Kyle might not show up, but I prayed he would.

Jim and I walked into John's room at the hotel. It was 6:45 p.m. John's first comment when he saw us was, "I just saw you." I didn't know what he meant, but then he added, "I have been viewing my video, *After Death Communication*, in which both of you are shown."

John sat down on a sofa, and Jim and I took our seats in chairs facing him. We talked about how the video was progressing and all the many appearances in John's busy life. John's unbelievable ability to connect to our loved ones who have died was spreading rapidly throughout the world. I remember feeling so good that Jim and I were having this private reading with John. He was becoming famous and his notoriety was making it increasingly difficult to get in touch with him.

It may sound a little abnormal, but I sometimes think Kyle chose a perfect time to cross over. I don't know where I would be right now, both physically and mentally, if it weren't for John and Mary Jo. Because of them, Jim and I have been able to move forward.

"Your biological father and your step-father Kenneth, who shot himself, are both here," John said, while looking at Jim.

We were literally shocked. We hadn't thought about them in years. John had never been told anything about Jim's family background. Jim's mother was pregnant with Jim when his father mysteriously disappeared. He had gone to work one day and was never seen again. Hazel had a three-year-old son, Pete, and was expecting her second child, Jim, in three months.

To this very day no one knows what happened to Jim's father. His showing up with John, however, did let us know he had indeed died. He made a few statements through John which we found to be true when we checked with Hazel later.

In hindsight, I wish we'd asked some questions to find out exactly how and when he died. I know Jim's mother would have liked this information. But we were really there in hopes of connecting with Kyle and were more or less caught off guard when Jim's biological father showed up.

Jim's step-father, Kenneth, had shot himself five years earlier. Kenneth fought in World War II where he lost one of his legs in battle. He was plagued throughout his life with pain and underwent numerous surgeries. Kenneth was a wonderful man and very considerate of others. But when I think of him, I picture him sitting on the sofa with bottles of pills on the table next to him. He was always in pain. I guess the pain became too much, because he drove off one day, got out of his station wagon and shot himself. Kenneth relayed to us that he clearly was not seeing straight when he took his life.

Even though I wanted Kyle to show up first, the appearance of Jim's biological father, whom he had never known, and his step-father gives additional credence to the fact that John doesn't have control over what happens. And again, there surely isn't any mind reading going on.

Kyle came through next, talking about being our son and his death as the result of an impact to his head in an auto accident. One thing that these ADC readings has proved to me is our loved ones are very aware of how they died.

Kyle has come through on three different occasions with John and James Van Praagh, saying he was irresponsible, he was driving fast and didn't have his seat belt on. He knows he was thrown from the vehicle and had major impact to his head. The back of his skull was opened. He has mentioned at least four different times this head injury cost him his life. Two times I remember him showing up during Mary Jo's Thursday night class, and showing her the hole in his head. Three times he told us he didn't suffer and that his soul left immediately. Twice he thanked us for taking him off life-support after two days. So our loved ones are very much aware of all the details concerning how they left the physical world and entered the spiritual world.

"He was born in March, and both he and his father have the same name, James. He wants you to know his big dog, a beagle named Walker, is with him," John continued.

As usual, John was very much on target again.

Then Kyle mentioned a large piece of property that was located north of us. Before he died we had bought five acres in Watson, Louisiana, and this property was being cleared for Kyle to live on. It was a beautiful wooded lot with a creek running through the back of it. One time, both Kyle and I were at the property, deciding which trees to cut down in order to have room for his home. I was traipsing around the muddy lot with boots on, trying to figure out which trees to tie ribbons around, when I looked up and Kyle was nowhere to be seen.

I couldn't imagine where he'd gone. I yelled out to him. I was actually mad. Here I was going to all this trouble to help him and where was he? Down by the creek bed, thinking about how he could build a bridge so the deer could get across easier. When we had walked on the property the first time, I remember how excited he was that he saw so many deer prints.

Since his death, I have been unable to go back and look at that property. It would be too painful. We bought it during the winter months when the trees were barren, but there were some magnolia trees and large live oaks that kept their foliage. I had looked forward to seeing the property with all the trees in green splendor. The trees were budding when Kyle died. For the longest time, I would be driving somewhere during the summer months and look at the scenery on the side of the road and try to visualize Kyle's property. It was heart-rending.

John Edward added, "Your son has created this property, and he is living on it with his dog."

This message from Kyle lets me know he lives there after all. He is able to enjoy the experience of seeing the trees in bloom. He has been able to landscape around his home, and I know he has built the bridge for the deer.

When our loved one dies, though, our first thought is usually, "Where are they?" It brings me a certain peace, being able to picture Kyle in his own heaven that he has created. I look forward to the day when I can travel there and see his home.

John said Jim had been hunting in October and November. Kyle often went with Jim when he went to the deer camp. "He says he validates he was there with you. There was a precious moment up there when you were able to tap into the value of life. He tells me you hunt for hours and he is with you. To further confirm he has been with you, he is bringing this elimination thing up. You had to do 'number 2' while on the deer stand. You didn't want to get off the stand, but you had no choice. You had to get off. He wants you to know he saw you do this."

Jim tells me he talks to Kyle the entire time he's at the camp. As I type this, I know he is having a conversation with Kyle. The solitude and beauty of nature create an environment in which Jim says he feels very connected and close to Kyle.

"He was a big kid, but not fat. He was very charismatic and smooth," John Edward went on.

I would often use the old cliché, "Kyle could sell ice to the Eskimos." He would have made a good actor. He could convince anyone of anything. My ex-son-in-law wrote me a letter after Kyle's death. The one thing he envied about Kyle was the way he could talk to girls, including his mother. "He had a way of being able to twist you around his little finger."

"His head was shaved before he passed," John added. This was true. John had never been told anything about Kyle's accident, injuries or death. As I stated earlier, I was very skeptical of this psychic thing, the ability to have our loved ones talk to us. I made a point from the very beginning not to ever bring up a name or discuss anything Kyle might want to bring up later. I was particularly "close-mouthed" when in the presence of John or Mary Jo.

Mary Jo had also told me Kyle said his head was shaved. When two different psychic/mediums say almost exactly the same words from Kyle, it gives me added proof it really is my son coming through. As a parent I knew my child well. I was familiar with his manner of speaking and the phrases he often used to describe things, his attitude concerning various issues, and what mattered most. The things Kyle has brought up during the readings are the things that Kyle would have brought up while here. It amazes me how quick our loved ones are on the Other Side to bring up specific things that could pertain only to them. No generalizations. It's mind-boggling.

Then Kathy's son, Barlow, showed up. He wanted us to let his mother know he is aware she is overwhelmed with depression. John said Barlow's death is "very weird."

"It's like he was found hanging from a ceiling, twice as high as a normal one. There is no way possible he could have gotten himself up there. Part of his family thinks he committed suicide, but he didn't."

John had no idea who this Barlow guy was who had shown up during our reading. Barlow's mother, Kathy, had already had a reading with John in Dallas. He was only confirming again what he had told Kathy then. There was foul play and Barlow had been murdered.

After this reading took place, Barlow's death and the circumstances surrounding it have been looked into further by forensic experts, and the evidence points to no possibility of Barlow's taking his own life.

John apologized to me, saying my son was directing most of his attention to his father. I told him I didn't mind at all, because Kyle had come to me many other times. This was only the second time Jim had been in the presence of a medium, which afforded Kyle the opportunity to connect with him.

"Did you have a tendency to be too hard on him? He knows you loved him and he doesn't want you to feel bad about how you felt about him."

Jim did have difficulty understanding Kyle's depression. He wasn't aware at the time of the devastating impact this illness had on Kyle. Kyle was unable to function at times and Jim had said he should just get busy and he'd feel better. Jim knows better now. Because of the increasing awareness of this hideous disease and more and more people's exposing their struggle with depression, Jim now understands how life altering it is.

"Because of his death, you have learned so much. He knows you miss him terribly, but what you have learned means a great deal to him. He's okay. He's content. He feels happy that you are better emotionally. It helps Kyle to know you are helping parents who have lost children. You have been an inspiration to others. Your son wants you to know this. It helps him in his transition. He's comparing you to another mother who lost her child, saying she hasn't progressed as much. He says he knows you have gotten to a point that you are okay."

This long message from Kyle stressing my helping others has given me added encouragement to continue what I believe I am supposed to do—why Jim and I have been given the opportunity to experience so many verifications that Kyle does live on and that he is happy. It not only brings us comfort, but I am also compelled to share what I know. Our loved ones may die, but they are still who they were, and they will always be with us, though we're separated physically for a little while.

A few days before this reading, I was talking with Jill on the phone. She has always listened to all my stories, never letting on that she is tired of hearing about her brother, his death, and his after-death communications. She lets me talk and talk for hours. She apparently inherited this trait from Jim. Of course, now that I think about it, how do I know she doesn't set the phone down and go about her business? It is awfully quiet on the other end sometimes. But I do believe she listens most of the time.

She has never criticized anything I've said or done. During this particular conversation, Jill told me about talking with Bob, her husband, the night before. She asked Bob if he thought it was bad for her to let me just keep on and on about Kyle? Bob supposedly replied, "It's better it is you than the checkout girl at Safeway."

John said, "Your son knows someone is tired of hearing about him. He's laughing. He finds it funny.

"He's reminding me that at a previous workshop you attended, you mentioned you carry swatches of fabric in your purse." This was true. At John's workshop in New Orleans, I had commented to the group that I wished I wasn't such a perfectionist. Everything has to match in my house. I always carry material and wallpaper samples in my purse, taking them everywhere I go. They are in my purse as I type this.

So Kyle remembered something I'd said at a workshop months before. John hadn't remembered. It amazes me how aware they are on the Other Side. Not that Kyle wasn't smart when he was here. But he's really smart now.

Kyle mentioned he had two sisters and one had a baby after he died. This was also true. Jill had given birth to Ty.

"He wants to remind you there is a birthday coming up. A birthday, next week."

This didn't make any sense. I quickly thought of family members, girlfriends, and others, but it didn't ring a bell to either Jim or me. We shook our heads no.

"Well, he wants you to know he's reminding you."

John said Kyle was beginning to step back, and he was losing the energy connection with him. I asked John if I could ask my son a question. He told me yes. I asked, "What does he spend most of his time doing?" Previously, I had been told he was living on the lot we'd bought him. I knew his animals were with him. I also knew some of the people who were with him. But I wanted to know what he did all day.

"He's helping people on the Other Side, mostly young people. He's also telling me he has something to do with parentless children in Europe. There is a kind of network of souls working with parentless children."

"Does he know when we'll be over and join him?" I asked.

"He won't tell us that. But don't worry about him. His transition was great."

We thanked John and stood up to leave. As we walked toward the door, John said, "He wants you to pass on to his sister he knows she's tired of hearing about him."

We passed Carl and his daughter, Kristé, on the way out. They were John's last scheduled reading for the day. I apologized to them for running over our time slot. But I was elated. As Janice remarked, "We got another Band-Aid."

It's truly an inexplicable feeling to be connected to your child again. Unless your child has died and you have experienced such profound knowledge that your child lives on, you would not understand.

Carl called me Friday evening. He wanted to share with me his reading with John. It was unbelievable, he told me. His daughter, Kristé, had wanted her mother to mention three things. The first three things that Debbie brought up were the three things that Kristé had asked for.

One of the things Debbie referred to was the "D" initial pendant that had been hers. She told Carl and Krysté to give it to her sister, Danette, who lived in Florida, because she would be able to wear it since her name also started with a "D."

How did John know that Carl's wife had a sister and how did he know her name and that she lived in Florida? This is proof that we don't die. Debbie was giving out this information.

When we arrived home from New Orleans, I pulled out my small book with the special occasion dates listed in it. I was wondering whose birthday Kyle was so adamant about my remembering. No one's birthday was next week. Maybe John misunderstood this one bit of information from Kyle. So I forgot about it.

When I came home from teaching on Friday, February 13, 1998, there was a message on my answering machine. It was from Kathy.

"Today is my birthday and tomorrow is the second anniversary of Barlow's death. I've been asking Kyle to tell you. I've been telling him to remind you." These were the exact words on my answering machine. I even recorded them so I could save them.

I had completely forgotten Kathy's birthday. I telephoned her after I heard her message and apologized for not having remembered. She told me for the past couple of weeks she had been telling Kyle to remind me, so I wouldn't be embarrassed if I forgot. I felt bad I had forgotten, especially since Kyle was trying to remind me. She hadn't forgotten my birthday and had sent me a card with a note saying that Kyle had helped her pick it out.

But I'm glad now that I did forget. Kyle's reminding me after Kathy had asked him to is just another affirmation of how aware and present our loved ones are in our lives. When Kyle was reminding me of not forgetting a birthday the next week, he was also correct. Our reading with John was on a Thursday. The following Friday of the next week was Kathy's birthday. Unbelievable, isn't it? What would the skeptics say about this?

A humorous incident happened the day Jim met Kathy. Kathy was planning a trip to Baton Rouge, and I'd invited her out to dinner with Jim and me. We took her to Sammy's, a neighborhood restaurant. Jim had often heard me talk about Kathy, so I was glad they were going to get to know one another.

We were enjoying our meal, and during the conversation Jim said, "Oh, yeah, Kyle needs some toothpaste." Kathy looked perplexed. Was Jim crazy or what, she likely thought.

To go back in time, whenever Kyle told me he was out of something or needed something, I would get it immediately for him. I'd even overnight mail it, if he were out of town. But with Jim, it was a different story. He might have to ask me two or three times and often ended up getting it for himself. So Jim finally figured it out. Say that Kyle needs it, and he'll get it immediately. It usually works, too.

It was Saturday, February 7, 1998. Mary Jo and John Edward were appearing together for the first time. They were appearing with Raymond Moody, author of *Life After Life, The Light Beyond,* and *Through Time Into Healing* and Robert Grant, author of *Love and Roses from David.* For five years, Robert Grant was part of a five-member team tasked to computerize and preserve the entire collection of 14,000 readings given by Edgar Cayce. Mr. Grant possesses a wealth of historical information of little-known facts of Edgar Cayce's life, work, and psychic readings.

I was seated next to Carl Harper who had a reading with John two nights earlier. At that time he had made contact with his wife Debbie who had died in an auto accident. We were seated near the back of the large room. While listening to Raymond Moody, Carl leaned over to me and said, "I'm lost." He was attending the program alone, and he was still searching for some comfort.

I reached inside my purse which I'd placed on the floor. I pulled out a paperback book, *Contacting the Spirit World* by Linda Williamson, and handed it to Carl. I whispered to him that it was something he might want to read. It might bring him some consolation.

Carl looked rather surprised. He reached in his shirt pocket and pulled out a sheet of paper with the title of only one book, *Contacting the Spirit World*, with the author's name on it. He told me he'd spent an hour at Barnes & Noble Book Store the day before looking for the exact book. He said he couldn't find it.

Another coincidence? I don't think so.

Earlier that afternoon, I was already seated in my car in the carport for the drive to New Orleans. I had put my car in reverse and had begun backing out of the driveway. Then I stopped and drove back into the carport. I got out of my car and walked back into the house. I walked over to the bookshelf where I keep many of my newly acquired readings and picked up the copy of *Contacting the Spirit World*. I had no idea why I was taking this book with me. Now I knew why.

24

"Your Son Is More Alive Now"

Judy LeSage was in Mary Jo's class for a short time. It was there that I'd become aware of Patti Brown, whose son Brandon died in an automobile accident four months before Kyle's death. He was also 26 years old. I knew her pain.

Mary Jo McCabe, Dr. Brian L. Weiss, Annie Kirkwood and James Van Praagh were scheduled to appear at a weekend intensive for spiritual enlightenment. It was going to be held in New Orleans, November 15th through the 17th. I had just returned from seeing James and John Edward in California the month before, and I was looking forward to attending this event.

Over the phone, I convinced Judy and Patti to go to New Orleans with me. I had never met Patti before, but I wanted to help her. I picked them up and we headed to New Orleans. On the way, we passed the site of Brandon's accident. It was very difficult for Patti. I encouraged her to look forward to what lay ahead and tried to convince her that after this "spiritual weekend," she would think differently about her son's death and more importantly his whereabouts.

Friday evening consisted of a "welcome" from each of the speakers, preparing us for what would take place the next two days. It gave everyone an opportunity to meet not only friends, but also others who were on their spiritual journey.

Mary Jo appeared first on Saturday morning from nine o'clock until noon. Her lecture consisted of how to hear your inner voice. She also spoke about each of us having guides and angels that accompany us throughout our lives. She then drew numbers from the audience and did ten random readings. As usual, she was very impressive. From watching the expressions of the people in assembly, I saw that most were overwhelmed with her ability. Mary Jo is such a natural, down-to-earth person. She never puts on any airs; she is who she is. This makes her gift and the work she does very believable. That's why when I speak of her to others who have neither met nor seen her, I always tell them I wish they could see her "in person." They'd never again think of a psychic as a lady in a turban, draped in jewelry, and staring into a crystal ball. Mary Jo McCabe is one very classy lady.

My younger brother, Steve, was greatly affected by Kyle's death. Steve and my sister-in-law, Linda, always showed an interest in Kyle's welfare. Their family often attended Kyle's college football games, and Kyle would drop by my brother's Subway restaurants when he was in Hot Springs. Steve told me after Kyle's funeral on their family drive back to Arkansas, their entire trip consisted of conversations about death, the reality of it, and what death really is.

Steve and Linda have heard me talk about Mary Jo numerous times since Kyle's death. One time, while visiting at their home, I asked them if they would like to view a short video tape of Mary Jo's being interviewed on a television segment. I wanted them to "see" her. I watched their faces as they watched the video. I could tell that Mary Jo's appearance and mannerisms shocked them. I knew they were impressed when Steve remarked, "It's a shame Dad can't go to her. He would feel differently about Mom and death."

My mother has been in a nursing home for over four years. She has Alzheimer's. For the last three and a half years, she has not recognized me. She may smile for a moment, but then any recollection quickly fades and she's back in her own world. One thing I'm thankful for is that she isn't aware of her grandson's death and the pain I've had to endure.

My father didn't come for Kyle's funeral. I had told him there was no need for him to come; it would be better if he stayed with Mom. I love him, but I didn't need any added worries about him and his needs at that time.

I spoke with my father on the telephone the evening of the funeral. "It's funny," he said, "but Mom said your name 'Judy, Judy' today." So on a soul level, my mother was aware of my deep, indescribable pain. She was just unable to express herself. What I've learned about death has given me such a different outlook concerning life that I will be happy for my mother when she finally gets to the Other Side and can once again enjoy life fully. She might even cook Kyle some good home cooked meals.

Dr. Brian L. Weiss, one of the foremost figures in past life regression therapy, and the author of the following books: *Many Lives, Many Masters*; *Only Love is Real*; and *Through Time into Healing* appeared during the two to five o'clock time slot. His lecture concerned learning techniques of meditation, healing and deep relaxation. He also spoke of regressing oneself in order to be aware of past lives. He chose a man at random and regressed him while he was seated on stage. It was very eye opening and interesting to watch.

A lot of people have difficulty accepting the concept of past lives. I know when I first became aware of the possibility of this, it upset me greatly. It would mean that Kyle could have other mothers, that others could also have this special bond and love that I have for Kyle.

But, then again, with all I've learned these past few years, why not? It surely would explain a lot of questions. My two daughters could not be any more different. They have entirely different interests, likes, dislikes, outlooks, and yet they grew up in the same household, with the same parents, and under the same circumstances. My two brothers are entirely different. I can't think of anything they have in common except for having the same parents. The same goes for my husband and his only brother. So what makes us so different? You can see it within your own family. We had to acquire our interests to pursue varying activities throughout our lifetime from somewhere.

Mary Jo had told me that Kyle's past life consisted of his trapping animals and selling his wares. She said he was very good at this. This was before she knew about his love for animals. When she said this, I knew immediately why he was preoccupied with catching animals throughout his life. He had never learned it from Jim or me. Jim couldn't stand snakes, and I wasn't fond of them either. Kyle had to have acquired this inborn love of snakes from somewhere. The argument for past lives is considerable. How about the people who are regressed and who can speak a foreign language? A language they knew nothing about during these lifetimes? There is truly no other explanation for such happenings.

There had been a short interlude during Weiss's presentation. Lu was seated next to Patti. "Your son is more alive now than he ever was while here," were the first words she leaned over and said to me. My thought when she said this, as I've told Lu, was "Who in the heck are you?"

Lu introduced herself saying that Patti had told her both of our sons had died in automobile accidents. Lu then said, "You don't die. Your physical self dies, but you soul doesn't die with it."

She asked me if we'd like to join her for something to eat during the two-hour break before James Van Praagh's lecture that evening. For some reason I felt drawn to Lu. I told her my car was parked in the hotel garage, and I'd drive us to get a bite to eat.

She said she knew the New Orleans area well and some-one had dropped her off at the event. So my driving would be a good idea.

"Do you always drive this slowly, or is it because of Kyle's accident?" Lu asked while sitting next to me. Patti was in the back. I responded that it was because I didn't know where I was going. Lu gave directions.

On the drive to La Madeleine's, I found out that Lu was a forensic consultant, whose field of specialty was medicolegal dynamics of death. Although most of her work dealt with crime scene reconstruction with police files and photo-graphs, on numerous occasions her investigative case work involved participation at autopsies with coroners and medi-cal examiners at the local morgue. Lu was quick to point out that she is not a coroner, medical examiner or medical doc-tor. She considers herself an independent consultant.

I asked Lu how she knew that the soul lives on and doesn't die with the body.

Lu recounted that in the late '70s she was a photogra-pher for a pathologist at a large hospital. While providing lab services to the local coroner's office, various investiga-tors would drop by and visit Lu while waiting to pick up lab reports. She became interested in death investigation after reading FBI publications that the investigators dropped off. Lu told me there were many articles concerning how to better process crime scenes, investigate homicides, and recover buried bodies. Then she related this story.

"One of the coroner investigators who came by to pick up lab reports became one of my most valuable spiritual mentors. RC had been a medic and had seen some Vietnam action, was wounded and came home a hero. He told me he saw so much useless death that he figured he'd get a job that tried to make some sense out of death. He became one of the best, most thorough death scene investigators in the area.

"RC informed me that human beings are born with a soul, and at death the soul leaves the body and crosses into the light on the Other Side." Lu said she wasn't prepared for what he said next.

"Don't be surprised if you see a panicky human soul at autopsy, but if you do, tell it to go to the light, because some of them do not know they are dead."

Lu then said, "Well, the human soul bit didn't surprise me. I had a Bible; I went to church and knew about the human soul. I attended funerals of loved ones and assumed their souls went back to God after death, but I was a little taken back by the 'panicky human soul' part or anyone's needing to go into the light. Although I was aware that in the 22nd chapter of the book of Revelations it talks about the light that God gives forever, I simply was clueless as to what RC was talking about. Besides, none of the other investigators ever told me any of this stuff. I had been present at many clinical autopsies and had not seen anything that looked like a 'panicky soul,' not that I would recognize one until I actually saw one several months later."

It's a good thing Lu kept giving directions, because I was paying no attention to where I was driving. I was only listening to her stories. I couldn't believe what I was hearing. I was in a car with a person I had never met until one hour before, and she was telling me that my son was more alive now than ever. I was loving it. The more time I spent in the presence of Lu, the less I wanted to hurry back to see James. I even remarked to Lu that she should get up on stage. She could comfort a lot of people. It was surprising to learn that until that afternoon, Lu had never known who Mary Jo or James Van Praagh were.

We each picked up a cold meat sandwich on a roll. Lu ordered some special soup. I knew she must have eaten at this place often; she knew what to order.

Every single word that came out of her mouth gave me more insight about death. She wasn't getting paid to say any of it either. Not that I believe for one minute that Mary Jo and John and the others aren't legitimate and from the heart. I know they are. But Lu's story was different.

We sat down to eat and Lu continued with her story. "Well, back to the panicky soul encounter on that fall afternoon in the morgue.

"Although I had witnessed autopsies at the morgue, I was told I would be able to 'assist' at the autopsy of a woman who had most likely overdosed on some kind of medication. The individual was found in a car in the parking lot of a shopping center. My duties would be to inventory personal items belonging to the deceased. I was told that the person was a woman, but I really couldn't tell by the size of the body bag when it arrived.

"After I emptied a small paper sack that held the deceased's belongings that were found on her person, I logged each item onto the required form. I had just completed the form and was looking at the photographs in her wallet when it happened.

"I saw the reflection of a very pretty young woman on the stainless steel table in front of me. I turned around, but no one was on either side. I turned back and looked at the table and the reflection was still there. I looked over my shoulder thinking it was one of the nurses, but no one was there. I looked back at the table and the reflection was gone.

"Then I distinctly heard someone say, 'What are you doing? What are you doing with my things?' I looked up from the photographs in my hand and could see the young

woman standing there in front of me on the other side of
the table. Some today would call it an apparition, but I
prefer to describe it as the spirit of the young woman. I
could see the spirit of this very pretty young woman very
clearly. I knew this had to be the spirit of the woman in the
body bag.

"I could see through her," Lu told me, "and there standing on the other side of the room making eye contact with
me was RC. He later told me that when he looked up and
saw the expression on my face, he pretty much knew that I
had my very first encounter with a 'panicky soul.'

"One of the nurses had unzipped the body bag and the
attendants were moving the gurney over to the stainless
table."

"What are you doing? What are you doing?" the woman
asked several times.

"I then realized that she must have recognized herself in
the body bag and everything RC had told me now made
some kind of rational sense . . . '*Some of them truly do not know
they are dead. . .tell them to go to the light.*'"

Lu said she told the young woman she was physically
dead, and that her body could no longer be of any use to
her. She told the deceased woman she should go into the
light.

"No, I am not dead. I am still very much aware of everything. I can't be dead," Lu heard the woman say very clearly.

Then Lu continued, "I found myself standing next to a
gurney with a deceased individual in the body bag whispering into thin air. I didn't know then if the light were there,
here, or anywhere, but I repeated to the woman to look for
the light and then to go toward it. The woman looked
around the room and back at me. She looked over her
shoulder, smiled, and quickly disappeared."

When Lu took a closer look at the body in the bag, she
recognized the woman immediately. Only this time the

woman was not so pretty, having been in the car for a few days before being discovered by a parking lot attendant.

The next day Lu discussed what had happened with the coroner himself. Apparently he humored her and told her not to worry about it. "Some people get really nervous around the deceased," he said.

"After this experience," Lu told me, "I knew then, if nothing else, that in reality our spirit doesn't die."

The stories Lu shared with Patti and me over the meal at La Madeleine's were incredible. She used analogies to describe many things. She said our families are like a huge sparkler. Each of us is a spark of light that makes up the whole. We always stay together, connected by love. There is a mission for each one of us while we are here, and when the mission is completed, we go back through the light to our "home" and are reunited again.

Her words were like music to my ears when she said, "I sincerely believe your son Kyle is drawing me to you to share this information with you."

25

I Stayed Glued to My Chair

I made sure Patti was sitting on the aisle seat. I was ecstatic after our meal with Lu, and I wanted Patti to experience some of the same feeling. I wanted Brandon to show up.

James Van Praagh looked in our direction. "I have this young man in his twenties who was irresponsible, and he died recently in an automobile accident."

I wanted to jump up and raise my hand, as James had told us to do if the message made sense to us, but in a way I was hoping it was Patti's son. The message pertained to both of us, so I waited for something else from James, hoping it would single either Patti or me out.

I was bewildered when a lady sitting a little behind us, across the aisle, jumped to her feet. James said, "Does this make sense to you?"

She responded, "Well, my sixteen-year-old nephew died thirteen years ago."

I couldn't believe it. Nothing James had said matched what she said. I *knew* it was Kyle. But I just sat there, watching this lady become very emotional. I thought to myself, "James will say something specific and she'll know it's not for her."

"He's telling me you just turned a rug around on your carpet." I was *positive* it was Kyle. I even leaned over to Patti and told her. Just the week before, I had rearranged the furniture in my wall-to-wall carpeted den to face toward the fireplace. I had turned the patterned area rug to accommodate the furniture. I found out later this lady who was standing up getting Kyle's messages had no carpet in her house and had not moved any rugs. But for some reason, I stayed seated in my chair.

Then James said, "He's telling me you are doing something with his pictures *now*." When he asked the lady if that made sense, she said she'd looked through the family photo album a few months back.

At that exact moment, while I was still glued to my chair, there were numerous group pictures of mine at a professional photographer's office. I had asked them to crop Kyle's picture out of the group pictures and enlarge just the pictures of him. They were also making copies of photographs of Kyle others had given to me after the funeral. As a matter of fact, the Monday immediately following this spiritual weekend, I picked up these pictures of Kyle.

Looking back on this episode, I know how frustrated Kyle must have been. John has often said how much energy our loved ones have to expend in order to connect with the physical. He has said many souls want to bring comfort to their loved ones, but only the strongest ones get through. He said to imagine a bunch of people jockeying for position to get to the front of the line. When they are able to succeed, it comforts them greatly. Sad to say, Kyle worked his way to the front of the line, and his mother just sat there.

Somehow, though the messages didn't fit, this lady kept standing, sobbing uncontrollably at times. I guess the comfort she was getting was meant to be. When I often talk about Kyle's coming through James, I don't even mention her, because I'm *certain* it was Kyle. Also, in a way, I guess I'm trying to make it up to Kyle. I know he is aware of everything, and I know he knows I know it was he. But I will always regret not standing up.

James went on. "He's telling me you have made one of your bedrooms a junk room."

Just two weeks before when Bobby came to visit for the first time, I showed him the bedroom where he would sleep. I took him on a small tour of our house. Opening the corner bedroom door where I had stored a lot of boxes and things I hadn't gone through since Kyle's death, I remember saying to Bobby, "And this is what has become my junk room." I couldn't even open the door the entire way. It was full of so much stuff.

Later that evening when I asked the lady who thought the message was for her if she had a junk room, she replied, "My entire house is always messy."

Then James mentioned something about a tree's falling down. I visualized Kyle's accident and knew Kyle didn't hit a tree. He had hit a bridge. But this lady's nephew didn't hit a tree either. Some additional short messages were given and the next thing I knew, James had directed messages to someone else in the room.

After James's presentation, he was seated at a table autographing photographs. I got in line. When I spoke with him, I told him I'd seen him in California and was very impressed with his gift. I then said I *knew* the young man who came and mentioned the rug turned around on the carpet was my son. I said the only thing that didn't match was the tree falling down.

James then said, "Well, he definitely showed me a large tree falling down."

I got James's autograph and walked away. I had difficulty sleeping that night. I kept asking Patti and Judy, "Why didn't I stand up? Why didn't I challenge that lady?"

The next morning, before Annie Kirkwood, author of *Mary's Message to the World*, took the stage, I was greeted by four different people at four different times who came up to me and said, "It was Kyle who came last night." They had no way of knowing how everything James had said was so specific and exact pertaining to Kyle. They had known it was he, yet I still didn't stand up.

On the drive home with Patti and Judy Sunday afternoon, a light went off in my head. I couldn't believe it. Here was evidence again about being "brain dead," as Mary Jo refers to it. How could I have forgotten?

The Friday we left to drive to the weekend retreat was November 15, 1996. We had left in the early afternoon. That very morning, the day before James had said something about a big tree's falling down, a tree surgeon was cutting down the huge tree right outside Kyle's bedroom window. I had even thought, "What would Kyle think of our cutting down this large tree that shaded his room?" Now I was even madder that I didn't stand up.

But again, we can't change the past. We can only learn from it. If I ever attend one of James's seminars in the future, he'll probably wonder what's going on with the daffy lady who keeps jumping up for every message.

Something that might be controversial happened during the weekend in New Orleans, though. Often I have been confronted by people who have found out I'd had a conversation with O.J. in California. How could I have had a picture taken of him and me, even with his arm around me? How could I even associate with a murderer?

I'm not the one to judge whether O.J. did it or didn't do it. I have my thoughts concerning Nicole and Ron's murders, but I guess I was more or less caught up in the celebrity status of the entire event. And O.J. had been in our lives, if only for a few minutes (picture at NCAA track meet), before all this happened. I knew I would have to be cautious concerning who I shared the story with. I knew it would be a questionable act on my part.

I was riding the elevator down to the first floor of the hotel, looking forward to the culmination of the wonderful, spiritually awakening weekend, even though I was still upset about not standing up. I spotted a local television personality. We struck up a short conversation after I mentioned I enjoyed watching her on TV. She said she had come because she'd heard so much about the presenters and had been impressed by what she'd seen and heard.

I told her I was there because my only son had died and I'd been comforted by Mary Jo and James who I'd seen in California. Then for some reason, don't ask me why, I said, "We even got to see O.J. while in California." I had no idea why that came out of my mouth. Why would I tell a complete stranger I'd seen O.J.?

But what came out of her mouth next literally shocked me. She said, in reality, from the spiritual perspective of what happened, O.J. may have done something good. "Just think of how many lives he may have saved. The awareness of spousal abuse and its impact on our society will no longer be looked at so lightly. O.J. gave up a lot. Not only did the mother of his children die, but he also lost his reputation and celebrity status." Then she added, "Though it appears so sad and tragic to us here, and the grief that both Nicole's and Ron's families have had to endure must be unthinkable, who is to say that it is not part of a much bigger plan?"

Why was she saying this? For a minute, it made me feel better about having my picture made with O.J. Maybe there was a reason.

Annie Kirkwood was introduced and she walked to the stage. She could not have been on the stage more than five minutes when she brought up the name of O.J. Simpson. I couldn't believe what I had just heard. She, of all people. She who converses with the Virgin Mary. My mouth dropped open when she repeated almost word for word what I had just heard on the elevator only minutes before. Annie said from the spiritual world, things appear differently than they often do to us here on earth. "We can't see the whole picture. They can."

Hearing the same message from two respected people in only a matter of minutes made me wonder. I've often thought of sharing what happened in New Orleans with O.J. because I know it happened for a reason. Maybe he'll read my book.

Marcia Clark, one of the prosecuting attorneys during the O.J. trial, appeared on the Fox News show, *The Edge*, hosted by Paula Zahn on Friday evening, June 2, 2000. Approaching the sixth anniversary of the murders of Nicole and Ron, Marcia and Paula were discussing the outcome of the trial and what good, if anything, came out of it.

"Because of the trial, people became more attuned to domestic violence," Marcia told Paula. "A lot of education took place, so that was a good thing."

This again confirms what I have come to believe. Everything does happen for a reason—to help us learn and grow.

26

Premonition of Death

I've always said that one hundred percent of my three readings with John Edward were accurate. And if any part of them did not make sense at the time, it would soon afterward.

Case in point. While in California during our reading, John had said that a "Thomas" was with Kyle. This didn't ring any bells at the time. Then the night of our return to Louisiana, while attending Mary Jo's class, she told me I'd received a miracle from Kyle and how easily Kyle was drawn to John Edward. All of a sudden, she changed the message. She said, "Thomas will be important. Kyle wants you to know this."

So within days, two different psychic/mediums brought up the name of "Thomas." I wondered what meaning it could have. Three days later I found out.

I opened the Sunday paper. On the front page was an article about an automobile accident that had occurred within a few blocks of our home the night before. The thirteen-year-old boy who lived directly behind our house, but across the street, had died. I didn't know him. But I did know his name. It was "Thomas." Did Kyle know about his death beforehand? Mary Jo told me he did. It was Kyle's way of letting me know that everything is already planned, even our time to die.

Weeks later, at The Compassionate Friends meeting, I talked with Thomas's grieving parents. After much soul searching, I decided there had to be a reason why Kyle had given this information to me. I showed Thomas's parents where I had written Thomas's name down two times, once with John and once with Mary Jo. I really don't know what they thought, but I felt obligated to tell them.

I guess sometimes people are not at a place to accept such things, though. When I'd offered to try to get them a reading with John Edward, they didn't pursue the issue. So I backed off. I had brought them a few comforting books, one by Billy Graham, along with a tray of sandwiches when I'd heard about the accident. But I didn't want to upset them and push them in a direction they didn't want to follow.

Thomas's parents have separated recently. Their grief has driven them apart. I wish I could have helped them, but apparently, for some reason, it wasn't meant to be.

Another premonition of death occurred with Cory. Janice had told me Cory had dreamt his exact death three nights before he died. He had shared it with his mother. In the dream, he was hit by a large vehicle while walking near a ditch. It ran over him, causing his death. Cory's body was found near a ditch where he fell after he was run down by a teenager in a van. He was taken by an ambulance to a hospital where he died. Janice has been in a deep depression since Cory's death. She has been unable to return to her teaching profession and yearns to be with Cory. I constantly remind her of Cory's premonition of his death. On a soul level, Cory was preparing to leave. There are no accidents and there are no victims. We are all playing out the roles that we subconsciously chose.

Another night while at The Compassionate Friends, Janice and I were talking about Cory's dream. A mother whose daughter had recently died overheard us. She joined the conversation. She said her twenty-one-year-old daughter had come to her one morning sharing her dream of the night before. She said in the dream she had died and was lying in a casket. Because it upset her so, this mother told her daughter, "I don't want to hear anymore."

Two weeks later after her daughter's funeral, a close friend of her daughter's confided that her daughter had shared the entire dream with her before her death in the automobile accident. She told her of the dress she was wearing while in the casket, the color of the flowers on the casket, and the songs that were sung during the funeral. Everything matched perfectly. The decisions the mother made concerning her daughter's funeral were exactly the same as her daughter had dreamed.

Carl Harper told me he dreamt of his wife's death and also the death of his father, who died at forty years of age, before their deaths.

When I told Kyle's former mother-in-law of these foretelling dreams, she confided she had dreamed of her twenty-year-old brother's death by drowning four days before he drowned.

Mary Jo has told me Kyle dreamed of his death. He never shared it with me, though, if he did. I'll only know when I get to the Other Side.

We decided to have an open casket at Kyle's funeral. He had suffered major head trauma, but there wasn't a scratch on his face. His head had been shaved, but a cap concealed that to some degree. Kyle always wore Tommy Hilfiger caps, so he looked as normal as possible. We knew some people might not want to remember him like that lying in the casket, but we also thought of those who might want to see him one more time and say their good-byes.

I've never had a problem with having kept the casket open. Jim has, though. He often gets teary eyed and says it's hard to get rid of the picture in his mind of his son in the casket. He can't seem to shake it. I'm different. When I think of Kyle, I picture him walking in the back door with a big grin on his face.

Jaclyn, Kyle's fourteen-year-old niece, had never been to a funeral before. I know it was very emotional for her to see Kyle in the casket. Soon after the funeral, Jaclyn called me from her home in Washington. She wanted to share the "very real" dream she'd had of Kyle. She said he was lying in the casket, and all of a sudden he sat up. He kept telling her over and over, "I'm okay."

To this day, I think this dream brings her a lot of comfort, because she still talks about it often.

Tuesday, August 19, 1997, was one of those days that Jim became emotional and said he could not stop picturing Kyle lying in the casket. That very night, Kortnee had a dream she shared with me the next day.

"There was going to be a memorial for Kyle. I asked you and Mr. Collier if I could come with you, because I didn't get to attend Kyle's funeral. After I looked at Kyle in the casket, you both turned and walked out. I saw Kyle sit up in the casket. He waved at me and had a big smile on his face. And his hair looked gorgeous."

Kortnee said this wasn't a dream; it was a "visit." It seemed so real.

While Mary Jo was explaining the meaning of Kortnee's dream of Kyle's sitting up in the casket, waving and smiling, she said, "He's trying to tell you something—'I'm alive.' There is no such thing as death."

I was seated in my chair during the August 21, 1997, Thursday night class. Mary Jo looked at me and continued, "You have not yet faced his death. I know that's a very hard thing for you to accept and understand, but you haven't faced it. Do you see the light that just went off, right up over your head at the door frame? Trust me, you're being led." These were the exact words Mary Jo spoke and I have them on tape. I knew, as Mary Jo knew, that Kyle was the one manipulating the light.

When I returned home from school on September 7, 1997, DeDee (Kortnee's sister) was seated at my kitchen table. She was writing down questions for her reading with Mary Jo scheduled for later that day. She had slept in Kyle's bed the night before and had a very vivid dream of him. He was dead, at a viewing, lying in the casket. She looked at him closely and was very sad. Kyle opened his eyes, smiled and said, "Shhhhh." He then closed his eyes and did it again. She could hear him laughing with his mouth closed. She said he was letting her know he was not dead. She said when she woke up, she knew it wasn't a dream; it was a "visit."

Three different people had dreamt of Kyle in his casket. He let each of them know he wasn't really dead. "I'm okay, I'm okay. That's not me, I'm not in there," were the words Wendi had heard throughout Kyle's funeral. So I guess Kyle is doing all he can so we don't picture him in the casket. I only wish Jim could have a dream like these. Maybe in time.

27

An Angel Gift from Kyle

Bert Fife was a classmate in Mary Jo's Thursday night class. She is a very spiritual mother of five, who I soon learned had quite a bit of psychic ability herself. She had moved into a new home and had invited me to a house-warming party on August 9, 1997. She told me that she was also inviting someone who she wanted me to meet, Judy LaCroix.

When Judy and I were introduced, she handed me a boxed gift. I opened it and inside found a gold guardian angel pin. I was totally in awe, first by the gift and then by Judy's having bought it for me—a person I had never met before. She told me it was a gift from Kyle.

Judy had a near-death experience in 1975. She hemorrhaged while giving birth to her only child. Her child died, but she told me that what she experienced made her not want to come back to her body and life on earth as she knew it.

We sat outside by the pool on a swing and talked for over three hours. Her story of her trip "to the Other Side" brought me comfort then, as it does today. I will be forever grateful to her for sharing it with me.

She told me how she was aware of everything's taking place in the hospital, how they said "Code Red" when they were losing her. She described her trip through the tunnel into such a beautiful place that was much more "real" to her than here on earth. She was able to see God who was holding her baby. "God's eyes are like no other's," she said.

Judy experienced the review of her life and even saw how her being mean to a girl on the playground when she was younger had affected the girl. The stories she told me about how wonderful heaven was were very moving. Upon returning to her body, she could see herself lying on the table and could feel herself going back into her body. She was mad that she had to come back.

From her NDE, Judy learned that all that matters is love and that we will be with those we love throughout eternity. She said Kyle can see everything that is going on here and can feel our pain and that it is best to let him go so that he can be happy.

After this visit with Judy, I purchased the Betty Malz book, *Heaven—A Bright and Glorious Place.* It's unbelievable how so much of what is in that book matches exactly what Judy experienced, even written in Judy's words, word for word.

I previously mentioned that Bert Fife has amazing psychic ability. She shared this experience during one of Mary Jo's classes in the spring of 1997. I remembered reading about the accident in the newspaper and the feeling of sadness I had for the father.

A teacher from LaPlace, Louisiana, which is south of Baton Rouge, and her two children were driving to school. It was the first day of school for the 1996-1997 school year. They were stopped at a stop sign, waiting to pull out onto the highway. While waiting patiently for an opening, a car traveling at a high rate of speed approached the intersection. The speeding car apparently veered across the highway, striking the median, then flipped and landed on the car carrying the teacher and her two children. They died instantly.

The husband and father of these three individuals was a client of Bert Fife's company. After being paged, he received the anguishing news just as the information of the horrific event was breaking over his car radio. The shock and grief this man experienced at that moment had to be one of indescribable pain. I can't even begin to imagine losing your spouse and two children at the same time.

Sunday night following this horrendous accident, the woman came to Bert and told her to tell her husband that she and the two children were fine. "It's like the physical world where we are, but it's even better because the kids don't fight with each other anymore."

Bert was afraid to tell her client of this after-death communication with his wife. She was afraid he would think she was crazy.

The woman appeared a couple of days later, and Bert communicated with her again. She said she knew that Bert had not relayed the message to her husband. She stressed that she wanted him to be told all three of them were all right. The woman then reached near her heart and pulled out a shiny piece of jewelry and showed it to Bert.

Bert questioned the Thursday night class about what she should do. Mary Jo and I told her to tell her client about his wife's appearance. I told her she could not imagine the comfort a loved one gets when an after-death communication experience is shared with them. I told her I didn't know how I could have gone on without all the people who told me of Kyle's visits with them. I told Bert she had no choice. The woman had come to her twice. It was her obligation to share this with the grieving husband and father. After two sleepless nights, Bert promised to share these ADCs, if she could sleep that night.

After a restful night, Bert got up enough courage and set up a meeting at a local motel restaurant where she felt more comfortable sharing the ADC with this man. After telling the stories of his wife's two appearances, the man became very emotional. He said the day before his wife first appeared to Bert, he had gone into his children's room. Talking out loud, he said, "Everyone says you are okay, but I want you to let me know that you're okay."

When Bert described the shiny piece of jewelry the deceased woman had shown her, the man *knew* he had been given the confirmation his family was indeed okay. As he pointed to the cubic zirconia tie tack he was wearing, he told Bert he had pinned one on each of his family members before they were buried.

After Bert relayed additional messages to this grieving man, he acknowledged his deceased wife answered all the questions he had voiced to himself on Sunday, the night his wife first appeared to Bert. He thanked Bert for the messages.

This story makes me wonder how many loved ones who have died are able to connect with someone like Bert, and for fear of being ostracized, fail to mention the ADC. The next story is further evidence of the amount of comfort that can be derived by sharing after-death communications.

Four months after Kyle's death on August 27th, I received a phone call from Nancy Wood. Mary Jo had given my name and phone number to Nancy. She wanted Nancy to share the following story with me.

Nancy's son, Michael, and his best friend, Michael Chadwick, both 21, had died as the result of an automobile accident caused by a drunk driver. The accident happened in 1993. Over two and a half years later, Nancy received a telephone call from a friend, Jim, whom her family had known when they lived in Maryland. She hadn't heard from this man in over ten years and was wondering why he was calling her.

Jim and Nancy carried on a rather general conversation, when all of a sudden, Jim asked about Nancy's two sons. Nancy told him about Michael's death. Jim then told Nancy he had a message for her.

Jim had been in a very serious automobile accident. He suffered critical injuries with almost every bone's being crushed or broken, including his back and neck. He lapsed in and out of consciousness. After the accident, he saw a young woman at the driver's side window. He asked her for help in making him more comfortable, but the young woman told him to stay still because his neck and back were broken. She then called 911 on Jim's car phone and told them she was an emergency trauma nurse. She said it was serious and for them to send a helicopter. Jim lost consciousness again.

When Jim came to, a policeman was at the window. Jim asked where the woman was, but the policeman said that there was no woman, that he was the first person at the scene of the accident. This woman's voice *is* on the 911 tape, though.

During the ride to the hospital, Jim died but was resuscitated. He died again while at the hospital, but the medical staff was able to revive him once more.

While on the Other Side when all Jim's vital organs had stopped, Jim saw a young man who said, "I am fine. I am very happy. This is a wonderful place." Jim didn't recognize the young man who kept telling him over and over that he was fine. When he asked who he was, the young man said, "Michael Wood."

Jim had not known of Michael's death. The months following Jim's near-death experience, he kept having recurring dreams of Michael's telling him that he was fine and very happy. Jim thought about calling Nancy but was afraid she might think he was crazy. These vivid dreams of Michael persisted. Michael's relentless determination persuaded Jim to call Nancy. Michael wanted to make sure that his mother knew he was okay. It was only after his phone conversation with Nancy that these messages from Michael stopped.

I remember meeting Nancy in New Orleans after she told me this story. She gave me the impression that she knew Michael was okay. I realize now she was in the place then that I am today. We both *know* our sons are okay, and we'll be with them one day.

28

Only the Good Die Young

Princess Diana's death was very emotional for me, another awakening that we never know how long we will be here. We can never take anything for granted. I was glued to the television set on August 31, 1997.

During Mary Jo's Thursday class, she talked about Diana's death and again said what she often says, "There are no accidents."

Judy, who had the near-death experience while giving birth, was visiting our class that night. One of my fellow classmates was unable to attend, and Mary Jo had invited Judy after I'd told the class about my experience with her. Judy told all of us she had dreamt of the exact accident that caused the death of Diana. When she saw the wrecked car on TV and diagrams of what had taken place, she said it was exactly the same.

The guest on *Larry King Live* on Friday, September 5th, was the woman who owns Tiffany's in London. She told Larry she was one of Diana's best friends. I don't remember her name, but I remember her telling Larry that while she was visiting the coffin, "I felt such energy in the room." She told Larry on her drive to Kensington Palace she could hear Diana whisper, "I can't believe all these flowers are for me."

Unless you are in deep grief over the loss of a loved one, you might not pick up on messages such as this from the spirit world.

During the morning, a psychic appeared on the *Regis and Kathie Lee* TV show. She had written a book which had been published. In the book she mentioned that Diana would be in an accident followed by a motorcycle. The psychic then said, "According to Catholic beliefs, Diana will be watching everything tomorrow."

DeDee was visiting us the weekend of Diana's death. She had gone with us to the LSU vs. Texas El Paso football game in Tiger Stadium on Saturday night. She knew Jim had coached there fifteen years and Kyle had grown up around the LSU campus. She wanted to experience some of what they had experienced.

In Dallas, DeDee attended the Unity Church. When we awoke Sunday morning, she asked me if I would attend the Unity Church in Baton Rouge with her. She got out the phone book, found the location, and convinced me to go.

When we entered the parking lot of the church, my mouth flew open. I spotted two of my classmates from Mary Jo's class. DeDee and I were welcomed as we walked in the door and took a seat. A woman was in the front of the sanctuary playing a guitar and singing. She had a beautiful voice. We were even more amazed when the church service began, and we found out the lady with the beautiful voice was Reverend Jan.

Reverend Jan also spoke about Diana's death and said we all have a time frame to be here on earth. She said, "You are more than your body, more than your thoughts. We incarnate into a body, but are often programmed by those in our life to be someone other than who we are. We pick the culture and number in the family when we come into the earth." She was saying the exact words I'd heard from Mary Jo.

I was glad that DeDee pushed me to go with her that first time. It reinforced that everything happens for a reason.

Sylvia Browne appears monthly on the *Montel Williams Show*. I try to watch her as often as possible and tape most of her shows. She says so much of what I know to be true. She also says that we "chart" our own lives, and we choose our parents, our circumstances, and the way in which we will leave this earth. She, as well as John and Mary Jo, says that there are no accidents. We all have to leave the earth, and we choose the way we die. When we have completed what we came here to do, then we are able to go home.

It is ironic, as I write this, that the U.S. Coast Guard is searching for John F. Kennedy, Jr.'s plane that crashed into the ocean off Martha's Vineyard. The sadness of the loss of three young lives is overwhelming, not only to their families but also to the nation and the world. The Kennedy mystique is still with us. I even have all the magazines and newspapers concerning President Kennedy's death in my attic.

The death of my own son has given me an entirely different perspective on John, Jr.'s death than I had when President Kennedy died. While watching television yesterday, a lady was being interviewed at the gravesite of President Kennedy and Jackie Kennedy Onassis at Arlington Cemetery. The lady commented, "It's so sad. Jackie has lost her baby."

Lost her baby? No. No way. She's found him. He's with his parents again. Just think of all the catching up John Jr. is doing now with his father while Carolyn, John's wife, is getting to meet her in-laws. I think of how happy they are to be together. The one I feel a sadness for is Caroline, John's sister. She has to endure the grief of losing her loved ones, but she will be with them again one day.

Too often our attitude toward death makes us appear to be hypocritical. We say we believe in a "Higher Being." We say heaven is a far better place than here on earth, then we are sad about our loved ones who have gone on before us. Because we are human, we miss them. In reality, though, we should be happy for them. If we believe in God and His heavenly home, then we should celebrate John's graduation as well as all who pass on.

I didn't intend to get on my soapbox concerning this. We are all going to die. We are all going to suffer. As I've heard both Mary Jo and Sylvia say, "There's no point in coming to earth if your life is perfect and without pain. You won't learn anything, so you might as well have stayed on the Other Side."

Reverend Billy Graham spoke with Katie Couric, host of the *Today* show on television this morning. When she questioned Reverend Graham about these young deaths, he said that God has a plan for each of us. "We may not understand while we are here, but we will one day." Then he said, "John's death, at the prime of his life, brings an awareness of the shortness of life, and the knowledge that we don't know the day when each of us will have to face our Maker, God."

Janice sent the following story to me. She had received it soon after Cory died. I'd like to share it with you.

> *When I was a little boy, my mother used to embroider a great deal. I would sit at her knee and look up from the floor and ask what she was doing. She informed me she was embroidering. I told her it looked like a mess from where I was. From the underside, I watched her work within the boundaries of the little round hoop she held in her hand. I complained to her that it sure looked messy from where I sat.*
>
> *She would smile at me, look down and gently say, "My son, you go about your playing for awhile and when I am finished with my embroidering, I will put you on my knee and let you see it from my side."*

I would wonder why she was using some dark threads along with the bright ones and why they seemed so jumbled from my view. A few minutes would pass and then I would hear mother's voice say, "Son, come and sit on my knee." This I did only to be surprised and thrilled to see a beautiful flower and sunset. I could not believe it, because from beneath it looked so messy.

Then mother would say to me, "My son, from beneath it did look messy and jumbled, but you did not realize there was a pre-drawn plan on the top. It was a design. I was only following it. Now look at it from my side and you will see what I was doing."

Many times through the years I have looked up to my Heavenly Father and said, "Father, what are You doing?" He has answered, "I am embroidering your life."

I say, "But it looks like a mess to me. It seems so jumbled. The threads seem so dark. Why can't they all be bright?"

The Father seems to tell me, "My child, you go about your business of doing My business and one day I will bring you to Heaven and put you on My knee and you will see the plan from My side."

Though I miss Kyle, I often think of all the wonderful souls who also get to call heaven "home." The idea that such loving caring souls leave this earth at a young age somehow brings me comfort. Knowing that Kyle is in the same place as Diana and JFK, Jr. also brings me comfort. Sometimes I relive the song, "Only the Good Die Young," over and over in my mind.

29

Trivial and Mundane Messages

Lisa Guidroz opened an angel store, "Bryson's Angel's" after the death of her son, Jason, in a motorcycle accident. I was drawn to these kinds of shops after Kyle's death. She had an angel lamp which caught my eye. While talking about the lamp, we struck up a conversation about our sons. I told her about Mary Jo and John Edward, and I gave her Mary Jo's personal card.

Evidently Lisa was impressed with what I'd told her because she attended one of Mary Jo's workshops. I knew she would also be interested in seeing John when he came to New Orleans. He was not scheduling any private readings, but I knew how moving an experience it was just being in the audience and watching him do spot readings.

Lisa and her husband, Terry, both attended John's seminar on Friday evening, June 12, 1998. I talked with them before the event in the restaurant of the hotel located on the top floor overlooking the city. Terry seemed rather skeptical of John and what he was supposed to be able to do. I hoped all would go well that evening and both Lisa and Terry would be glad they had come.

When I finally took a seat, I looked for Lisa and Terry. They were seated near the front of the room, across the aisle from me. I was seated farther in the back. John explained how the spirits come through to him and asked for those to whom the message is being directed to only say yes or no. He began walking in the direction of Lisa and Terry.

I was thrilled when Jason, Lisa and Terry's son, was the first one from the Other Side to come through. John said, rather embarrassingly, "I don't know what this means, but he's talking about farting. He's saying, 'Fart.'"

Though I couldn't see their faces, I knew Lisa and Terry were emotional. I could see them both shaking their heads as if in disbelief. Jason mentioned his girlfriend's name and gave his parents other messages. And then John said their son was stepping back.

Terry spoke up. He told John and the audience that he was probably the most skeptical person in the room that evening. But after what John had just told him, he wouldn't be skeptical anymore. Lisa hadn't even been aware of it, but Terry had told Jason beforehand, if this were for real and he could speak through John, for him to "bust to the front of the line" and come through first. Also, Jason's father often called him "Rat Poot" or "Fart."

I phoned Lisa and Terry's room the next morning while still at the hotel. She told me the entire message from Jason made sense and was unbelievable. She and Terry had been discussing how they could tell everyone what had happened without their thinking they had lost their minds.

That's why most of the people I now associate with are people I did not even know before Kyle's death. I feel a lot more comfortable being with people who don't think I've become loony. My life, as I knew it, can never be the same. I've learned too much. I'm on a different plane.

One time when John was giving private readings in New Orleans, I was waiting in the lobby of the hotel for one of the parents I brought to see John. I struck up a conversation with Mary Adams whose daughter had died. Kimmie, as only her immediate family called her, was twenty-one years old and three and a half months away from graduating with honors in engineering from Florida State University. Kim had died as the result of an allergic reaction to an allergy shot, anaphylaxis, which caused a complete systemic shut-down of her body.

Mary told me that she, her husband and two adult sons were going to have a private reading with John. She then told me a little bit about the private reading she had with George Anderson, another renowned medium. Mary said, "Before my reading with George, I was nervous and scared that Kim wouldn't be there. I asked God to please let her come, and then I said to my daughter if George tells me 'Kimmie' is here then I will know for sure that it is really you."

In the course of the reading, George told Mary there were eight letters in her daughter's name (Kimberly), but he couldn't quite come up with it. A bit later George said, "I see the Rudyard Kipling book, *Kim*. Ahhhh that's it, that's her name. Kim, Kimberly, Kimmie. She says to tell you 'Kimmie is here.'"

For over twenty-five years, George has worked with be-reaved families to facilitate contact with their deceased loved ones. He has written many wonderful books: *Our Children Forever, We Don't Die, We Are Not Forgotten,* and most recently, *Lessons From the Light.* Mary told me her reading with George had been a turning point in her grief process, and that she had "absolute proof that Kimmie still lived and is still a part of my life." She told me she was greatly antici-pating this reading with John.

I was still in the lobby after Mary's reading. She said John was as good as George and that Kimmie had come through. John began the reading by saying, "Kim is here. No, she's correcting me to say Kimmie." During the reading Kimmie brought up a tattoo that one of her brothers had on his leg. Both men shook their heads "no" when their parents looked at them rather perplexed. A tattoo was something their parents wouldn't have approved of, but Kimmie was persistent that one of her brothers had a tattoo on his leg.

At John's seminar the following night, I found out about the tattoo. On the family's drive home, Kim's brothers, Chris and Chad, were seated in the back seat and they began chuckling. Chad pushed up his pants' leg and exposed the tattoo of his fraternity emblem on his ankle. The entire family laughed as Chris said, "Kimmie busted you, Chad, from the Other Side." Kim and Chad were only eighteen months apart and were very close while growing up. Apparently Kim had been the only person Chad had shown his tattoo to after having it done. She was able to let her parents know about it even from the spirit world.

These instances, though seemingly trivial, illustrate anew the way our loved ones attempt to let us know they are still very much alive.

30

Cemetery Chip & Dip Party

Kathy and I were headed to East Feliciana Parish. We were going to our first ever cemetery party. We didn't know what to expect. How many graveyard parties have you been to? We had been to the same number.

The month before, after retrieving the mail from our mailbox one day, it entered my mind that in the near future the postman might not think anyone lives at our address because of the deteriorating condition of our front yard. I voiced my concern to Jim that night, and he told me he had met a man awhile back in his muffler shop who did yard work. He said he'd check it out for me.

A few days later, George showed up at my front doorstep and I introduced myself. I noticed the trailer behind his old truck was full of lawn mowers and other lawn manicuring tools. I figured he'd need all the stuff to get our lawn back in shape.

After a few hours I poured a big glass of ice water and brought it out to George. He stood up, with sweat running down his face, and I felt bad that he was having to go to so much trouble helping me. I apologized for the condition of our yard and to make myself feel better I said, "It would probably be hard for you to believe that a few years back we had a sign in our yard that read, "Yard of the Month." George looked surprised and laughed, which made me know it was hard for him to believe.

I told him our lives had become so busy and hectic that we got behind on everything. I even mentioned that I was writing a book.

When he asked me what the book was about, I told him our son had died and the book was about Kyle.

"You know he's really not dead," George said. "I'm around dead people all the time, and I know you don't really die."

I looked at George in amazement. He was the last person I would have expected to get this message from. Then he told me he did maintenance work at a cemetery in another parish.

He said one year he was cleaning the grave markers at the cemetery. There were some old markers in deplorable condition, and he had decided to paint them to make them look better. After a long day of sprucing up the grave markers, he headed home. He told me he was lying in bed and his wife's cat was lying at the foot of their bed. All at once, the cat scampered out of the room. It was then that George noticed a young man dressed in black clothes enter his doorway. He walked in and sat on the foot of the bed.

George pushed down on the bush we were standing next to, showing me how the man dented the mattress when he sat down. George and this young man carried on a conversation. George asked who he was. The man told him he had died in the 19th century and was buried at the cemetery where George was working. George told me, "I've been open and able to connect to the spirit world all my life, so I was used to this kind of communication."

I couldn't believe what I was hearing from the yard man Jim had sent to our house.

This deceased man told George that his gravestone had been neglected, because it was separated from the other graves, and was difficult to see. He told George where he could find his grave, then disappeared.

George told me the following day when he arrived at the cemetery, he checked out what his visitor had told him. Sure enough, there was a gravestone separated from the others that was in dire condition.

The visit by the deceased man had intrigued George. He checked around with the families who were buried there and was able to acquire a photograph of the man who had been buried at this particular gravesite. When he looked at the picture, he recognized the man as being identical to the man who appeared in his bedroom.

When I told George how much his story comforted me, he asked if I might want to help in a few weeks when a number of people were going to show up at the cemetery and give it a good cleaning up. I asked what I needed to bring, and he said, "Just bring some chips and dip and the drinks you prefer. We take a break every now and then, and that's when we do our partying."

Upon hearing this story, many people ask me how we could spend the day at a cemetery, especially since both Kathy and I had lost our sons. In all honesty, it was a comfort. If George had not shared his story beforehand, I would not have even gone. But I had enough proof that these people weren't dead . . . just their bodies had died.

This story is added affirmation that even though we are on the Other Side, no matter for how long, we are still a part of this earthly world.

31

Spreading the Truth

As I mentioned previously because Kyle brought it up in my reading with John Edward, I stuttered when I was younger. I was terrified of speaking in public. In high school, I never tried out for cheerleader, school plays, or even called people on the phone. In college, I tried to sit near the back of the classroom, hoping I'd be more obscure and not get called on.

I was very embarrassed by my stuttering. Fortunately, it was something I gradually outgrew, though to this very day, I'm still aware of the possibility of this speech impediment surfacing now and then.

That is why it is amazing to me that I have phoned in on radio talk shows four different times and have even recorded a commercial. Kyle's death and my awareness of an afterlife have enabled me to overcome this fear of speaking. The need to spread my message has become my primary focus.

WJBO, the local talk radio station in Baton Rouge is a very popular station. It not only carries the nationally syndicated shows of Rush Limbaugh, Dr. Laura Schlessinger, and Art Bell, but it also carries many local hosts whose programs are unusually interesting and mind stimulating. Mary Jo

McCabe now has her own program on this station. She has a one-hour time slot which is broadcast weekly.

Ed Buggs has the drive-home slot between four and six o'clock, each weekday. In the promos for his show one day, he said that James Van Praagh, a well-known psychic from California, would be the guest that day. So I made sure I was tuned in at four o'clock.

Ed asked if anyone in the listening audience had experienced being with a psychic, and if so, to call in. I didn't even hesitate, though I had no idea what I was going to say. When I told the screener that I'd seen James Van Praagh perform in California, they put me on the air next. I was mortified. Because I had already planned to tape the show, I have a copy of what transpired.

I told Ed my son had died, and my husband and I had sought help by going to see James. He seemed rather surprised that someone from Baton Rouge had been to California to see his guest who would be appearing later in the show. I explained that James was able to bring comfort to those in grief by communicating with their loved one who had died. I also said James was not giving private readings anymore but that he appeared with John Edward, a young psychic from New York. I then spoke about how unbelievable our private reading with John had been.

Mary Jo also appeared on this show about psychics, which was the beginning of her local radio exposure. The intense interest shown concerning this psychic radio broadcast shows how desperately people seek to know more about the spiritual life. We want to know what really happens when we die.

When Ed was speaking with James, he brought up the conversation he'd had with me. Ed said a lady from Baton Rouge had seen both him and John Edward appear together. James acknowledged he had appeared with John.

This little validation by James helped me, because it gave whatever I had said more credibility.

Later, because of the growing interest in this psychic phenomenon, Mary Jo was scheduled as a guest on Ed's program for an entire hour. Before she came on the show, I didn't hesitate. I phoned in and was put on hold to be the next caller on the air. I was mortified again. Even though I was still very aware of my stuttering, I knew I had to tell my story.

I never told Mary Jo of my plans to write a book about Kyle and our experiences with him after his death. I often thought about mentioning it during many of our Thursday night classes, but I didn't. Usually, we were allowed to ask questions, but for some reason I never brought up the subject. Now, I'm thankful I didn't. You'll see why.

Mary Jo had apparently heard my comments about her while on her drive to the radio station. When she arrived at the station, Ed asked if she'd heard me and said my comments were very impressive.

Needless to say, I was very surprised when Mary Jo phoned me later that evening. She told me I *had* to write a book. She said it should be called, "The Search for Kyle," (You can see that I didn't follow this one suggestion of hers.) and it would be a bestseller. She will never know how much that phone call meant to me. I was not able to sleep that night, I was so excited.

After her phone call, the guides through Mary Jo have told me three different times I needed to get started on this book. They said it must come from my heart and not my head.

I actually started jotting down things one year after Kyle's death, but more or less got sidetracked because so many things kept happening. But I documented everything. Thank heavens I did. There is no way I could have remembered every little detail without keeping records. I even kept every ticket stub for every seminar I attended and saved the directions I scribbled on a piece of paper when I went to John's home on Long Island. I don't get sentimentally attached to things like some people, but something made me keep everything concerning Kyle's death and his new home, the spiritual world.

This push by Mary Jo gave me the inspiration to begin fulfilling my plan to share with you my unbelievable spiritual journey.

It's so important to stress that all of these wonderful people who have contributed to my growth in spirituality are not "kooks." They are some of the most compassionate, God loving people I have ever met. They are members of normal families and try to live normal lives. If you passed Mary Jo or John on the street, you wouldn't have a clue they talk to the dead. They're attractive, well-balanced individuals.

When *People Magazine* ran a story about the movie, *The Sixth Sense*, I became upset. A skeptic, James Randi, commented that mediumship was all a scam and they just played on the weaknesses of those in grief. I was so mad I actually e-mailed a letter to *People* for them to put in the "Mailbag" section of the magazine where people respond to previous articles. First, I told them they left out a picture of the best medium ever, John Edward. Then I asked James Randi if he had a child to die, and if so, if he had been to see John Edward. I knew they wouldn't print the letter, but it made me feel better.

So many people raise their eyebrows and often make comments when they know I sought help by going to Mary Jo and John. I've learned to say one thing. "Have you had a child to die?"

Not that I want to be ugly or mean to people, but unless you have lost a child, you cannot possibly begin to understand the pain that a parent experiences. It has to be the worst imaginable pain. I've learned there's really no sense in trying to explain it to others. Unless you've been there, you have no idea. It's an ache that never goes away. And there never will be any closure. I hate that word. What is closure? The dictionary says that closure is a finish, a conclusion. How do you reach a point in your grief when you come to a conclusion? Trust me, it never ends; there is no finish. The pain of your loss will always be with you. But it does ease some with time and with the assurance through faith that there is no such thing as death. Knowing your loved one lives on, as I have been given proof of over and over again, makes Kyle's not being here with us more tolerable. But the death of a loved one who is a part of your life can never, ever reach complete peace. Your heart will always ache.

Because of Mary Jo's accuracy and impact on people's lives while appearing as a guest on talk radio, she earned her own radio show. I was ecstatic when she shared the news. The more people she can reach, the more people she can touch, and the more people she can help. The very night she told me about her upcoming show, I awoke at 2:00 a.m. and went to my kitchen table and began writing. I wrote a commercial to be broadcast the first twenty-six weeks of her show. When I went to the studio to record the commercial, it was exactly sixty seconds long. It never ceases to amaze me how powerful our guides are.

I would like to quote part of the commercial: "I never thought I would be recording a commercial, but I could not pass up this opportunity to share our story. Two and a half years ago, our only son died in an automobile accident. Two months later, I met Mary Jo McCabe. After a thirty minute visit with Mary Jo, I knew my son's soul lived on and I would one day be with him again. The comfort Mary Jo has brought to our family is indescribable. She truly does have a gift from God. Needless to say, our lives have been changed forever. Because of our devastating loss, we were led to Mary Jo and have experienced a spiritual growth beyond expression."

As I type this, on October 3, 1999, I have just viewed a television promotion of an upcoming special on Mary Jo McCabe. It will be aired tomorrow night on a local television station in Baton Rouge, WAFB-TV. I am eagerly waiting for it to be broadcast. I know she did a wonderful job in presenting her "gift." I know how impressed many of her radio listeners will be when they are able to put a face to the voice they hear each week. I know how surprised they will be when they see for the first time how attractive she is.

But I'm worried about my appearance. Mary Jo phoned me before filming the special and asked if I would appear on the show with her. Again, I cannot tell you how good I feel to be given the opportunity not only to share Mary Jo's gift, but my story as well. I realize many viewers will be people who know me, either from my being a teacher for over twenty years, or from my living in the Baton Rouge area for over thirty-four years. Many, however, are not aware of my spiritual awakening. I anticipate many comments.

But I know I am doing the right thing. If I can help bring comfort to one individual, it is the right thing for me to do. I've received far too many blessings these past three years for me not to share them with others.

Mary Jo's radio broadcast was instantly popular. There were callers phoning far in advance of the air time hoping to get on the show. They even announced during the preceding show when callers could begin calling in, because the radio station was being bombarded with so many calls. Whether the death of a loved one and the concern we have for them, or the prospect of a new job opportunity, or a health concern, Mary Jo always has an answer that is quite remarkable. I am amazed at her accuracy in stating facts and occurrences that have taken place. Her audience has continued to grow.

On the evening of June 6, 2000, from 6:00 until 7:00, Mary Jo appeared on the first weekly broadcast of her own television show. Now the callers are able to see her as she continues to bring comfort to others through their journey in the physical world.

A growing awareness of our spirit is brought to the forefront every weekday during the highly successful and nationally popular *Oprah* television show. Oprah Winfrey, a trailblazer during her own journey, has exposed to her many viewers an understanding and sense of who we *really* are. Her "Remembering Your Spirit" segment presented at the end of each day's program, gives the audiences both at home and in the studio a deeper introspection of the spirituality within each living being.

I admire Oprah for her initiative and drive in stressing the spiritual side of our existence. When we can accept our spirit as the main focus of our lives, we will in turn make our physical journeys all the more meaningful. Oprah has contributed not only to my spiritual growth, but to millions of others as well. And I am thankful to her for that.

For those of you reading this book, I know you are on a spiritual pilgrimage. I truly believe one has to endure pain, suffering, or loss in order to learn and grow. When everything in life is calm, peaceful, and flowing smoothly, we are more apt to feel safe, and we can function well in that space. But when our lives are confronted with obstacles as emotional and permanent as the loss of a loved one, we choose either of two paths. We bury ourselves in sorrow and continue to hurt not only ourselves but also those we love, or we choose to accept the pain, grieve, and then become more compassionate and loving. Our acceptance is evident in the way we help others which in turn helps ourselves. This is clearly shown through the activity of MADD parents who try to prevent future alcohol-related deaths. Through their grief, they reach out to others. They illustrate the fact that we cannot change the past, but we can change the future by the way we accept what has happened to us and move forward.

Too often, however, we have a tendency to wish our lives away. For example, have you thought of how often in your life you looked forward to something? As a child, you looked forward to holidays and vacations. As a teenager, you looked forward to being able to date and drive a car. Then you looked forward to going away to college, to having a career, to being married, and to having your own family. You couldn't wait to see your child's first smile and take his or her first steps. And your children continue the cycle of "looking forward" throughout their lives. In reality, all we are certain of is the "now." We do not know what the future holds for us. We must enjoy and be at peace with the present, or we waste much of our lives.

It often takes the sudden death of a young person to awaken us to this reality—to know that the here and now is what is important. How well do I know this? I've learned it well, trust me. Not that I still don't look forward to things, because I do; I am human. But I definitely notice the small things, the things we often take for granted. I am more in awe of the beauty that surrounds us, the colors of the flowers, the variety of trees, the cascading waterfalls, the majestic mountains and the rumbling rivers. I often think if God made such beauty here where we live temporarily, just imagine how wondrous He has made the home where we will live with Him eternally. I no longer fear death. Though I feel a certain contentment in my life now, and I believe I know my purpose for being here, I still look forward to the day I will see Kyle again.

32

Do Your Own Thing

I have just returned from my 40th high school reunion. I had no intention of including this event, but because of all that happened and what I learned, I feel compelled to share some of it with you. Perhaps these lessons may be of benefit to you someday.

First, let me backtrack a little. At the beginning of my summer break from teaching school, I had planned on doing three things. First, I would visit Jill in Anacortes, Washington, and become acquainted with my newest grandchild, Jordyn, born June 1st. Then when I returned home after a ten-day visit, I would begin writing this book. During August, I would attend my reunion in Hot Springs, Arkansas.

While in Washington, a light went off in my head as I was putting on my make-up one morning. My upper eyelids had become very saggy, and no eye make-up would stay on. So I thought, why not kill two birds with one stone? I'd have the fat removed from my upper eyelids and recuperate while I was working on my book.

Lesson number one: Do not *ever* schedule elective cosmetic surgery two weeks before a very important event like a wedding or 40th reunion.

Dr. Reilley assured me it would only take two weeks for my new face to be presentable. She said any discoloration and swelling could easily be concealed with make-up by that time. So I went "under the knife" for the first time ever, exactly sixteen days before my reunion. Now you have to understand, I'd looked forward to this big event. I had begun dieting and suntanning and had bought all new clothes and accessories.

I knew, however, I must really look bad when I went to take a bath two days after the surgery. Jim had taped towels over all of the mirrors in the bathroom. I would have been too scared to look anyway, but this was not an encouraging sign. The next day Jim commented if I should happen to cross over now to the Other Side, I would have to have a name tag, because Kyle wouldn't know who I was. I was upset with this comment but laughed, trying to have some sense of humor about the situation, but it hurt when I laughed.

Forget about killing two birds with one stone. I spent the first three days lying on the couch with my head elevated and with frozen peas in a Ziploc bag on my eyes. Yes, Dr. Reilley told me to do this because the peas can conform easily to the contour of your face, unlike ice cubes which are harder and heavier. When the "putting on the peas to inhibit the swelling" time frame elapsed, I was still unable to work on this book. Not that I couldn't type on the keyboard. I just couldn't see if I were hitting the correct keys.

Lesson number two: Do everything you need to do before surgery. Pretend you are going to prison for two weeks and you'll be in solitary confinement.

Dumb me. I wear contact lens for near-sightedness. I'm as blind as a bat without my contacts. But did I get some prescription sunglasses made before the surgery? No. I don't know what I was thinking. If I had wanted to go out in public those first two weeks, I would have to have dark glasses on.

Not only for the glare and my comfort but so I wouldn't scare anyone. When I finally got up the nerve to look in a mirror one week later, I saw stitches hanging from my eyelids. Surgical tape was on my forehead and in the corner of both eyes. I was black and blue and yellow. Trust me, I wasn't a pretty sight.

Ten days into this fiasco, Dr. Reilley assured me I'd be able to make the reunion. I asked her who she knew who sold designer sacks for over the head.

But I tried to stay positive. I phoned Susan Barry, my "hairdresser and psychiatrist," to schedule a haircut the day before I would leave, just in case Dr. Reilley was right and I would be able to go. I asked Susan if she'd had any experience cutting hair with a sack in place. She asked if it were that bad and I told her yes.

The day before my intended departure was the first time I applied make-up. I actually got a little excited, looking somewhat human and recognizable again. I went to see Dr. Reilley. She called in another doctor. She figured I needed additional encouragement. When this new doctor told me I was about average in my post-operative progress, I immediately thought, "Pity the poor below average person."

They again took pictures. This was the fourth picture-taking session. I wondered if they do this with all their patients or if I were just an extreme case and they needed documentation if they were ever faced with another situation like mine again. I was afraid to ask.

With Dr. Reilley's encouragement, along with the rest of the office staff saying I looked "wonderful," I headed for the door. But I was thinking to myself, how many patients have they told, "You don't look too good," as they walked out the door?

By now, I had gotten up enough nerve to go to the eyeglass place. I would expose my face and get a pair of "ready in an hour" prescription sunglasses. That was probably the quickest purchase I ever made. I picked up the first pair of frames I saw and put them on my face. I squinted. I couldn't tell what they looked like. I was desperate though. I handed my eyeglass prescription to the saleslady and told her I'd be back for them in an hour.

I walked into Susan's beauty shop with my new sunglasses in place.

"Let me see," she said.

I hesitated. I removed the sunglasses.

"You look just like Jamie. It looks good. Your eyes look so open."

When her customer asked what she was talking about and Susan told her that I had plastic surgery, the lady said she never would have known. So it was exactly at that moment, and only at that moment, that I knew I would go home and pack my car for the reunion.

"Just how long is this reunion going to last?" Jim asked as I kept filling up the car with suitcases.

So I headed off in my packed car, driving along listening to all the '50s CDs I had put in the car CD player to get in the mood for my class of '59 reunion.

It had become a very emotional drive for me to Arkansas. I often think while driving that Kyle drove on these exact roads, stopped at these same gas stations, ate at these same places, and saw the same sunsets. It's funny how everything now either happened "before Kyle died or after Kyle died." That will always be the frame of reference for any occurrence in my life. Those of you who have lost a very special loved one know what I am talking about. I am no longer the same person. This new person relates to everything differently, as I'm sure you do as well.

So I'm getting in the mood with Fats Domino, Conway Twitty and Elvis, and I drive on anxiously awaiting what lies ahead. The one CD that didn't apply to the '50s music was the Rod Stewart CD with "Forever Young" on it. Let me explain why it was included.

One day in the spring of the year, I had dropped by Albertsons, the neighborhood grocery store, to pick up a few things. While hurrying down one aisle, I ran into Linda Hullinger. She had been a classmate in Mary Jo's Thursday night class. We exchanged greetings. She said she hardly ever shopped at that particular store and never when she was on her way to pick up her children from school. She said somehow she knew she would see me.

I must let you know that Linda was the one in Mary Jo's class who was very "gifted." She has psychic and healing abilities. I have heard many people speak of her ability to heal their pains and physical problems. She is a very happily married mother of three, and I was often overwhelmed with what she shared in class.

Linda's father had died in an automobile accident. On five different occasions, he came to her while she was in a dream state. He was always in a car and had picked up a person. Within one week, the person her father picked up was dead. She often saw dead people and could carry on conversations with them.

So Linda's telling me she knew she would see me didn't surprise me. When I asked how she was doing, she said she was beginning to do private readings, and from the response she was getting, they were going well. We cut the conversation short, because both of us were in a hurry.

The very next day I received a typed letter in the mail from Linda. I will quote part of that letter.

> Then as soon as I got home, I could barely put the groceries away . . . I had to go type this message. I asked if I were sent to Albertsons by Kyle. Kyle said, "Of course, I sent you there. I sent you there for my mother. Her voice carries to others in unreachable lengths and so it is as if she is the messenger on the mountain top shouting to

others her need to express that there is an afterlife. Tell her to put her heart into her work. Become a public speaker. It will benefit many."

Linda was never told of my plans to write a book. So this message from her has given me additional encouragement in my endeavor to share Kyle's story.

I immediately phoned Linda to thank her, and she told me something that had happened. While she was mailing my letter, the car radio came on. She said she never listens to the radio; she only plays tapes when she is in her car. "Forever Young" played. She knew it was a sign from Kyle. She then asked me if Kyle hadn't died in 1996? When I told her he had, she said, "Well, that's the year Rod Stewart recorded that song."

So that is the reason why I picked out Rod Stewart's CD and put in the CD changer with the other five '50s CDs.

Ironically, only the night before I bumped into Linda at the grocery store, Jim and I were talking about how we would always think of Kyle and picture him as being twenty-six years old, young and good-looking—"forever young."

I had just crossed over the Louisiana-Arkansas border. I was listening to "Forever Young." Both of my hands were on the steering wheel when I heard the right rear window go down. I immediately thought Kyle was responsible and said something to him out loud. Then the left rear window went down all by itself. That confirmed Kyle was with me, and I thanked him for letting me know.

I walked into the hotel lobby and removed my prescription sunglasses. I found the front desk and checked in. I noticed a long table on the other side of the room with what looked like three people sitting behind it. I couldn't read what the signs said but assumed these people had something to do with my reunion.

I approached the table and said lots of "so nice to see you again" phrases. I was handed a copy of the reunion booklet. It not only listed the events and their scheduled times but also included each former classmate's up-to-date autobiography in a condensed form.

I had received a blank questionnaire in the mail about three months earlier. There were places for names of children, grandchildren, life since graduation, hobbies, most exciting moment, and other pertinent information. When I filled out my form, I thought of how easy it would be to exaggerate a little. Maybe not that I became a doctor when in reality I was a schoolteacher. That might be too hard to hide, especially if someone collapsed on the dance floor while doing the fifties moves, and I had to scream for help. But maybe little exaggerations like one of my hobbies is comparing different cruise lines and the food they served while on excursions throughout the world would be all right. It was like going to a strange city where nobody knows you. You can become anybody. They'll never know. And after all, it's been at least ten years since any of these people have seen you. I could have invented Post Its and had an affair with Tom Cruise. What would they know? But I relented and was truthful. I didn't have to lie to make my answers memorable. I mentioned I had to endure the most profound grief imaginable, and I spoke of Kyle's death. Because of my sharing this devastating loss, three former classmates approached me at the reunion and shared their stories of the deaths of their children. These were people who probably wouldn't have even spoken to me if I had not shared my experiences. They had not included their loss in their autobiography.

When I asked Mary, whose thirty-two-year-old son had died the previous year where he was buried, her response surprised me. She told me the place but quickly added she had only been to his grave one time, the day he was buried.

She said she knew he wasn't really there, that he'd gone to a much better place. My kind of person. She already had this part figured out. She was very open to signs from him and had "visits" while she was in a dream state.

I was getting ready for my first public appearance at the reunion. I had showered, washed and blow dried my hair. But I was still concerned. It was nighttime. I would be inside. I would look out of place with sunglasses on.

All of you contact wearers will know what I am talking about. It never fails to happen. You're in a hurry. You put the contact on your index finger. You open your eye wide. You move your finger and touch your eyeball. You move your finger away. Surprise! The contact is still on your finger. Often it's not on your finger, and you get excited thinking you've been successful. But you soon know differently when you look and realize you still can't see. You've only dropped the contact and you begin your search.

It was much worse for me that first night. I hadn't worn contacts or even attempted to wear contacts for sixteen days. I had been told by Dr. Reilley it would be all right to try to wear them for a few hours. If it were at all painful, I should immediately take them out. So I said a little prayer, talking to God, to my angels, to my guides, to Kyle or whoever might be around.

"Please let me see during this big reunion I had so looked forward to." After all, what good would the new clothes I'd been able to buy in a smaller size and my new "you look wonderful" face be if I didn't know who was at the party and who could see this "new" me?

The contact was on my finger and I moved it toward my eye. I pulled my finger away and looked in the mirror. I realized I could see across the room while looking at the reflection in the mirror. I blinked once, then twice. It didn't hurt. I thanked God that I could see. Not wanting to push my luck, I didn't attempt to put in the second contact. I headed for the party. I would make my grand entrance.

I felt rather stupid right away. I approached someone I thought I recognized and said the usual, "So glad to see you" stuff. I was embarrassed when she said, "Judy, I spoke with you when you checked in this afternoon."

I quickly explained that I had been driving with my prescription sunglasses and hadn't put my contacts in, so I didn't see whom I was speaking with earlier.

Could she see my stitches, I wondered? I had jokingly told Dr. Reilley if it were obvious I'd had eye surgery, I could always say I had been cutting my yard, and a sharp stick had struck my eye area from the lawnmower. When I went to her, I told her I might as well have both eyes done since I had to have surgery anyway.

"Sounds good to me," was Dr. Reilley's response.

But I didn't want to have to use this excuse. I wanted to keep my surgery a secret if at all possible.

I walked up to Paula. She had a scarf tied around her head, turban style. We gave each other a hug. I then said, "Do you have cancer?"

Paula said she'd had a mastectomy and she didn't yet know the prognosis. She talked about God's plan for us and that she would be able to accept whatever happened. We spoke about death and the meaning of life. I felt very connected to her. Throughout the remainder of the reunion, we never really talked again but would see each other and hug.

Here I go again, but before Kyle died, I don't think I would ever have been able to approach Paula and talk about her illness. I know I would definitely not have been able to talk about death. But because of Kyle's death and what I have learned, I feel drawn to those in pain in hopes of being able to bring them some comfort.

Saturday morning there was a memorial service for the thirty-three classmates who had died. I walked into the room and looked around the room for a seat. I spotted Bob whose wife, Linda, had died the previous year. They had dated steadily throughout high school and had attended the same college that Kyle attended. I had read Linda's obituary in the quarterly magazine that we continue to receive from Ouachita Baptist University.

I headed toward the empty seat next to Bob. Now, here again, before Kyle's death, I would have avoided Bob. Now I felt I had to sit in that seat. We hugged, talked a little, and the service began.

In the front of the room, there was a table with thirty-three candles of different sizes and shapes. Two classmates were standing on either side of a long table, with a candle lighter. A name would be read, one candle lit, and we'd all say, "For blessed memories, Oh Lord, I thank you." Two bells would ring and the next name would be called out.

When Charles's name was called, his candle wouldn't light. Even the candle thing that was supposed to light it would go out. They finally got it lit, but it went out again. We were sitting there, seemingly for ages, watching them unable to light Charles's candle. I leaned over to Bob and whispered, "You know, Charles is probably blowing it out." I could never have done this before Kyle died. Here Bob had just lost the love of his life and I was joking. Charles's candle finally stayed lit.

After the service, we were encouraged to form a line and walk past the lit candles, and then look at the display of class pictures of the fellow students who were no longer with us. While in line Fred remarked, "You know I almost made that list."

I asked Fred what he meant, and he told me he'd had five heart bypasses a few months earlier. I told him I didn't fear death, that in a way I was looking forward to it, to being with Kyle again. I said I wouldn't jump in front of a car, but when it was my time, I was ready.

I specified to those who were in line with me if by any chance I was one of those candles at the next reunion, I wanted mine to be the biggest, with glitter on it. I do know I'll be able to drop by and see if they were listening to me.

When we got to the picture display, I asked how Bobbie Sue had died. Apparently her husband had died in an accident. While at his wake, she was holding his hand in the casket and collapsed and died. Talk about going to the Other Side together!

It was the last night of the reunion. Everything had been wonderful. After the final party ended, around nine of us headed for the bar area of the hotel. I was drinking water on the rocks and having so much fun, I didn't want the evening to end.

Sue told us to join her on the dance floor and form a circle. I had no idea what she had in mind. Two of us followed her. I said, "We're not a circle, we're a triangle." I motioned for someone else to come and make a circle.

Sue then told us to get in the middle one at a time and do our thing. What a "thing" was, I had no clue. I told her to show us what a thing was. Sue went to the middle and did a wild dance with lots of moves.

I remarked, "You're doing a good 'thing,' Sue." Then it was my turn. At the time, I'd wished that I hadn't been drinking water on the rocks. I was aware of what I was about to do. I did this "thing" I'd never done before.

They all said, "Good." So I felt good.

We were laughing so hard, I wasn't even concerned about anyone's being aware of my plastic surgery. Of course, it helped being in a dark room, with little colored lights rotating across the dance floor. We didn't have to drink alcohol to get dizzy.

Lesson number three: Go to all your class reunions. You'll never know who or what you missed if you don't go.

I checked out of the hotel and stopped by the Western Sizzler for a buffet salad before embarking on my family visits. While eating, I recognized one of my fellow classmates from the night before. He approached my table but I had no idea who he was. We no longer had our name tags on. He said he hoped to see me at the next reunion. I responded, "There's no way they could keep me away. Even if I'm one of the candles, I'll be there." He probably thought I was nuts, but I *knew* I was telling the truth.

After visiting a number of friends on my way home, I ended up in Hope, Arkansas. I stopped in to see CeCe. I had phoned her earlier and knew it was a busy time for her. Her grandson was scheduled to have tonsil surgery, and her daughter, Kortnee, was due to give birth to her first child at any moment. But I hadn't seen CeCe during the summer, so I dropped in.

CeCe handed me a church program from their Easter Service. In the "Remembering Our Loved Ones" part of the program I spotted Kyle Collier's name. This tribute was given by Don and CeCe Tye and DeDee McDonald. This gesture moved me deeply. Then CeCe asked me to go to the church with her. She wanted to get me something.

My car was parked out front, so we took it. While on the way to the church, the rear right window behind CeCe rolled down all by itself.

"I didn't touch anything!" CeCe said, startled.

I said, "I know. Kyle did it."

When she walked out of the church, she handed me the church program for the Mother's Day Service. In the "Given in Honor of" section, my name, Judy Collier was listed. This gift was given by DeDee McDonald and Kyle. I cried. I'm glad I stopped by to see them on my way home.

33

My Students Teach Me

I am thankful every day for the job I have. I entered
college in the late fifties, thinking I had two options. I could
become a secretary or a teacher. I liked to play school when
I was a child, so my choosing to become a teacher came
as no real surprise. I always thought I'd get married, have
children and live happily ever after. Whatever that is. My
mother was a stay-at-home mom, so the idea of my having to
work really never entered my mind. I graduated from high
school, went off to college, and like many young adults,
never really had a plan past that.

I substitute taught when the children were young, and
when Kyle entered school I returned to college full-time
and received my teaching degree. Jim was coaching at
L.S.U., and we lived a few miles from campus, so it worked
out well.

My first teaching job was a physical education teacher
at Istrouma High School. Not only did I have to teach PE
and health classes, but I was put in charge of sponsoring the
cheerleaders and coaching the girls' track team.

I can't begin to tell you how frustrated I became when
the cheerleaders made the run-through signs for the football games each week. Those are the big paper signs the

football team runs through when they run onto the field. You had better not blink, or you won't be able to see what the sign says before it gets all torn up. The cheerleaders spent hours after school working on each sign. They had to make it perfect, they would tell me. I would try to hurry them, saying it looked great, as I repeatedly looked at my watch noticing the hours passing by, hours I wasn't being paid for.

Then to top it off, I had to go to all the games. The only McDonald's I felt safe parking at after the games was the McDonald's at the local mall. Forget that it wasn't on the way back to school. I knew I could find an open spot and maneuver the bus there. Driving a school bus was quite an experience in itself. The first time I tried to move the driver's seat forward, the entire seat fell to the floor. Obviously, it wasn't a new bus. The entrance door wouldn't even open or close. It just stayed open all the time so we had air-conditioning whether we needed it or not.

And they had to be desperate when they hired me as the track coach. What did I know about coaching track? When I went to the sporting goods store to order uniforms and equipment for the upcoming track season, I ordered four batons for the relay team. When I remembered we only needed one, to hide my embarrassment, I joked, "That way we won't drop it." Needless to say, the administration relieved me of my track duties the following year.

Then I was "let go" as a teacher at Istrouma after three years because of the beginning of the integration movement. I had to look elsewhere for a job. In retrospect, it was a blessing in disguise. It enabled me to have the opportunity to work with "exceptional children," those in special education.

Not a day goes by when I work with these children, that I don't realize how very "special" they really are. God has indeed given their souls a unique opportunity to teach the rest of us so much.

Each of them is different, yet they are alike in many ways. Though they might not be able to function normally physically and often mentally, they seem to possess a far greater awareness of what our soul really is. The material world is not important to them. They seem happy with the moment and often smile and laugh. Little things mean a lot to them, and it doesn't take much to bring a smile to their faces. But the one thing I've noticed more than anything else is they never complain. They never complain of the body they have been given. On a soul level, I believe they are very advanced. They teach me something every day I am privileged to be with them.

I enjoyed being with my students before Kyle's death. But because of the pain I have endured in losing Kyle, I feel even more connected to these children now. I remember the time I was speaking with Christie. She was fifteen and had been confined to a wheelchair throughout her entire life because of cerebral palsy. She told me she dreams every night. And in these dreams, she is always running. I told her one day we would be able to race each other. She nodded yes.

I am fortunate to have my own classroom. Often itinerant teachers have to teach out of their cars, not having a place to keep their equipment. My classroom is referred to as the "Toys R Us" room. I have acquired a lot of neat things over the years, mostly by going to garage sales.

When you enter my room and turn on the light, a cat meows, a bird starts talking, and a moose head hanging on the wall repeats what you say. I was embarrassed one time recently, though, when the principal was seated in my classroom, pen and paper in hand evaluating my teaching performance. Suddenly, Elmo, the Sesame Street character, started yelling, "Help! Help!" He was sitting on the chalk-board eraser holder. His batteries were not turned on and even when I picked him up to hopefully quiet him, he wouldn't quit. The principal couldn't figure out what was happening, but I knew Kyle was there.

Many things happen in my classroom that I believe are signs from Kyle or from one of my students who have died. Just this past year, two of my students passed away. Brent was a fifteen-year-old who the day before his death shot basket-balls for me. He died the next day at home as a result of a seizure. Ashley, a thirteen-year-old student, whom I also taught, died of a seizure unexpectedly during the summer. I know the pain their parents are going through, a pain that will hopefully lessen, though it will remain with them throughout their lives.

One day, the light kept going off and on in my class-room. I opened the door and asked two teachers who were standing in the hallway if the light out there had gone off? They told me no. I immediately thought of Kyle, Brent, and Ashley. Then a little later, I walked out into the hall. The light in the hallway started going off and on, but I could see through the window above my door the lights in my room were staying on.

Just this past Halloween I was working with Noel, a blind student who is confined to a wheelchair with cerebral palsy. She is a very intelligent girl but is quite limited in her physical abilities. The cat began meowing on its own, and another battery operated toy turned on by itself. Miss Norma, Noel's full-time aide, remarked to Noel, "Mrs. Col-lier has ghosts in here." I smiled and nodded my head yes. Little did she know how true her statement was.

One time I entered my classroom with three students who had been outside with me doing an activity. When we entered the room, battery operated games that we had not touched in days were operating. And one that was turned on did not even have all the batteries in it. Strange things do happen in Room C-5. I always thank Kyle, Ashley and Brent.

These special students help me learn more each day I am with them. I love them dearly and will be forever grateful for all they have taught me. I am truly blessed being in a profession I love so much.

At the beginning of each school year, all of the parish teachers (we don't have counties in Louisiana) get together for a "pep rally," in hopes of instilling some enthusiasm for the upcoming year. On August 28, 1997, we boarded school buses at our schools and headed for the Bethany World Prayer Center where the Teacher Conclave would be held.

An added benefit this trip provides is that it definitely gives each teacher sympathy for the students who have to ride these buses every day. Talk about hot! Driving in muggy Baton Rouge in August on an old, bumpy, non-air-conditioned bus is definitely not something you want to do more than one time. No wonder we have so many discipline problems at school. But that's another story.

It's always fun to see teachers you no longer teach with and haven't seen in a while. Susan Samson taught with me at Ryan Elementary about six years before. She knew that Kyle had died. She told me her mother had recently died and her young son, Georgie, often says, "Grandma came last night and said. . . ."

When the superintendent of the school system was about three quarters of the way through his speech, trying to build teacher morale, all the lights went out. There are no windows in this large room, and it was dark. Over the loudspeaker system, they told us to remain calm, and they turned on the generator so the lights would come back on. They did come on, but immediately went out again. My mind raced to Kyle. Was he telling me something or just letting me know he was there? The person sitting behind me said, "An omen from God."

I've shared this story with you because I want you to know that no matter where you are or what's going on, if you are open to connections from the spiritual world, these experiences can bring you great comfort. Just keep your eyes, ears and mind open. Trust me, they will happen, as the next encounter shows.

I was attending an Adapted Physical Education meeting at the beginning of the school year. It was August 21, 1998. It was there that I met Jim Miller for the first time. He was a new teacher, and we struck up a conversation. For some reason I mentioned Kyle. Jim told me he'd lost a very close friend six months before. He said the night his friend died, he came to him in a "visit." He said it definitely was not a dream, that his friend was happy, and he was able to feel him and hug him. He then told me his friend has "visited" him more than once since that first time. He also said another friend died this year, and he has "visited" him, too.

When I think back, Jim had never met me before, nor did he know anything about me. What made him share these very personal and spiritual happenings with me? Most people would have inhibitions about sharing such things. But Jim's opening up to me was just another reassurance that Kyle still lives. I marvel at all of these confirmations of the other life that are continually given to me.

34

Kyle Helps Put This Book Together

Never, never, never in my wildest dreams could I envision the comfort I would receive by writing this book. It is further validation to me of Kyle's strength and unrelenting determination to help me cope.

While talking with Mary Jo at her office one day, the topic of my book came up. I told her I'd almost completed writing it, but I didn't know what the next step would be. I had no idea what was involved in trying to get a book published. Like so many things in life, you just take for granted the finished product, never having any idea about how much is really involved. So I'm definitely on a learning path.

Mary Jo told me she herself was writing a new book and that Linda Hullinger, a former classmate in the Thursday night class, was editing it for her. "You should have Linda do your book. She's very good at it," she said.

I told Mary Jo I didn't want to interfere with her book, but she encouraged me to phone Linda and talk with her about it.

Linda convinced me she could work on both Mary Jo's book and mine at the same time. She assured me it would be good for her to trade off on the two, that it would give her a break since both books were entirely different. We agreed to meet at my house the following day.

After Linda and I greeted each other, she followed me into the kitchen. One of the first things she said was, "Kyle wants me to ask you about the difficulty you had this morning putting your right earring in your pierced ear."

I was sort of taken aback by this statement. That very morning before I left for school, I had attempted to put my pierced earrings in while I was standing in the den. I had put my left earring in without any problem, but I kept missing the hole while putting the earring in my right ear. After about six attempts, I finally hit the hole with the post.

"I did have trouble. So Kyle is here with us?"

"Yes, he's very excited that I am doing his book," she responded.

Before Mary Jo told me about Linda, I had been a little uneasy about who I should contact about working on my story. After all, communication from dead people is not the topic of most people's conversations at the dinner table. A lot of people might not be receptive to all that has happened to me. I felt good Linda was willing to help me tell Kyle's story.

Linda took a copy of my rough "rough" draft home with her after our first meeting. We agreed when she was finished with a number of pages, we'd get together again and go over what she had done.

A few days later, Linda called and wanted to come over. She was due to come by in about ten minutes. I'd just arrived home from a day of teaching. I was hungry so I opened the fridge, grabbed the cheese, cut a few slices and put them on chips and heated some nachos in the microwave. I had just finished putting the plate with the melted cheese on it in the dishwasher when I heard Linda's knock on my front door (door bell is broken).

The very first thing she said after telling me "Hi" was "Kyle wants me to ask you about the cheese."

I shook my head. I asked her if she'd like me to fix her some nachos. I felt a little guilty knowing she knew I'd eaten something and had not waited to share it with her. Knowing that people we can't see know everything we are doing is kind of eerie to me. I don't mind dead people knowing the good things about me, but there are some things I'd like to keep private. It's as if there's a hidden camera on everything I do and say and a computer translating everything I think. I often find myself explaining things out loud even though no one is with me.

As Linda and I began discussing the book and what we hoped to do with it, it became apparent to her that Kyle was trying to put his two cents worth in the endeavor. She said he came to her when she was working on the book and tried to encourage her. She also said Kyle wanted me to invite mothers whose children had died to come to my house so she could give them messages from their children. I called Janice and Jean who had both lost a son. At the beginning of our get-together, which I have on tape, Linda said Kyle wanted everyone to know he was in charge of the meeting. He went on to give meaningful messages, and both sons of Janice and Jean showed up.

Linda told me later she really felt her purpose in life was to help comfort parents and bring messages from their children on the Other Side. Mary Jo has always encouraged Linda to use her special gift. It was very evident through the two years of the Thursday night class that Linda was psychic, and she could communicate with those who have died. I really found it ironic that she wanted to work with me on my book. Through her messages, Kyle has been able to continue to communicate with me and I love it.

I put two Christmas trees up last year because Jamie and the boys would be home. The tree in the dining room is called a "nature" tree, because it doesn't have any Christmas things on it—only butterflies, birds, nests, feathers, pine cones, and acorns. They are all done in shades of brown, copper, and gold, so the tree doesn't really look Christmassy. I got tired of putting the Christmas decorations away and decided this tree would stay up year-round. Linda was leaving my house one afternoon, and after talking about the tree she said, "Kyle wants to know why there is not a fish on the tree?"

I spent over five hours that weekend going to the Christmas shops that stay open year round. "Do you have any fish ornaments in brown, copper or gold?" I'd ask when I entered each store. I'm glad they didn't ask why I had to have a fish. Saying that my dead son told me to put one on the tree that I still had up in March might have been a little controversial. Luckily, I found two small gold and brown glass blown fish that fit in perfectly with the other things on the tree.

After pointing out my two new additions to Linda during her next visit, I told her in the future she had my permission to censor any messages from Kyle that might be unreasonable. She knows anything he wants me to do, I will do.

During the meeting at my house with Janice and Jean, the meeting that "Kyle was in charge of," I asked Linda why Kyle had never come to me in a dream. She told me if I did have a "visit" from him while in the dream state, I'd want to sleep all the time. I'd read this before concerning another mother who had lost her child, and it did make sense.

Two days later I received a note from Linda by mail. I will share it.

Dear Judy,

> *This afternoon while working on your book, I remembered the question you asked last night about why*

you never dream of Kyle. He came through with the message that you would want to sleep all the time; just like you had said in your book. So I asked him for further clarification on that question since I hate repeating what someone already knows.

And his response was this: He feels no need to come to you during your sleep since you are so aware of him during your waking hours. When he sends you a message, you respond immediately. Dreams are for people who aren't as aware as you are. It is an attention-getter for those who are not as spiritually attuned to the Other Side.

He knows you know he is around. He doesn't have to get your attention in that manner.

Well, I just thought I'd share that with you since he took the time to share it with me.

Have a good weekend.

Love,
Linda

Linda's message from Kyle made a lot of sense to me. I do talk to Kyle all the time, acknowledging I know he is responsible for all the signs and things going on in my life. His special concern for me makes me love and miss him all the more, but I keep pressing on, trying to fulfill my life's mission. I know Kyle planned his death to teach not only me, but you as well. By your reading this book, I hope you have been made more aware of how our loved ones continue to live and how they communicate with us.

35

Kyle Thanks Me for Letting Him Go

On April 25, 2000, I received a call from Linda. She asked me if it would be convenient for her to drop by and see me the next day, that she had something to give me.

"Do you know that today is the fourth anniversary of Kyle's death?" I asked her.

Her response baffled me. "I thought he died two days from now; that's why I need to come to see you. Kyle had me pick something out to give to you on the 27th," the actual date of his death.

"What?" I couldn't believe what she had just said.

"While I was in a Hallmark store today picking out a card for someone else, Kyle made his presence known and said he wanted to give you a gift in celebration of your letting him go to the Other Side. He wants to thank you."

Needless to say, I was on a high, wondering what Kyle was up to. Jim and I always release balloons and have a cake on the 25th because Mary Jo and John had told us his soul left his body on the 25th. Now Kyle wanted to thank us for giving him his freedom from an earthly existence. I left the front door ajar so I could hear Linda when she came. When I heard "Judy," I rushed to greet her.

Linda was carrying a small decorated bag that I could see had tissue and a colored envelope protruding from the top. After she followed me to the kitchen table, she handed the bag to me and told me Kyle didn't want me to open it until the following day, on the 27th.

When I was able to focus on what was on the outside of the bag, I couldn't believe what I saw. I said, "That's Walker, Kyle's dog, and Walker was his birthday present on his 11th birthday." I then told Linda, "Wait, I want to show you something." I ran to the bedroom to retrieve a photo album. I skimmed through the pages, all of them containing pictures of Kyle. Linda seemed flabbergasted when she glanced at some of the pictures with Kyle holding snakes, lizards, pigeons, rabbits and turtles. I stopped turning the pages and gave the album to Linda.

"Oh my gosh!" was Linda's reaction. She was looking at a picture of Kyle holding Walker, who looked *identical* to the dog on the bag. Kyle was sitting at the kitchen table with his birthday candles lit, just like the birthday cake on the bag she had given to me.

"The funny thing," Linda said, "is that when he made me pick out this gift and card for you at the Hallmark store, I didn't buy the bag then, as I should have. For some reason, it slipped my mind that I needed something to put the present in. After I left the Hallmark store, I drove to the Winn Dixie grocery store, and when I was walking down the aisles of the store I kept hearing Kyle say, 'What about the bag? What about the bag to put the present in?' I said, Okay, Kyle, I'll go and get one right now. So I pushed my buggy to the gift-wrap section of the store."

I was all ears by this time. Here it had been four years since the most devastating event in my life had taken place, and Kyle was letting me know how much a part of my life he still is able to be.

"That bag is not an appropriate bag for the occasion," Linda told me. "But Kyle insisted it was the one to buy and it would make sense to you."

"Mom will understand," was apparently Kyle's response to Linda when she said it wasn't a good choice.

"Besides," Linda tried to convince Kyle, "your gift won't even fit in that bag."

"Mom won't care," Kyle tried to reassure Linda. "She'll understand immediately the meaning of the picture on the bag."

Apparently Kyle was pretty persuasive, as he was so often when he was here physically. Linda finally agreed to purchase "that" bag, the one Kyle had insisted she buy. I plan to frame the bag. The picture of the dog is so much like Walker that it appears as if Walker actually posed for the drawing. Every marking on the dog is identical to the markings on Walker. Even the build of the dog is exactly like Walker's build.

When I rushed out to greet Jim that evening with the bag in my hand, I showed it to him. "It's Walker," was Jim's first comment.

I guess Linda was relieved she'd listened to Kyle and had chosen that particular bag for my gift, but she reiterated that Kyle didn't want me to open the present from him until the following day, the anniversary of our letting him go. I assured her I wouldn't. I knew in the back of my mind that Kyle would definitely know if I didn't follow his instructions.

"Can you believe I have a present from Kyle sitting on my kitchen table?" I kept repeating to Jim throughout the evening and when we were in bed. How many parents are so lucky?

Jim was already seated at the kitchen table reading the morning paper when I awoke and walked into the room, the room where my present was from Kyle. We both sang

"Happy Birthday" to Kyle and I picked up the present. You can only imagine my feelings at that moment. I opened the card first. Linda had told me that even though the card was placed in the wrong section of the card display, Kyle found it and definitely picked it out for me. She had wondered if it would also make sense to me. The front of the card is burgundy with gold footprints (even matches my color scheme). It read:

> MAY THE FOOTPRINTS
> WE LEAVE BEHIND
> SHOW THAT WE'VE
> WALKED IN KINDNESS
> TOWARD THE EARTH
> AND EVERY
> LIVING THING

And inside the card it read:

> *Congratulations on the success*
> *You have achieved.*
> *You are an inspiration.*

So this message from Kyle lets me know he is aware of my involvement in helping others. I guess the part about bringing kindness to every living thing means I'll keep buying the big bags of Meow Mix (crows keep cawing loudly as I type this) to feed the animals—raccoons, possums, ducks, and crows that were never seen in our yard until after Kyle died. If I ever calculated the cost of all the bags of Meow Mix, I might be upset, so I will just think of Kyle's card and his message of my showing kindness to every living thing. Hopefully he won't bring an elephant.

As I unwrapped the tissue on the present that didn't quite fit into the "Walker, birthday cake bag," I couldn't believe what I saw. I knew Linda did not know when Kyle instructed her to select the gift for me what a special meaning it had.

It was a small picture frame, laid out in an envelope motif, with a message beside the glass opening for the photo. Linda had no idea I had this exact message done in needlework hanging in my utility room. The words have given me much to ponder and think about each time I read it.

Count your garden by the flowers,
Never by the leaves that fall,
Count your days by golden hours,
Don't remember clouds at all,
Count your nights by stars not shadows,
Count your years with smiles not tears,
Count your blessings not your troubles,
Count your age by friends not years.

This message reminds me of the full life Kyle had. Though he was here only twenty-six years, I don't know of many people who have had more friends or touched more lives than Kyle.

Kyle must have known about the new refrigerator that Sears was delivering on the 25th. Apparently he figured it was time to take down the only picture I had on the door of the old fridge. I often wondered what Kyle thought of my keeping this picture in such a prominent place. I figured he thought it was time for me to "move on" and put this picture, one of the few taken of just the two of us, in another place. His gift of the picture frame which fit the picture perfectly, was the needed incentive to do just that. Even the frame coordinates with my decorative scheme, so Kyle is helping me move along.

The magnet that held this picture on the refrigerator was bought at the book store in the Unity Church. It helps to read it from time to time, giving me added encouragement.

> *Remember that no matter how difficult the present circumstances of your life are . . . they will not last forever. This is just one phase that you must pass through. And someday when you come closer to the top of the majestic mountain that you are ever ascending, you will look back at this particular stopping point along the way, knowing that it was here that you gained a certain essential strength, a perspective and wisdom, that sustained you throughout the rest of the journey. . . .*

Mary Jo held a weekend intensive entitled, "Learning to Soar: Teachings from the Other Side," held at the Radisson Hotel in Baton Rouge, April 14–16, 2000. From noon until late Sunday afternoon, Mary Jo's messages concerned "Putting Death in Its Place." Anything concerning death gets my added attention.

One of the most beautiful visions of death was presented by Mary Jo that afternoon. She had her eyes closed and was in a trance. I always tell people I know she's for real, because there is no way she could come up with the things she says if she were not getting help from somewhere. I hope this doesn't offend her, but it is true. She uses words when she is in trance, I, as well as others know she doesn't even know the meaning of while she is in her physical body. It is very evident she definitely has a spiritual body connecting her to her higher self.

I will attempt to interpret Mary Jo's portentous words with my everyday language. She told us to think of our loved ones who have died as climbing to the top of the highest mountain. Picture them leaning over, out over the vast expanse below where they can see no end, just space. Think of them as finally having the courage to take that leap of faith and be able to fly and be free. Think how wonderful that must have been for them to have the courage to experience such a spiritual awakening, one that we will all experience one day.

So now I have attained yet another picture of Kyle. He's yelling, "Geronimo!" as he jumps off, and I think of how exhilarated he must have been at that moment. As John Edward told us, "He's like Peter Pan, his limits are endless." And then as Mary Jo told me, "He feels like a bird let out of a cage."

Let me ask a favor of you. Close your eyes. WAIT! First, I should explain what I want you to do when your eyes are closed. I want you to answer these questions. Do you still love the same people? Do you still have the same interests? And do you still have the same emotions? Of course, you do. The only difference is that your eyes are closed, and you can't "see" your body. But you're the same person inside in your soul.

This is how I think of Kyle now. He's exactly the same as when he was here; it's just that I can't see him. But I *know* he can see me. Then I think about all of the good things that no longer having a physical body has enabled him to do. He no longer gets depressed. He no longer has to work out at the health club and watch his diet to have a perfect body. He no longer needs money to travel. He can go wherever he wants at just a thought. He doesn't worry about his future, and he *knows* he will be with us again.

I realize everyone of us will die. Yet, we don't like to think of our own deaths. But I assure you it will happen, and you will climb up that high mountain. Maybe tomorrow, maybe years away. We don't know. Only God and our soul knows.

36

Am I Normal?

I feel it is important to let you know a little about who I am. When I read a book, I find that knowing something about the author makes the story more personal and real. I feel more connected to what is taking place.

I think of myself as an average person, whatever that is. Of course, depending on who you ask, they might have a different opinion of me.

I was born on October 13, 1941, in Evanston, Illinois. I was the second of three children born to Dorothy and Joseph White. My brother, Chuck, is sixteen months older and Steve is seven years younger. Both my parents were raised on the North Shore of Chicago. My father received his degree in engineering from the University of Michigan where he was a cheerleader. My mother is five years younger and was modeling when she met and married my father.

My father commuted to Chicago from the suburbs to work. Apparently, my parents opted for a lower keyed lifestyle, and we moved to Hot Springs, Arkansas, when I was in the seventh grade. We lived at a resort, which my parents bought, with eight rental cabins on Lake Hamilton. I loved it because I thought I was on vacation all of the time. Of course, I didn't have to worry about cleaning the cabins and sprucing up the place to entice vacationers. But my parents did. They soon felt it was too much work, too little privacy, and no future for our family. They sold the resort and Dad became employed with Reynolds Metals in Jones Mill, Arkansas. He worked there until his retirement.

Luckily, my parents also enjoyed being near the water, so we moved into a home located on Lake Hamilton. I attended Hot Springs Senior High School. President Clinton later attended this same school when my brother, Steve, was there.

I was a good student. I enjoyed studying and was proud of my grades. I was on the pep squad, had a steady boy-friend, and memories of my high school years are mostly good.

There is one thing, though, I need to mention about myself, because it has had a profound effect on most of my life. For some unknown reason I was always impressed with football players. None of my family had ever played football, so I don't really know where this obsession came from. I remember cutting out pictures of football players from sports magazines and carrying them around in my wallet when I was in the fourth grade. It wasn't that I even knew anything about who the players were. In high school, my boyfriend was on the football team, but he wasn't a star. I was still following the careers of college and professional players. To this day I can name a lot of the players who played when I was younger, and I know whom they played for, and what position they played. Kind of strange, isn't it? Maybe this is another non-normal part of my life.

On my first day at the University of Arkansas in Fayette-ville, I met Kathy Hawkins in the freshman dormitory. She was from El Dorado, Arkansas, and I knew nothing about her other than being sent her name in a letter telling me she would be my roommate.

I had picked up a copy of the *Razorback*, The University of Arkansas yearbook that was on display in the hallway just outside our room in Fulbright Hall. I took the yearbook to our room, sat on my bed, and turned to the sports section. I had not unpacked and I hadn't put up anything. The boxes filled with my college stuff were also sitting on my bed. For some reason, it was more important to check out the pictures of the athletes. After scanning a few pages, I saw Jimmy Collier's football picture. I said to Kathy who was putting up her things, "I'll bet you one dollar I marry this guy, Jimmy Collier." She said something like "Okay." But thinking back on it later, she probably thought what a weirdo for a roommate she was getting.

Jim and I have been happily married for thirty-nine years. But I never collected the dollar. Just think how much interest I could have earned over all this time.

Jim finished his college career at Arkansas where he was ALL-SWC for two years and was chosen most valuable player in the conference in 1961. He played two years of professional football with the New York Giants and the Washington Redskins. Kyle Rote was a teammate of Jim's on the championship Giants' team, and I knew if we ever had a son, we would name him Kyle. Both Jim and I liked that name.

After Jim's professional stint, he accepted a college coaching position at Louisiana State University, which is what brought us to Baton Rouge. My life as the wife of a college football coach was one of varying emotions. It was often exciting. I was able to travel with the team on some occasions, and being given the red carpet treatment was quite an experience. I remember LSU often lost the bowl games, but we always won the parties. Whether at the Sun Bowl in El Paso or the Orange Bowl in Miami, the bowl sponsors always told us they liked having LSU. They said they always knew it would be exciting, because the Tiger fans really knew how to have a good time.

At the Orange Bowl one year, Miss America was in attendance at one of the parties. Jim asked her to dance and led her onto the dance floor. I felt left out. I approached Joe Paterno (we were playing Penn State) and led him out to the dance floor. He kept saying over and over, "I don't dance. I don't dance." But I kept dancing anyway. Now, to this day, when I see him on TV coaching from the sidelines, I wonder if he has learned to dance.

But there are a lot of downs associated with the life of a college football coach. When Jim was at home, the kids would say, "What is he doing here?" He was either on the road scouting teams, looking for future prospects at high school games, promoting LSU with public appearances, grading films, or attending practices, not to mention the coaches' meetings into the wee hours of the morning.

Some people asked me what else Jim did for a living. He was only earning about twenty-five cents an hour, so I guess they figured he did need extra income. It's amazing how many people not associated with college football know so little about what is really involved in getting ready for what they do know, which is the game that's played on Saturday.

Since football season is in the fall, Jim missed most of the Halloween, Thanksgiving, and Christmas programs and events that our children participated in while growing up. Luckily, one Halloween, LSU had an open date. There was not going to be a game that Saturday, so Jim would be able to come home earlier in the evening.

Kyle was five years old and all excited about going trick-or-treating. We had decided on his costume together. He was going to wear one of his sister's ballet tutus, put on girl make-up, and wear a wig I had. That picture of him is one of my favorites. He was so cute. He didn't look anything like

Kyle. Not that Kyle wasn't cute, but I want you to know he was a cute "girl."

Back in those days, when Halloween candy didn't have to be x-rayed before being eaten, there was no specified time period for trick-or-treaters. Jim had come home and Kyle was still out filling up his bag. The doorbell rang and Jim went to the front door and opened it.

"What a cute little girl we have here," I heard Jim say. I peeked around the corner and spotted Kyle. Jim kept talking to the "little girl" and began to shut the door after putting candy in the bag.

"It's Kyle," I said quickly. "Let him in!"

Jim had no idea it was his son.

So a football coach's family misses out on a lot. In many ways, I was happy that Jim was "let go" (a nice way of saying fired) after sixteen years of coaching at LSU. They won seven games, lost three and went to the Tangerine Bowl his final year, but he and the other coaches were still fired because the fans wanted more. Of course, LSU has gone through five head coaches since then, and the current coach is in the hot seat now after losing the last two games, but that's an entirely different book.

Getting out of the coaching profession enabled Jim to attend all of Kyle's high school and college games. He was also able to hunt and fish with Kyle. They could spend time together that would not have been possible had Jim still been coaching. This is something that both Jim and I are very grateful for, especially since Kyle left us at such a young age.

I resumed my college education when Kyle began kindergarten. I had attended the University of Arkansas for two years and was able to get my teaching certificate from LSU in two years. I have been a special education teacher in the East Baton Rouge Parish school system for the past twenty years.

My husband opened an automotive franchise, Meineke Discount Mufflers and Brakes, in September of 1986. We love the Baton Rouge area and didn't want to uproot the children when Jim finished coaching. We were in the process of building our second Meineke when Kyle died. Kyle was going to run one of the businesses. We have since sold our first Meineke. It was too time consuming and stressful to have two shops located at different ends of the city. We've learned that life is too short. Operating one place of business gives Jim a little more free time. Jim loves to hunt and fish. I used to joke that if Jim died, I knew I could live well for at least a year. I could always sell his fishing tackle.

Currently, we have nine grandchildren. Jill lives in Washington state with her husband, Bob and her six children, Jaclyn, Cole, Dane, Brant, Ty and Jordyn. Jill has earned her Master's degree, but is presently concentrating on being a stay-at-home mom. Dr. Laura would be impressed.

Jamie also has her Master's degree. She lives in Massachusetts with her two sons, Jared and Joshua. She is presently going through a divorce. But I know everything in our lives happens for a reason and is a learning process. Jamie is aware of this, also. Mary Jo has told me when we have learned what we need to learn from a relationship, we move on. I guess that means that Jim and I aren't learning anything, because I think we'll always be together.

And Cain, Kyle's son, lives in Little Rock. Needless to say, he is a very "special" boy.

37

Kyle Spies on His Sister

Jamie phoned from her home in Massachusetts. "Guess who came by this week?" were her first words after, "Hey Mom."

Before I could guess, she said, "Kyle was here!" This caught me off guard, but I was happy that she phoned and shared his visit with me.

She said she was home alone, sitting on the sofa in the den while watching television. Out of the corner of her eye she saw someone. She said she turned to look and saw Kyle.

I asked, "Are you sure it was Kyle?"

"Oh yeah, I know it was." She continued, "I started talking to him and kept talking to him. I know it was Kyle."

So this was Jamie's fourth appearance of Kyle. Even though I wish desperately I could see him again, it helps to know others are able to see him. I know he still exists and I know he knows I am being told about others who see him.

It was Monday, January 17, 2000, and I was home from school in celebration of Dr. Martin Luther King's birthday. The phone rang early in the morning. I picked up the phone after noticing the call was from North Easton, Massachusetts, where Jamie lives. That's the good thing about caller ID; you can be choosy about whom you speak with. I'm always concerned when either of my daughters phones, though, especially if it's early in the morning or late at night. After losing Kyle, I don't take anything for granted. I know the possibility of getting heartbreaking news is always present.

But this call was good news. Kyle had dropped by the night before! Jamie had spotted him moving about her kitchen, where she had seen him twice before, and where John Edward had told us that Kyle hung out often, trying to grab Jamie's attention. This time he succeeded in grabbing not only Jamie's attention, but also a friend who was visiting her.

Apparently, Jared and Josh were in bed for the night, and Jamie and Brian were seated on the sofa talking. Both of them kept hearing noises. Twice, Jamie ran upstairs to check on the boys to see what they were up to. Both times the boys were sound asleep. Jamie even checked on the cat, wondering if maybe he was up to something, but Magic was sound asleep, curled up in a ball on a chair. The noises continued.

"Someone is in the house," Jamie said. She turned to look toward the kitchen, and saw Kyle moving around. "Kyle is here!" Jamie exclaimed.

"Can you imagine what Brian must have thought," Jamie told me. "He must have thought I was nuts. But it *was* Kyle. I can't believe he was making so much noise trying to get my attention, and he finally had to create himself so I would know that he was here."

Thursday evening after talking with Jamie, I attended one of Mary Jo's lectures. I asked her why Jamie was able to see Kyle and I have never been able to see him or have him "visit" with me in a dream?

Mary Jo was in a trance and responded, "It's like some people have green eyes and some people have blue eyes. Your daughter is able to see him, and you will never be able to see him. You know he is around, though, and you do not have to see him, in order to know he still lives. Besides, he wants you to tell your daughter he enjoys spying on her."

When I told Jamie about Kyle's spying on her, she just laughed. She then told me she'd even phoned her sister to let her know their brother dropped by again.

38

I Will Always Count the Days

Today is Tuesday, February 20, 2001. It has been 1,759 days since Kyle died. Not one of those days have I not thought of Kyle the first thing when I woke up each morning. Not one night was I not thinking of and praying for Kyle when I went to sleep. Not to mention the many sleepless nights when he was constantly on my mind. Every day he is often in my thoughts and prayers. I can never imagine its being any different.

Kyle's death has taught me much. As Mary Jo once told me, "It's a shame Kyle had to die for you to learn what you have." But in reflection, it is only because of the deep love I have for Kyle and my concern for his happiness, that I have been able to experience this inconceivable and enlightening journey.

Because of my loss I have become a more emotional person. Not that I haven't always been emotional. I have often embarrassed myself crying at the airport watching others whom I did not know say good-bye to each other. I have difficulty watching anything on TV having to do with human or animal suffering. I often use the throw on our sofa to hide under.

But now more than ever before, when I hear or see a newsbreaking story of yet another tragedy, I cry. I can relate to the anguish the loved ones must be going through. I don't know how a person can experience pain over losing someone unexpectedly or young and not become a more compassionate person.

Probably the most significant message I want you to accept and believe after reading *Quit Kissing My Ashes* is that *your* loved ones have *not* gone away from you. They are still very much aware of you and what is going on in your life. They have an abiding concern for your well-being and happiness. And, trust me, they definitely know if you are happy or sad. They want you to be happy.

Jill and Jamie live far from me, and I miss not being with them more often, but knowing they are happy is what is important. Though we can't always have what we wish for, we can try to be happy with what we do have.

Because of Sister Rita Coco, Mary Jo McCabe, John Edward, Linda Hullinger, Kyle's friends, and Kyle's many messages from heaven, I *know* Kyle is happy. I can function and be happy in my life, knowing my three children are happy.

Of course, I realize I have reached this certain peace in my life because of all that has transpired these past 1,759 days. Granted, there have been many difficult times and difficult days. It has been a struggle, and I know it will always be a struggle. But I live each day, hoping to bring some of the comfort that has been given me to someone else.

When people I've just met find out through conversation my son died, they often seem uncomfortable and at a loss for words, not knowing what to say. I understand this completely, because before Kyle's death, I didn't know what to say or do either.

When Bunny and Scooter's son, Jeff, died, and when my sister-in-law, Jean Ellen's son, Jason, died, I was not able to relate to them the way I wished I could. I ignored talking about their children, believing the less said, the better. That is the farthest thing from the truth. And those of you who have lost a very special loved one know this.

You want to talk about your loved ones, you want others to talk about them, and no matter what is taking place, they are often in your thoughts as they always will be. Time doesn't change this longing. They were a big part of your life when they were here, and they will continue to be a big part of your life.

It's odd how I actually feel more connected to Kyle now that he is in the spirit world. But I always tell people that even though I know how happy he is and I know I will be with him again, I would change all of that to see him sitting in my kitchen one more time, for just five minutes. We all know that's not possible. We can't change reality. We accept it.

The special closeness I feel to Kyle both spiritually and physically is truly indescribable. Both Jim and I feel very fortunate for all Kyle has been able to do to help us.

Deepak Chopra, author of *How to Know God; Ageless Body, Timeless Mind; The Seven Spiritual Laws of Success,* and many other best-selling books, was appearing on *Larry King Live* just the other night. I will never forget the conversation Larry and Deepak had. Larry had just asked Mr. Chopra if he were religious.

'No," Deepak responded, "religion is for those afraid of going to hell. Spirituality is for those who have already been to hell."

That comment jumped out at me. And that comment made sense to me. Seeking knowledge of what life and death is all about, because of such unbearable and excruciating pain over the loss of a loved one, definitely can lead one on a spiritual path.

We are all going to the same place . . . to our home with God. Whether you are Buddhist, Hindu. Catholic, Protestant, Jewish or atheist, you have a soul. Your soul was created by God, a God that loves us all. Our journey here on earth is only for our soul's growth. The situations and circumstances that you confront throughout your life, whether good or bad, are all teachings we came here to earth to learn.

In reference to the different religions and beliefs, I'll never forget what John Edward said. "If you're flying from New York to Los Angeles, it doesn't really matter which airline you choose; they are all going to end up at the same place."

I often tell people the pain and grief I am enduring because of Kyle's death is too deep to even describe. But in the next breath, I tell them these past five years have been the most blessed of my life. I know those two statements seem contradictory, but my love for God and my love for others on this earth path have reached heights that I know would not have been attainable without my loss. I hope that by sharing my story with you, you will not only be more aware of the spiritual world where your loved one now lives, but you will also find some of the peace I have found.

Everything I've shared with you happened and is the truth. Because two individuals asked to remain anonymous, though, their names and a few minor details have been changed to protect their identity. Many, many more "happenings" had to be left out. Jim often jokes, "You could write an encyclopedia."

And because of the many, many happenings that Kyle has managed to orchestrate into a script that tells such a beautiful story, I no longer think of each day as a day without Kyle. I think of each day as being one day closer to being with him again. And that helps.

42

Just Because

On four different occasions I have picked up the local newspaper and read a message from Kyle. In the *Sunday Advocate* on May 11, 1997, I read the following message under the "LOVELINES for MOTHER'S DAY" section.

MOM
Although I've been out of sight a year, I've been at your side.
I'm fine. On-Off. Doors locked. Dad's socks.
Jamie's friends. Your backyard. O.J.'s house.
One day we'll be together forever.
KYLE

Then I spotted the following on Monday, February 14, 2000, under the "VALENTINE'S DAY LOVELINES."

MOM
I LOVE YOU
Time has gone by so fast. This is a better place.
All the good ones are here.
Tell Dad I brought him the 9 point.
KYLE

These messages from Kyle have a very special meaning to me. Though I knew immediately that Jim had phoned them in to the newspaper, it made me realize how much Jim is aware of Kyle's continued presence in our lives.

I had been so touched by these messages that I decided to reciprocate and surprise Jim. So I phoned the newspaper and told them to put the following in the "VALENTINE'S DAY LOVELINES" on February 14, 2001.

42
DAD, Thanks for putting up with Mom!
The deer here have bigger racks
and more points.
Love,
Kyle

I kept waking up during the night of the 13th. I was excited about Jim's spotting the ad in the paper in the morning. I finally crawled out of bed around 4:30, turned off the security alarm and headed out to retrieve the paper so I could check out my ad.

When I pulled out the classified section with the LOVELINES, I was shocked to see a **HUGE** red heart at the very top of the paper that took up two entire columns and was 24 lines long with a big number **42** in the middle of the heart. My first thoughts were that they didn't follow my instructions and how much was this big ad going to cost me? And they didn't even write the message I had requested. After contemplating what could have happened, I unfolded the newspaper and spotted my smaller number 42 at the bottom of the page. I then realized that *both* Jim and I had put a number 42 ad in the paper from Kyle. Knowing Kyle, he's probably greatly amused by his parents' antics.

By the way, in case you are wondering, I *did* quit kissing Kyle's ashes. I *know* he lives elsewhere.

Am I Blessed or What?!!!!

Mary Jo McCabe, John J. Edward, and Linda Hullinger have literally *changed my life.* Because of the very special souls they are and the God-given gifts each so openly and willingly exhibits, countless individuals such as I have grown spiritually to new heights.

I will forever be grateful to Mary Jo, John, and Linda for all they have taught me, and in turn how they have helped me. And I know they can help you as well.

Mary Jo McCabe, widely acclaimed intuitive soul interpreter, visionary, teacher, and author.

    Books: *Learn to See,* Blue Dolphin Publishing, 1994
                 Come This Way, Unitis Press, 2000
    Website: www.mjmccabe.com

John J. Edward, internationally acclaimed psychic/medium, host of TV's *Crossing Over,* and author.

    Books: *One Last Time,* Berkley Press, 1998
                 What If God Were the Sun, Jodere Group, 2000
                 Crossing Over, Jodere Group, 2001
    Website: www.johnedward.net

Linda Hullinger, psychic/medium, who says, "I work with Kyle on a regular basis helping grieving parents unite with their children."

    Book: *A Puzzle Without a Box,* 2002
    Email: puzzlewithoutabox@yahoo.com